Taking as their point of departure general theoretical debates in the theory of ethnicity, the authors of this book present a wide-ranging and up-to-date analysis of the characteristics and interrelationships of ethnicity, religion, and class in Israeli society. While much has been written about the basic division between Jews from Europe and from North Africa and Asia, this book puts forward a more nuanced survey than the rather crude division which has formed the basis of most works on the subject. By focusing on four groups of Jewish origin in Israel (from Morocco, Iraq, Poland, and Rumania), and by including from each group both white- and blue-collar workers, the authors demonstrate the importance of breaking down simplistic categories of ethnicity. The work thus takes much further the analysis of ethnic identities and relations in Israeli society, and the data acquired from a rich ethnic mix lead to the analysis of a wide range of theoretical issues, which casts fresh light on social cleavages within Israel in particular and society in general.

Ethnicity, religion, and
class in Israeli society

Ethnicity, religion and class in Israeli society

ELIEZER BEN-RAFAEL AND STEPHEN SHAROT

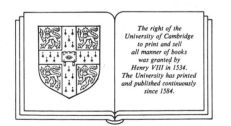

The right of the
University of Cambridge
to print and sell
all manner of books
was granted by
Henry VIII in 1534.
The University has printed
and published continuously
since 1584.

CAMBRIDGE UNIVERSITY PRESS

Cambridge

New York   Port Chester   Melbourne   Sydney

Published by the Press Syndicate of the University of Cambridge
The Pitt Building, Trumpington Street, Cambridge CB2 1RP
40 West 20th Street, New York, NY 10011, USA
10 Stamford Road, Oakleigh, Melbourne 3166, Australia

© Cambridge University Press 1991

First published 1991

Designed by Claire Brodmann
Printed in Great Britain by the University Press, Cambridge

British Library cataloguing in publication data
Ben-Rafael, Eliezer
Ethnicity, religion, and class in Israeli society.
1. Israel. Social stratification
I. Title   II. Sharot, Stephen

Library of Congress cataloguing in publication data
Ben-Rafael, Eliezer.
Ethnicity, religion, and class in Israeli society/
Eliezer Ben-Rafael and Stephen Sharot.
p.   cm.
Includes bibliographical references.
ISBN 0 521 39229 2
1. Ethnicity–Israel.   2. Israel–Ethnic relations.
3. Social classes–Israel.   4. Judaism–Israel.
I. Sharot, Stephen.   II. Title.
D113.2.B464   1991
305.8'0095694–dc20   89-78199   CIP

ISBN 0 521 39229 2 hardback

Contents

Contents

Acknowledgments

The names of the authors appear in alphabetical order; there is no senior author.

We wish to thank the Ford Foundation for the major funding, received through the Israel Foundations Trustees, of this research. A supplementary grant was provided by a Research Fund (anonymously donated) of Ben-Gurion University of the Negev.

We are greatly in debt to Dr. Hanna Ayalon who joined the study at an early stage and contributed her talents, including a considerable methodological expertise, to our analysis of the data. Five of the chapters of this book (6, 7, 10, 11, 13), and parts of two others (8, 9), first appeared as articles that were co-authored with Hanna. In addition, Hanna prepared additional tables for chapters 7, 8, and 9.

A grateful acknowledgment is due to Modi'in Ezrahi, the survey research company, that provided an excellent team of interviewers and administered the two surveys on which a large part of this work is based.

We are grateful to the following students for their assistance. Barbara Lavron helped in the compiling of lists for the sample. Shelley Shenhav gathered material on neighborhood committees for chapter 5, and Shmuel Bar-Gil and Uri Hamo gathered material on the synagogue congregations that are discussed in that chapter. Aida Dynia assisted in the processing of data from the second smaller survey on which chapter 12 is based. We wish to thank Alex Wright, our editor at the Cambridge University Press, for his interest and valuable help in seeing the manuscript through to publication. And many thanks are due to Margaret Jean Acland, our subeditor, for her most careful scrutiny of our work and expert editing.

Chapters 1 to 4, 12, 14 to 16, and large parts of 8 and 9, appear in print for the first time, but a number of chapters were originally prepared for publication as articles, and thanks are due to the editors and publishers for permission to use material as follows: a short section of chapter 1 was adapted from an article we wrote with Hanna Ayalon published in the *British Journal of Sociology*, volume 37, 1986, edited by Christopher

Acknowledgments

Badcock and Percy S. Cohen; chapter 5: *Ethnic Groups*, volume 7, 1987, edited by Anthony L. La Ruffa; chapter 6: *Review of Religious Research*, volume 27, 1986, edited by Edward C. Lehman; chapter 7: *International Sociology*, 1989, edited by Martin Albrow; part of chapter 8: *Ethnic and Racial Studies*, volume 8, 1985, edited by John Stone, Norman Fainstein, Susan Fainstein, and Henri Giordan; part of chapter 9: *International Journal for Sociology*, volume 28, 1987, edited by K. Iswaran; chapter 10 appears in *Tradition, Innovation, Conflict: Judaism in Contemporary Israel*, edited by Zvi Sobel and Benjamin Beit-Hallahmi, SUNY Press, Albany, New York, 1991; chapter 11: Hebrew version, *Megamot*, volume 20, 1987, edited by Kalman Benyamini and Nurit Ronel; English version, *Israel Social Science Research*, volume 4, 1986, edited by Paul Hare; chapter 13: *Research in Stratification and Social Mobility*, volume 7, 1988, edited by Arne Kalleberg.

We would like to thank the various anonymous reviewers of the above articles for their criticisms and suggestions. We also greatly benefited from the careful reading and valuable suggestions of the academic reviewers of Cambridge University Press.

Finally, we wish to express our heartfelt gratitude to our wives, Miriam and Tami, and to our children who make it all worthwhile.

I

Theoretical and empirical background

Ethnicity, class, and religion provide important foci for social cleavages, identifications, and consciousness in many societies, including Israeli society. They differ in many respects but they also converge and interrelate in complex ways. An empirical study of these divisions, including their institutional, behavioral, and subjective forms, is the centerpiece of this book. The dimensions that we decided to study and the questions that we asked can be best understood within the theoretical and empirical framework provided in this part. Here we give the greatest amount of attention to ethnicity, and chapter 1 provides an overview of the definitions, concepts, and theoretical perspectives in the sociological study of ethnicity. The intention is not to provide a complete review of the literature in one chapter but to focus on those topics in the general literature on ethnicity that we believe are relevant to an analysis of ethnicity in Israel. A short review of the relationships between ethnicity and class and between ethnicity and religion is also provided. Chapter 2 sets out the general historical development and present state of ethnic divisions among the Israeli-Jewish population, and chapter 3 discusses critically the theoretical perspectives on ethnicity in Israeli sociology. Our study focuses on four of the largest groups of origin in Israel: Jews from Morocco, Iraq, Rumania, and Poland. Chapter 4 describes the cultural and social background of these groups in the diaspora, their cultural and social profiles in Israeli society, and their position in Beer Sheva, the specific setting of our empirical research.

1

Ethnicity and society

Many social scientists have perceived a "resurgence" or "revival" of ethnicity in recent decades in many societies. The analysis of the reassertion of ethnic identities, the emergence and growth of ethnic movements, and the pervasiveness of ethnic conflicts has been one of the most important growth areas of sociology in the last two decades. It is admitted that sociologists and political scientists in the 1950s and early 1960s had assumed that ethnicity was declining in importance, and that it would continue to decline in the future. Western states had been held up as "nation states" that had succeeded over the centuries to assimilate and amalgamate diverse peoples, and many expected that the newly independent states in Africa and Asia would follow suit. Ethnicity was often associated with traditional societies, and it was expected that the process of modernization would weaken such ascription-based groups.

The growth of ethnicity and ethnic conflict has been analyzed as a universal or world-wide phenomenon. Not only have "tribal" or ethnic differences posed acute obstacles to the "nation-building" of newly independent states, but ethnic groups have appeared to endanger what had been considered the accomplished unity of European states. In multinational states, such as the Soviet Union and Yugoslavia, ethnic divisions and conflicts have perhaps only become more manifest and politicized, but indigenous ethnic movements have also appeared in countries, such as Britain and France, which had been considered unified nations. Post-Second World War immigrants, such as Indians, Pakistanis, and West Indians in Britain, North Africans in France, and "guest workers" in other western and central European states, have added to the number of "race relations" predicaments. The "nation of immigrants," the United States, has also received new waves of immigrants, especially from Central America and from South East Asia, but ethnic conflicts have taken their most violent forms among American blacks in the ghetto riots of the late 1960s, and there was also what many termed an "ethnic revivalism" among white ethnic groups who were well into their third or even fourth generations in America.

Some authors have emphasized that the recent ethnic upsurge is only a wave in a long historical process, but the apparently global nature of the "revival" has brought forth global explanations. Intensified ethnicity is said to be a response to the decline of traditional groups, such as the extended family and the local community in modern mass society. It is claimed that, in the impersonal modern society, people still have the need to identify with a social unit that is larger than the nuclear family and smaller than the state, and that the ethnic group provides such an identity (Glazer, 1983: ch. 12). Ethnic problems become more acute in the process of "nation-building," because modern states aspire to national integration and some groups have objected to becoming an integral part of a single order (Orans, 1971; Alexander, 1980). By becoming the major distributor of national resources, the state has unintentionally encouraged ethnic groups to mobilize in order to seek concessions (Glazer and Moynihan, 1975). Urbanization and mobility have increased contacts among ethnic groups, some of whom feel relatively deprived in comparison with other groups or have come to feel that their cultural distinctiveness is threatened. The development of communications has also had a "demonstration effect"; an awareness of ethnic groups who have achieved special rights or independence encourages other groups to seek the same for themselves (Connor, 1977).

Although the global explanations may explain part of the phenomenon in many cases, they tend to fit some cases better than others where they may be much less important or totally irrelevant. Ethnicity as a response to alienation in mass society is hardly a factor in undeveloped countries, and explanations such as relative economic deprivation or cultural deprivation are belied by a case such as the Basques who are relatively prosperous in comparison with other groups in Spain and demonstrate little interest in using their own language (Connor, 1977). The problems of finding common explanations point to the complexity and multi-dimensionality of ethnicity and the variety of ethnic situations and relations. Different causes and combinations of causes will be found because what is defined as ethnicity covers a very wide range of phenomena with many different characteristics.

One important difference among forms of ethnicity is that between nationalist and non-nationalist forms; the former, ethnonationalism, includes a demand for an independent state or at least considerable political autonomy. Ethnonationalism is a widespread phenomenon in a world where there are very few nation-states; that is to say, there are few states or territorial-political units in which the great majority of the population identify with a single nation or people who believe that they have a common ancestry (Connor, 1978). Since the French Revolution, in which the demand for popular sovereignty and national identity were fused, nationalism as an ideology and social movement has spread throughout most of the world. In many countries, the recent revival of ethnicity would appear to be related to the widespread acceptance of nationalist ideologies (Smith, 1981; Connor, 1977).

A nation is a particular type of ethnic group or community; its members, or a significant proportion of them, live within a definable territory, and if they are nationalists, they maintain or aspire to some degree of political autonomy. Not all ethnic groups are nations, and ethnonationalism is only one form of ethnicity. There are important differences, for example, between the ethnicity of Italian-Americans or Polish-Americans in the United States, and the ethnicity of separatist and irredentist movements in many multinational states.

Although there may be many alternative explanations of ethno-nationalism, its strength and characteristics are often very evident. The same cannot be said of the non-nationalist forms of ethnicity whose features appear to be far more problematic and have occasioned many disputes among sociologists, not only over appropriate models and theories, but also over empirical issues regarding the forms and directions that ethnic group identities and strategies are taking. For example, the "new ethnicity" of white ethnic groups in the United States has been viewed as an important phenomenon by some, and as such it has been both celebrated and condemned (Novak, 1972; Stein and Hill, 1977), whereas others have judged it a "myth" or a phenomenon with little real content (Gans, 1979; Steinberg, 1981; Patterson, 1979).

Disagreement among sociologists over the characterization and conceptualization of ethnicity among different Jewish groups of origin in Israel is at least as great as that among sociologists of ethnicity in the United States. Sociologists of Israeli society might agree that ethnonationalism is confined to the division between Jews and Arabs, and that the form of ethnicity that divides Israeli-Jewish groups remains within the boundaries of Israeli and Jewish identities shared by the vast majority of Israeli Jews, but they have hotly disputed the nature and forms of those identities that relate to the countries and continents of origin of Israeli Jews. Although the ethnic division between Jews and Arabs in Israel may be thought of as a more important problem, in the sense of separation and divisiveness, the problematical and possibly paradoxical nature of ethnic divisions among Israeli Jews have made it a more intricate puzzle for sociological inquiry.

5

Definition of ethnicity

A few sociologists have questioned the appropriateness of the terms ethnicity and ethnic groups to the Israeli-Jewish context. The term *edah* (plural, *edot*), meaning community, is used in Israel to distinguish Israeli-Jewish groups according to their country of origin. The term is used more commonly to refer to the Jewish groups from North Africa and Asia ("Moroccan *edah*," "Yemenite *edah*," etc.) who are often referred to collectively as *edot ha'Mizrach* (communities of the East) or Mizrachim (Easterners). Less commonly, the term *edah* is applied to Jews from Europe and America ("Poles," "Anglo-Saxons," etc.), who are collectively known as *edot Ashkenaz* or Ashkenazim. When they have written in English, most Israeli sociologists have used the term "ethnic group" interchangeable with *edah*, and have referred to the communal consciousness of these groups as "ethnicity." Ernest Krausz (1986) objects to this usage as misleading and suggests that the term "subcultures" is sufficient in order to delineate the differences among Jewish groups of origin in Israel. Our disagreement with Krausz is not only a semantic or definitional quibble, but reflects our different understanding of the phenomenon in question. However, some discussion of definitions would be useful at this point.

Many recent definitions of "ethnic group" have included both objective and subjective components (Marger, 1985: 7–8). The objective elements refer to the distinctive cultural and symbolic characteristics of the group. These may include "core" elements such as language or religion, but a distinctive language or religion is not generally regarded as a necessary condition; subcultural differences may be sufficient, or physical appearance, such as color, may also provide the major symbolic differentiation. The subjective element is the sense of kinship and community, the "we" feeling that relates to a belief in a common ancestry and group history. There may be little or no objective evidence of common ancestors, and it is possible that the presumed history of the group is largely fictitious, but myths can be potent and it is the group's representations of itself that are important here.

When defining and characterizing the ethnic group, some social scientists have focused exclusively on one or the other of these two elements. Barth (1969), for example, wrote that ethnic groups can only be understood in terms of boundary creation and maintenance, and that a shared culture should be regarded as a result rather than a primary or definitional characteristic. According to this conception, ethnicity is a corporate identity that exists independently of any particular cultural features. The latter may be used to indicate the boundary, but they are likely to change in accordance with boundary maintenance. Alternative definitions, focusing on culture, have emphasized that phenomena such as religion and language are "primordial" or "natural" attachments on a par with kinship; they are absolute ties that can not be reduced to or explained by other factors (Geertz, 1963).

There is no need to accept either of these extreme positions. Cultural factors need not be characterized as primordial, but, without some reference to cultural similarities and differences, it would not be possible to locate ethnic categories or groups (Smith, 1984). With regard to the subjective element, some knowledge or awareness of common characteristics would not be sufficient to characterize an ethnic group; another term such as "ethnic aggregate" or "category" might be used instead. The term "ethnic group" is more usefully limited to cases where members attribute importance to such characteristics, and these feelings have implications for their social interaction with others. Ethnicity or an ethnic consciousness implies an affective identification with the group and a commitment to the group's cultural heritage (cf. McKay and Lewis, 1978).

In his critique of the application of the term "ethnic group" to refer to Jewish groups of origin in Israel, Krausz takes as his point of reference Ben-Rafael's (1982: 24) definition. According to this definition, a group qualifies as ethnic when it has some primordial attributes, particular socio-cultural features, and a consciousness of constituting a group different from others in the same setting. Krausz admits that Israeli Jews may be divided by these characteristics, but he argues that with respect to all three attributes, what unifies Israeli Jews is stronger and more important than what divides them.

Even though Krausz refers to Israeli-Jewish groups as having "primordial bonds," he states that the primordial element of the definition is the most problematic in the Israeli-Jewish case. He writes that Israeli Jews share a common religion, trace their origins to a common source and, in addition to the ancient history of their common ancestors, they share parallel historical experiences of dispersion and persecution. These commonalities represent the deepest level of primordialism upon which are superimposed the "subcultural" differences in communal histories, languages, and culture that were brought from the more immediate countries of origin.

Krausz does not address Ben-Rafael's argument that the ethnicity of the *edot* from North Africa and Asia stems from the fact that they do not differentiate between their Judaism (what Krausz terms the deeper primordialism) and their specific cultural legacies (what Krausz terms the superimposed primordial elements). Krausz implies that the *edot* from Asia and North America consider their "subcultures" as only variations of a common core, and they are not, therefore, interested in perpetuating their separateness; their aspirations are limited to achieving socio-economic equality and finding acceptance on equal terms in Israeli society. The implications of Ben-Rafael's argument are different. He acknowledges that there is almost unanimous acceptance of the ideology of the "fusion of the exiles," but the groups' identification of their Judaism with their cultural heritage is likely to perpetuate differences, at least in the lower strata of the North African and Asian *edot* who have little social interaction with Ashkenazim at the primary group level.

Krausz argues that relations among Israeli-Jewish groups are not a variation of, but quite different from, the type known as interethnic relations. However, his comparisons with other societies point to differences in degree rather than kind. He admits that boundaries exist but argues that they are less rigid than among ethnic groups in other societies, pluralism exists but it is less divisive because of the overall unifying bonds, and conflicts exist but they are less fundamental than elsewhere. But if these are only differences in degree, it is not clear at what point it is possible to distinguish between ethnic differences and those that are merely "subcultural." Pointing to examples, such as black–white relations in South Africa and England, emphasizes the differences, but other examples, such as the relations among white ethnic groups in the United States, appear much less evidently different in type. Socio-cultural differences and consciousness of kind among some American ethnic groups may even be weaker than among some Israeli-Jewish groups.

In a case such as the United States, it might also be argued that the factors that unify most of the groups of origin are stronger than the factors that divide them. Of course, the factors that unify in the United States are not as "ethnic" as those that unify Israeli Jews; most Americans do not lay claim to a common ancient ancestry or history. However, most Americans do identify with the "founding fathers" and the history of the American "nation," even if their own particular ancestors were not among the participants. In a sense Americans adopt (and are adopted by) common ancestors and the national history, and this adopted nationhood is not generally considered less fundamental than the particular ancestry and history of the ethnic groups.

Just as it is too general to understand ethnic groups in the United States, the term "subcultural" is too general to understand the specific character of Israeli-Jewish groups of origin. We can agree that the differences are subcultural (as they are among ethnic groups in some other societies), but there are also subcultural differences among socio-economic strata and among communities that differ in their levels and forms of religiosity. How then should the subcultures of groups from different recent origins be characterized? We submit that "ethnic sub-culture" is a suitable characterization.

General statements that the common cultural and identificational components among Israeli Jews are more fundamental than their cultural and identificational differences are true in a sense, but they lack contex-tual qualifications. If the context is the Israeli-Arab conflicts or Jewish-Arab relations within Israel and the occupied territories, such statements are likely to be accepted. If the contextual frame is limited to the Israeli-Jewish population, such general statements are far more conten-tious. Most Israeli Jews will rank their Jewish and Israeli identifications before any subethnic identification based on country or area of origin – and these ethnonational identities have no doubt been reinforced by the protracted conflict of Israeli Jews with Arab countries and with the Arab population in the West Bank and Gaza – but in their perceptions and interactions with each other these identities often remain in the back-ground and it is the subethnic identities that become the focus of differentiation and symbolization.

Krausz implies that the common Jewish ethnic identity of Israeli Jews rules out the possibility of ethnic identities based on communities of origin. Our position is that it is possible for people to have more than one identification based on common descent. National and ethnic identifica-tions contain cultural definitions of kinship, and they can vary, like bio-logical kin, in terms of "closeness" and "distance" and in their relative importance with regard to loyalty, pride, social activities, and cultural orientations. It is possible for a national-ethnic identification, encompas-sing the entire "extended family," to coexist with ethnic or subethnic identifications that encompass branches of that "family." All Jews are said to stem from one family that began with the Patriarch Abraham and many Israeli Jews do conceive of themselves as kinsmen, but the association of recent geographical origins with cultural and socio-economic divisions has led many of them to distinguish these ties of putative kinship in terms of "closeness" and "distance" (cf. Shokeid and Deshen, 1982).

Dimensions of ethnicity and ethnic group relations

The concepts and theories in the field of ethnic relations and ethnicity have been usefully applied to the study of *edot* in Israel. A recent typology (George, 1984) that distinguishes four sociological approaches in the general field will be shown in chapter 3 to describe the different theoretical orientations among Israeli sociologists. The first approach, that was largely initiated by the Chicago school in the 1920s and 1930s (e.g. Park, 1928), focuses on the problems of immigrant groups and their difficulties in adapting to their environment. The second, a socio-psychological orientation that was classically formulated in the Authoritarian Personality study (Adorno *et al.*, 1950), focuses on prejudice and attitudes toward minorities. The third, the pluralist approach, emphasizes power and relationships of dominance and conflict (e.g. Kuper, 1965; van den Berghe, 1978). Finally, the fourth approach considers ethnicity as a reflection of class interests and divisions (Bonacich, 1980).

This typology may not be exhaustive, but perhaps the major concern of all approaches in the field has been to describe and explain the degrees and modes of integration and separation of ethnic groups. The recognition of the complexity of ethnicity has led a number of scholars to propose typologies of dimensions. One of the best known is that of Gordon (1964) who distinguished a number of variables of assimilation, among the most important being acculturation, structural assimilation, and identificational assimilation. Acculturation refers to the process when an immigrant or ethnic group changes its cultural patterns to those of another group or the host society. Structural assimilation refers to the entrance of members of an ethnic group into the institutions, organizations, and primary groups of the host society. Identificational assimilation refers to the development of a sense of peoplehood based on that of the host society.

The relationships among these variables can vary considerably, but Gordon argued that, whereas acculturation could occur without any of the other types of assimilation, if structural assimilation occurs, the other types of assimilation will accompany or follow it. Extensive acculturation and assimilation are likely to weaken a group's identity, but studies of white ethnic groups in the United States indicate that this process often falls short of deleting ethnic affinity entirely. Whether through food, the naming of the newborn, or participating in ethnic festivals, the ethnic identity often survives, even though it may appear to many as shallow or merely symbolic (Gans, 1979).

Gordon did not suggest that assimilation is inevitable, and it is quite possible for the processes discussed to move in an opposite direction. For example, the term deacculturation might be used to refer to a situation where an ethnic group reinforces or extends its cultural distinctiveness and moves culturally further away from the host society (Sharot, 1976: 2).

However, Gordon's major empirical reference was the United States, and his discussion tended to stress the varying degrees and forms of assimilation of immigrant groups into the host American society. Other authors, using the term pluralism rather than assimilation, have emphasized the continuation or emergence of group divisions in a variety of settings. Their conceptual distinctions largely parallel those of Gordon. An important distinction is made between cultural pluralism, that refers to differences in values, norms, and customs, and social pluralism, that refers to the social boundaries or limited social interaction among groups. Further distinctions within these dimensions are sometimes made, such as the distinction between secondary or formal pluralism, referring to the level of separation in impersonal frameworks or institutions, and primary or informal pluralism, referring to the level of separation in areas such as friendship and marriage (Marger, 1985: 79–84).

A further dimension of the integration or separation of ethnic groups is ethnic stratification or inequality. In Gordon's discussion there was an emphasis on the "criss-crossing" of class and ethnic groups, and he suggested the term "ethclass" to refer to the subsociety that was created by the intersection of the vertical line of ethnicity and the horizontal line of social class. He noted that those of the same ethnic group will share a historical identification or sense of peoplehood, but only within the ethclass will there be behavioral similarities and primary social interaction. Sociologists advocating the pluralist and class approaches to ethnicity have tended to emphasize the overlap of ethnic and class divisions. It is evident, however, that the relationships of ethnic and class differences vary greatly. They range from cases, such as those in Switzerland, where the ethnic lines approximate to the vertical crossing of the class structure, to cases, such as those in South Africa, where the ethnic lines converge largely with class differences.

In discussing ethnic stratification, it is important to distinguish socio-economic or class differences, that refer to the ethnic groups' relative distributions of wealth, income, occupations, and education, and ethnic status, that refers to the relative prestige of an ethnic group within a society. The class distribution and status of an ethnic group are likely to be related, but in many cases they can also be differentiated (cf. Weber, 1968: ch. 9). A combination of factors may result in an ethnic stigma, so that economic or occupational mobility will not be accompanied by an equivalent rise in status. The status of an ethnic group may be evaluated by other groups with reference to physical characteristics, such as color, or cultural characteristics, such as the degree of "westernization" or closeness to the dominant culture. A further dimension of ethnic stratification is the distribution of power in the political arena, and this may involve factors such as the right to vote, the possibility of becoming political leaders, and the ability to organize and to put pressure on political authorities.

Explanations

Explanations of ethnic group relations cannot be divorced from a discussion of the relationships among the dimensions of ethnicity. For example, if there is a substantial inequality between an ethnic group and others, there is likely to be substantial social pluralism, at least at the informal or primary levels of social interaction. Substantial social and cultural pluralism does not, however, necessarily imply substantial inequality. And although in some cases a decline in ethnic inequality may be accompanied by, or result in, less pluralism, as, for example, among white ethnic groups in the United States, in other cases pluralism has remained strong, as in Belgium.

The varied relationships among the cultural, social, and stratificational dimensions of ethnicity have at least two important implications. Firstly, no one factor, material or cultural, is likely to provide an adequate explanation of ethnic relations and ethnicity. And secondly, ethnicity can only be understood by analyzing the interaction between the ethnic group and the wider society which may be constituted by other ethnic or non-ethnic groups.

Discussions of ethnicity have tended to present a number of overlapping sets of alternative explanations: as an expressive, non-rational sense of loyalty to putative kinsmen or as an instrumental rational response to socio-economic conditions; as a repository of primordial components or as a strategy for pursuing interests; as a concern with cultural distinctiveness or as a facilitating condition of political mobilization. Many have analyzed ethnicity in terms of one of these alternatives, but the recent tendency is to recognize that ethnicity can combine these features; it is both expressive and instrumental, non-rational and rational, primordial and socio-economic, cultural and political (McKay, 1982; Burgess, 1978; Lal, 1983). In recent decades there may have been a shift among ethnic groups in some countries from the cultural to the socio-economic and political components of their ethnicity (Glazer and Moynihan, 1975), but a categorization of contemporary ethnic manifestations on a primordial-mobilization continuum was able to locate examples along the entire range (McKay, 1982).

The instrumental component of ethnicity has been emphasized in two recent perspectives, the division of labor model and the resource competition model. Both of these perspectives have been presented by their exponents as alternatives to the assimilationist-developmental model found in the works of Parsons and Smelser (1956) and Lipset and Rokkan (1967). The main thrust of the criticism of the assimilationist model has been directed against the view that modernization and, in particular occupational differentiation, will be accompanied by a decline in the importance of ethnicity (Hechter, 1975; Nielsen, 1985; Leifer, 1981).

The proponents of the cultural division of labor perspective have argued that modernization or economic development can strengthen the distinction and the inequality between the culturally distinctive periphery and the core that exploits it; ethnic solidarity and mobilization will develop in the periphery as a reaction to its relative disadvantage and exploitation (Hechter, 1975, 1978; McRoberts, 1979; Palloni, 1979). Proponents of the competition perspective have argued that ethnic solidarity or mobilization will increase when there is an improvement in the socio-economic profile of an ethnic group and a decline in the ethnic division of labor; individuals will turn to their ethnic group for support, and will seek relative advantage through collective ethnic group action when they come into increased competition with individuals from other groups over resources, occupations, and roles (Nielsen, 1980, 1985; Nagel and Olzak, 1982; Olzak, 1982). This perspective emphasizes that occupational differentiation within ethnic groups is likely to increase the groups' organizational capacity.

The extent to which the two recent perspectives conflict with the assimilationist model cannot be easily determined; not only have they investigated different cases, they have also focused on different dimensions of ethnicity. Whereas the assimilationist perspective has focused on primary social assimilation, especially intermarriage (Hirschman, 1983), both the cultural division of labor and the competition perspective have focused on differential voting patterns, support for ethnic parties, ethnic mobilization (Hechter, 1975; Olzak, 1983; Nielsen, 1980, 1985; Ragin, 1979), and perceptions of discrimination and social distance (Portes, 1984; Portes *et al.*, 1980).

Despite its objections to the assimilationist view, the cultural division of labor perspective shares with it an emphasis on a negative association between the socio-economic status of an ethnic group and its ethnic solidarity. The assimilationist and cultural division of labor models may here be considered as two sides of the same coin; the former emphasizes that relative economic improvement reduces ethnicity, and the latter emphasizes that relative economic disadvantage increases ethnicity.

13

Some proponents of competition theory acknowledge that the development of an ethnic group's collective action may be preceded or accompanied by its acculturation or even assimilation to the group with which it is engaged in conflict. Nielsen (1985) writes, for example, that ethnic collective action can occur "even though, and perhaps especially when, ethnicity becomes a weaker predictor of individual life-style."

It is apparent that, when the different facets of ethnicity are considered, neither the cultural division of labor perspective nor the competition perspective need necessarily be in conflict with the assimilationist approach. The two more recent perspectives have appeared to contradict each other in their divergent explanations of collective ethnic action, but because both can point to empirical support Nielsen (1985) has concluded that they may both be correct. In one society or period ethnic solidarity may rest on the homogeneity of its members' economic interests, whereas in another society or another period in the same society ethnic solidarity is the result of the ethnic group's greater wealth and occupational differentiation and consequent greater organizational potential. Why this is so was not clarified, and we suggest that cultural factors may need to be taken into account in accounting for the effects of either economic homogeneity or heterogeneity on ethnicity.

If perspectives on ethnicity are divided according to the extent to which they emphasize instrumental or cultural factors, all three perspectives may be classified as primarily instrumental approaches: ethnicity will be abandoned because of the greater status benefits associated with achievement roles and identities (the assimilationist perspective); ethnicity will be emphasized because of the economic and political benefits to be gained by promoting common economic interests (the division of labor approach); or ethnicity will be emphasized because greater economic and political benefits can be gained by using the diverse skills and resources of an economically heterogeneous group (the competition approach).

The assimilationist perspective has often been associated by its critics with an emphasis on cultural factors, but cultural references were mostly to the differences or distance between the values and norms of the minority and majority which impeded the assimilation of the former. The assimilationist perspective paid little attention to variations in cultural meanings of ethnicity. This is also true of the cultural division of labor approach despite the word "cultural" in its title; cultural factors, such as language, dialect, or region are treated as markers and convenient signs which are used in the process of economic differentiation. The exponents of the competition perspective were influenced by Barth (1969) who argued that, according to circumstances, cultural items may be used to signal differences or be underplayed or denied.

As Smith (1984) has argued, culture is not entirely malleable; some symbols are by their nature more important than others, and they are not only used to exclude others, but are also repertoires of attachment and expression. Groups attribute diverse cultural meanings to "sharing descent" and to other characteristics that are indicative of belongingness (Keyes, 1981; McKay, 1982). These meanings may be bound to ethnic myths and legacies of the past that are periodically strengthened by ritual re-enactment or remembrance. The importance of such symbols and myths may be traced back to past structural factors, but they can assume an autonomy that makes them relatively impervious to situational variables, and they may play a part in the definition of those situations. The relative importance of instrumental and cultural factors can vary from case to case (McKay, 1982; Smith, 1984), and a consideration of cultural elements may explain why the cultural division of labor perspective predicts correctly in one case and the competition perspective predicts correctly in another.

The point that some cultural meanings of ethnicity are less susceptible than others to instrumental considerations is an important consideration, not only in a comparison of ethnic solidarity or assimilation among ethnic groups, but also in a study of differential ethnic allegiance within ethnic groups. Sociologists presenting an assimilation perspective have found negative relationships between ethnic identity and socio-economic status (Sandberg, 1974; Gans, 1982). It is suggested that the ethnicity of mobiles from low-status ethnic groups will be weakened by their participation in non-segregated work markets, by their knowledge of the values and culture of the wider society, and by their more intimate contacts with individuals from other groups. Other research, however, has found either an insignificant or positive relationship between ethnicity and socio-economic status among United States blacks (Dillingham, 1981; cf. Willie, 1983), white ethnic groups (Pavlak, 1976), and Jews (Himmelfarb, 1980; Lazerwitz, 1977).

The relationship between ethnic stratification and ethnic solidarity has been an important part of the debate between the cultural division of labor and competition perspectives, but neither has paid much attention to the relationship between ethnicity and socio-economic or class differences *within* ethnic groups. Their focus has been on ethnic "resurgences," but there has been little discussion on whether the resurgence is evenly distributed among socio-economic strata within a group or is stronger in the lower or upper strata. It is possible, however, to deduce from the perspectives divergent expectations regarding the relationship between ethnicity and socio-economic status within ethnic groups.

The cultural division of labor perspective implies that since ethnicity is a reaction to exploitation, mobiles from the disadvantaged periphery will be less ethnically minded. Because it is believed to be rare for individuals from low-status ethnic groups to achieve high-status occupational roles, little attention is given to this matter. Hechter (1975: 41) writes that such individuals will either be co-opted by the advantaged group or become ethnic leaders and act as brokers between the two groups.

As for the competition perspective, it may be deduced that because higher occupational status members of a subordinate ethnic group will enter into more competitive relationships with members of the dominant group, they will be more ethnically conscious than others in their groups. Nielsen (1985) writes that this will depend on the rate of modernization of the group; when there is a rapid level of modernization, the opportunities for leadership in the core may not keep pace, and frustrated mobiles from the subordinate group may turn to ethnic leadership as an alternative. Portes (1984; Portes *et al.*, 1980) found that the more educated and higher status Cuban immigrants in the United States were more likely to express greater distance from, and to perceive greater discrimination in, American society.

The relative importance of ethnic symbols can influence the extent to which both the subordinate and superordinate groups are open or closed to others, and these variables can have important consequences for the reaction of mobiles from the subordinate group. The assimilationist perspective has often assumed that individuals from the lower ethnic groups want to assimilate and that the problem was the barriers imposed by the dominant group. If cultural meanings of ethnicity are considered, the costs of disaffiliation are likely to be greater for individuals in some groups than in others, and the same status benefits of assimilation will consequently pull mobiles from some groups less than others. Where there is a considerable division of labor according to ethnic origin, the cultural meanings of ethnicity will influence the readiness of the dominant group to co-opt mobiles and the decisions of mobiles to allow themselves to be co-opted or become ethnic leaders. Where there is considerable occupational competition between members of a low-status ethnic group and a high-status group, the cultural meanings of ethnicity will influence the extent to which competitors define their competition as one between members of different ethnic groups, or whether they simply see competition in individual terms without reference to ethnic background. In the latter case, competition will reduce ethnicity, not increase it.

The dialectics of ethnicity

Instrumental considerations or calculations of the costs and benefits of ethnicity are made through cultural "spectacles." The cultural meanings of ethnicity of an immigrant or subordinate ethnic group may in part be traced back to its history prior to its immigration or contact with the superordinate group, but they are also likely to be influenced by the features of the dominant group's culture. A dominant culture consists of beliefs, values, and outlooks that are widespread in the superordinate group, and represented and diffused by the political center. It includes the general rules and normative arrangements that relate to the entry of an ethnic group into the social order. These depend on the extent to which the dominant group stresses the exclusiveness of the cultural identity that it represents, and its images, which are not necessarily uniform, of the cultural, economic, and political characteristics of the subordinate groups. A position of cultural closure and social segregation may encourage a dominant group to emphasize ethnic differences and encourage their perpetuation. On the other hand, the openness of a dominant group or its general aspiration for a unified society may lead it to deny the importance of ethnic heterogeneity, and to emphasize the non-ethnic character of those strata that identify with the dominant culture.

The religion of dominant groups has been a major factor in their attitudes and policies toward immigrant and subordinate ethnic groups. Both Islam and Catholicism have been seen to have universalistic outlooks that transcend nations and ethnic groups, but they have clearly differentiated between believers and non-believers. Muslims of many origins, including those who were previously enslaved, have enjoyed formal equality in Islamic empires and states (Fernea, 1973), whereas Jews and Christians have been subject to special laws and have been separated in their semi-autonomous communities. The official Catholic doctrine of the equal theological status of all Christians has been one factor in accounting for the more diffuse color lines in Central and South America compared with the rigid lines of Protestant America and Calvinist South Africa (Hoetinck, 1972; van den Berghe, 1978). The influence of the Church in Latin America has diminished over time, but the organic image of the social order has remained, and this has strengthened an assimilationist rather than pluralist orientation toward immigrant groups. In the United States, the dominant Protestant ethos gave way to an acceptance of religious pluralism, but ethnic pluralism continued to be discouraged until the 1960s. France since the Revolution has provided an example of an assimilationist stance based on largely secularist premises of French civilization and language. Communist states have also demonstrated strong assimilationist aspirations.

The official ideology of a dominant group may, however, be inconsistent with, and even undermined by, unofficial but widespread beliefs among the dominant group. Not only doctrines of ethnic separation, but also doctrines of assimilationism or amalgamation, may be found together with widespread beliefs among the dominant group that the subordinate ethnic group is inferior, genetically and/or culturally, and that association with them is to be avoided or restricted to non-intimate settings. An inconsistency between stated doctrine and widespread beliefs and behavior may stem from fears of the dominant group that the absorption of the subordinate group will endanger the dominant culture. Such ambiguous situations are likely to be frustrating for members of ethnic groups who may have taken the official doctrine at face value and sought entrance into the dominant group.

Even if the dominant group is relatively consistent in its policy of assimilationism, it should not be assumed that a subordinate ethnic group will exploit the openings, especially if the consequence appears to be the loss of a highly valued cultural heritage and identity. The openness or closure of the boundaries have, therefore, to be related to cultural, socio-economic, and political conditions that relate to the interaction of the groups. A comparison of cases points to differences in the relative importance of these dimensions.

The Jewish-Arab cleavage in Israel (Lustick, 1980; Zureik, 1979) and the Protestant-Catholic division in Northern Ireland (Curran, 1979) are examples of mutual exclusion and rejection at all levels of the socio-economic hierarchy. Arabs are heavily concentrated in the lower social strata in Israel, but there is a significant Arab professional stratum. In Northern Ireland, Catholics are disproportionately represented in the lower strata, but the socio-economic disparity of the two religious groups is not acute and Protestants make up the majority of lower as well as upper strata. In both societies, religion and nationalism are more important to boundary maintenance than intergroup socio-economic differentiation.

Differences in ethnic identification among socio-economic strata within an ethnic group are found where the ethnic boundary is viewed by both dominant and subordinate groups as open. White Catholic groups in the United States, such as the Polish-Americans (Sandberg, 1974) and the Italian-Americans (Gans, 1982; Roche, 1984), include substantial urban working-class communities who perceive benefits of ethnicity in their competition or comparisons with minorities such as blacks. The mobiles from these white groups who move to hetero-geneous suburban communities may express a symbolic ethnicity, but because they assimilate with other groups and define competition in individual rather than group terms, their ethnic identifications will have little saliency.

Perhaps an even better illustration of the effects of socio-economic status on ethnicity within ethnic groups is the situation in Brazil (Wade, 1985). Here there is a clear overlap between color and socio-economic distribution, but the Brazilian ideology has favored the amalgamation of all groups of origin and color categories. The various European ethnic groups in Brazil have met few obstacles in assimilation, and although certain immigrant groups began with attempts at closure, by the third generation the upwardly mobile sectors became part of the Brazilian economic and political elites. There is discrimination against non-whites, but blacks and mulattoes have been able to rise in the class hierarchy and those with the "appropriate" occupational and cultural credentials have been accepted into the dominant white society. Thus, the upper strata of the subordinate ethnic group have been assimilated into the dominant groups and, although the openness of groups has weakened ethnicity in all strata, indications of ethnic identification and consciousness are most apparent in the lower strata.

Black–white divisions in the United States (Bowser, 1985) and Britain (Arnold, 1984; Wilson, 1984) represent another pattern. Cultural features and material interests have interacted to create a heavy historical baggage (slavery, colonialism) and continue to interact to reinforce a dominant culture that is essentially segregative. This orientation is especially endorsed within the dominant group by the lower stratum, some of whom compete with members of the black minority for jobs and housing. The minority groups have aspired to an open ethnic boundary, but as a reaction to their rejection by whites, ethnic consciousness and a militancy have developed among lower-class blacks, especially as their power resources and expectations of benefits through ethnic mobilization have grown. A syndrome of marginality has often characterized the middle class of the subordinate ethnic group in this context. The American "black bourgeoisie" in the 1950s separated themselves from the majority of their ethnic group and constructed an exclusive social world in which there was considerable imitation of the culture of the dominant ethnic group which was closed to them (Frazier, 1957).

The relationships of Canadians of British and French origin exemplify another pattern (Theriault, 1979). Here, it is the dominant culture that has encouraged an open boundary and the minority group that has been relatively closed. In Quebec, the French Canadians, who are concentrated in the lower strata, have resisted integration and fought for their language and cultural legacy. The dominant British group of origin has been open to the participation of the French and this situation has produced a division within the middle-class French, between assimilationists, who move into the dominant group, and ethnic activists, who have sought to mobilize the lower strata. A similar pattern is found with respect to the Basques in Spain (Heiberg, 1979).

The model of a dominant culture and a single subordinate ethnic group is obviously a simplification. There may be a number of subordinate ethnic groups – some may be more subordinate than others – and their relationships with each other are likely to influence their relationships with the dominant group or culture. More than one pattern may exist in a single society as, for example, in the case of blacks and white non-Protestant ethnic groups in the United States. Another example of a mixture of patterns in a single society is that of the relationships of the British, Afrikaners, and the blacks in South Africa. Like the French in Canada, the ethnonationalism of the Afrikaners was in part a response to the pressures of Anglo assimilationism. Their first strategy was withdrawal, but they turned to political mobilization in order to wrest political or economic power from the dominant Anglo group (Baker, 1983). In South Africa, the Afrikaners eventually became the dominant group, and the majority joined those of British origin in the middle and upper socio-economic strata. The black population makes up the great majority of the lower strata, and although a small black middle class has emerged, the rigid racial separation and the clear convergence of ethnic and socio-economic status have meant that there is little likelihood of intra-group differences in ethnic identification among socio-economic strata.

The levels of closure and openness of these various patterns can only be explained by a variety of socio-historical factors – religious, territorial, and linguistic, as well as material interests. The emergent structural and cultural features will determine the relative costs and benefits of ethnicity for different ethnic groups and for socio-economic strata within ethnic groups. Instrumental calculations may in turn affect the development of structures, especially group boundaries. For example, mobiles from a low prestige ethnic group may find that the benefits that they expected from ethnic disaffiliation are not forthcoming, and that solidarity with their group of origin and ethnic mobilization is likely to bring greater benefits or lower costs. The boundary of the group as a whole may then move toward closure, but if socio-economic and political benefits are gained through ethnic solidarity and mobilization, the orientations of the dominant group to the subordinate group may also begin to change.

In sum, objective features account, at least partially, for subjective phenomena, but these in turn are bound to behavior patterns and social action that are carriers of change. These changes may involve the socio-economic and political divisions, the premises of the social order, and the very definitions of the ethnic situations. Ethnicity that starts with the problems implied by the location of a given group within the social order may evolve to become a questioning of the structure and premises of the society. It thereby constitutes a focus of social dialectics involving culture, socio-economic interests, and power.

Ethnicity, class, and religion

Some authors have seen a relationship between the "resurgence" of ethnicity in the post-war period and a decline in the importance of class and class conflict. It is argued that in advanced western societies, class no longer carries affective ties (Bell, 1975), class differences are less rigid and invidious (Burgess, 1978), and class conflict has lost its bitterness (Beer, 1980). Ethnicity is seen as a more effective means of advancing interests because it often combines common interests and already existent affective ties (Glazer and Moynihan, 1975). The socio-biological approach emphasizes that ethnicity is an extension of kinship and as such is considered more elementary, basic, and permanent than class (van den Berghe, 1981). In sharp contrast are those perspectives that conflate ethnic groups and classes, or account for ethnicity in terms of class interests (Bonacich, 1980). Unlike ethnic cleavages, class is seen to be embedded in the structural features of society, and as such it may be considered more elementary than ethnicity (Miles, 1982).

Many accounts of ethnicity, although not necessarily reductionist, have considered class to be an important component. An emphasis on the overlap between class and ethnic divisions is found in pluralist approaches (Smooha, 1978), as well as in internal colonialism and dependency theories (Blauner, 1972; Hechter, 1975; Zureik, 1979). Some Marxist writers have pointed to ethnic divisions within classes as a hindrance to class consciousness and solidarity. It has been argued that

21

capitalists have encouraged or sharpened ethnic differences in order to divide the proletariat and obtain cheap labor (Cox, 1948). The split-market approach has pointed to the existence of two labor markets; the working class of the dominant ethnic group obtain higher wages and more secure work than the subordinate ethnic group, and they reinforce their privileges by excluding the latter from their unions (Bonacich, 1972).

We have already noted that the relationships between ethnic groups and classes or socio-economic strata vary greatly empirically. Where class and ethnic divisions crosscut each other and are clearly differentiated, the relative importance of class and ethnic allegiances and consciousness are also likely to vary. It would be a mistake to assume that this is simply a matter of the relative importance of material as opposed to ideal interests, or of economic interests as opposed to cultural concerns. An ethnic group may have economic interests, such as the benefits from an affirmative action program, regardless of the class position of its members (Thompson, 1983). Class and ethnic identities may be held simultaneously, and one need not necessarily suppress the other. Each may be activated according to situational exigencies (Goyder, 1983). It makes little sense, therefore, to make generalizations that reduce ethnicity to class interests, or to assume that ethnic allegiance and consciousness will always be more important than class allegiance and consciousness.

There are far more general discussions of the relationships between class and ethnicity than there are of the relationships between ethnicity and religion (Enloe, 1976, is an exception). Religion is, however, considered to be one of the most important symbolic foci that provide bases for ethnicity. The others are language, territory, and color. One of these attributes is rarely sufficient in itself to sustain an ethnic group, and ethnicity is likely to involve a cluster of attributes rather than a single cultural characteristic, but in many cases religion largely determines the maintenance, expression, and mobilization of ethnicity.

Although the world religions crosscut many national and ethnic divisions, there are few ethnic groups which are divided by different religious traditions. An exception is the Czechs who, despite the Catholic–Protestant division, maintain a strong sense of ethnicity. But if religious divisions are not necessarily expressed ethnically, cases where two ethnic groups confess different religions are among the most conflictual and deadly. The religious differences may be based on entirely different traditions, such as Islam and Christianity in Lebanon, and Islam and Hinduism in India, or there may be different streams within a world religion, such as Protestant and Catholic in Northern Ireland. The religious differences in Israel between Jews and Arabs, most of whom are Muslim, are clearly of great importance.

The case of Israeli-Jewish groups has been seen as an example of the existence of ethnic boundaries where religion is a constant (Enloe, 1976). There is, of course, an essential tie between Judaism and the Jewish people, and there are very few Israelis who both identify as Jewish and confess a non-Jewish religion. Moreover, the dominant form of Judaism in Israel among all groups of origin is Orthodoxy; the two largest Jewish denominations in the United States, Conservative and Reform Judaism, are very small in Israel and are associated with comparatively recent immigrants from English-speaking countries, especially the United States. This does not mean, however, that religion is an insignificant factor in ethnic differences among Israeli-Jewish groups. Different orientations toward the religious tradition as well as subcultural religious differences, such as specific religious customs, festivals, and prayer styles, are important components of the ethnic differences among the Israeli-Jewish population.

Thus, ethnicity overlaps, crosscuts, and interacts in complex ways with both classes and religious differentiation. In this study we focus on the interrelationships of the three cleavages in Israeli society. Our major primary source of data is a sample of the Israeli-Jewish population, but in the penultimate chapter we incorporate a discussion of the Jewish-Arab ethnonational cleavage, and in the final chapter we make some tentative suggestions as to how all these cleavages may be analyzed within a single conceptual framework.

2

Divisions in Israeli society

More than forty years after its establishment as a state, Israel may still be considered the youngest society in the world because nearly 40% of its Jewish citizens were not born in the country. No single group from a particular country or origin is dominant demographically. The largest group of origin is the Moroccans; the Moroccan first and second generation make up 13% of the population. They are followed by the Russians, Poles, Rumanians, and Iraqis (each group comprising 7% to 8%). Various other groups, such as the Yemenites, Germans, and Hungarians each account for between 2% and 5% of the population, while still others, such as the Bulgarians and the Greeks, reach only 1% or 2%. Israel's English, French, or North American Jews number even less. Of the Jewish population, 21% is third generation or more, and Jews of eastern European descent are likely to be the largest group in the adult section of this category.

The Israeli-Jewish ethnic landscape is an intricate one, but it has been simplified (and often oversimplified) by collapsing the various groups into two broad categories: Ashkenazim, who came mainly from European countries, and Mizrachim or *edot ha'Mizrach*, who came from North African and Asian countries. The term "Ashkenaz" came to be applied by Jews in medieval times to Germany, and Jews originating from there were called Ashkenazim. The major distinction that came to be made among European Jews was between Ashkenazim, the Jews of western, central, and eastern Europe, and Sephardim, the Jews of the Iberian Peninsula. Today, the term "Sephardim," used in its most strict sense, refers to the descendants of the Spanish Jews who left the Iberian Peninsula from the time of the expulsion of Jews from Spain in 1492. Many of the Jews in Spain and Portugal who avoided death or expulsion by converting to Christianity later fled those countries and returned to Judaism. Some Sephardim settled in major European cities, especially in Italy, the south of France, Hamburg, and Amsterdam, but the majority settled in the Ottoman Empire where they came to have a dominant cultural influence on a number of Jewish communities, including many in North Africa, Palestine, and the Balkans. The term "Sephardim" may, therefore, be used to refer to all Jewish communities that came under the Sephardic cultural influence or adopted the Sephardic religious forms and style. However, in popular Israeli parlance, the term is often used to refer to all non-Ashkenazim.

In state publications of censuses and other statistical reports, the Jewish population is usually categorized according to continent of origin: European and American origins are grouped together; Asian and African origins are sometimes listed separately but are more often grouped together. These statistics are often used to represent the demographic, economic, and social profiles of "Ashkenazim" and "Mizrachim" or "Sephardim." This categorization may ignore the exceptions: Jews from South Africa are Ashkenazim, and Jews from the European Balkans are mostly Sephardim. These exceptions are numerically small, and the broad statistical division does give a rough approximation of the profiles of Ashkenazim and Mizrachim.

Other terms used to make a dichotomous classification also have problems. The term "Afro-Asians" has occasionally been used for Jews born in North Africa and Asia, but it conveys inappropriate racial connotations. "Oriental" has been the most commonly used term in the English literature to refer to Mizrachim, but the term often has negative connotations, and its opposite "Occidental" is hardly an appropriate term for Israeli Ashkenazim, most of whom are from eastern Europe. In this work, when we wish to make a broad distinction in terms of origin, we will refer to Europeans (most American immigrants to Israel are descendants of European Jews) and Middle Easterners (the Middle East is understood to include North Africa). However, when we refer to respondents' identifications and opinions regarding these categories, we will use the terms Ashkenazim and *edot ha'Mizrach*. These terms are common in every day parlance in Israel and we used them in our questionnaires.

The appropriateness of a dichotomous classification of the Israeli-Jewish population will be questioned in this study with respect to a number of ethnic dimensions, but the distinction between European and Middle Eastern Israeli Jews does pertain to a number of broad historical, demographic, and socio-economic differences. Historical differences in the patterns of migration of Jews from Europe and the Middle East have had important social repercussions. The motives of migration to the Land of Israel and the cultural and socio-economic characteristics of immigrants have changed from those during the period of the "Old Yishuv" (Old Settlement), to those of the "New

Yishuv," beginning in the 1880s, and to those after the founding of the State of Israel.

For centuries small numbers of Jews migrated to the Land of Israel, primarily for religious reasons. The Old Yishuv was a religious community, devoted to religious prayer and study, and dependent financially on the contributions from the diaspora communities. Up to the middle of the nineteenth century, the Sephardim made up the majority of the Jewish population in Palestine, but they came to be outnumbered by religiously inspired Ashkenazi immigrants, some of whom migrated to the Holy Land in order to escape the secular trends in Europe. It was the Ashkenazi community that created the basic patterns of ultra-Orthodox Judaism in Palestine; they did not have to concern themselves with making a living, and this enabled them to maintain a way of life that was resistent to worldly matters and secular influences. A higher proportion of the Sephardim of the Old Yishuv were engaged in trade or worked as artisans and, conversant as they were with the Arabic language and culture, they were far more integrated in the wider milieu. Many Sephardim subsequently integrated into the New Yishuv (Abramov, 1976; Eliav, 1982).

What came to be known as the New Yishuv was founded by Jews from eastern Europe whose *aliyah* (ascent, referring to immigration to the Land of Israel) was motivated by Zionism, a secular Jewish nationalism. During the emergence of the New Yishuv there was some migration of Jews from Muslim countries, such as the messianically inspired migrations of Yemenite Jews at the end of the nineteenth century (Klorman-Eraqi, 1981), but they were neither integrated into the Old Yishuv nor into the New. Although radically different in their cultures and ideologies, the Old and New Yishuv represented the cultural expressions of eastern European Jews.

The Jewish population of Palestine numbered less than 25,000 in 1880. It reached 85,000 by 1914, declined during World War I, and was back to 85,000 in 1922. A large proportion of the immigrants during this period were idealistic pioneers from Russia. The settlers of the first *aliyah* (1882–1903) wished to create a society based on social justice and Jewish labor, but they became conventional farmers, often employing Arab labor, and they came to enjoy a comfortable living by Palestinian standards. Far more important in the development of the New Yishuv were the second (1904–14) and third (1919–23) *aliyot* which included many individuals and groups who wished to fuse Zionism and various forms of Socialism. They rejected the "bourgeois" and traditional religious life of the diaspora Jewish communities from which they came, and they saw themselves as pioneers of an entirely different Jewish society to be based on a life of labor in the Land of Israel. These "founders" established agricultural settlements, especially the *kibbutzim*, the various Socialist-Zionist political parties, the self-defence forces, and the Histadrut, the Federation of Labor, which combined trade-union activities, building and industry, banking and insurance, marketing, transport, housing, and various social services.

The restriction on immigration to the United States, imposed by the American government in the early 1920s, and the worsening situation of the Jews in Poland meant that "push" factors were more important than "pull" factors among the 82,000 immigrants of the fourth *aliyah* (1924–31), half of whom came from Poland. "Push" factors continued to be important in the fifth *aliyah* (1932–6) of about 200,000; over 15% were from Germany, but Polish Jews continued to be the largest immigrant group. The majority in these *aliyot* wished to continue the urban, "middle-class" life that they had known in the diaspora. The stratum of merchants, artisans, shopkeepers, teachers, and other professionals from eastern Europe was reinforced by the German immigrants, some of whom brought considerable capital and helped to develop trade and industry on a larger scale. Thus, a private sector or capitalist mode of production, with accompanying values emphasizing individual achievement and private consumption, developed alongside the socialist and public modes of production. Interrelationships among these sectors, especially public-sector aid for private-sector industry, developed in the 1930s and 1940s, and increased considerably after the establishment of the state. This was accompanied by a decline in the revolutionary zeal of the immigrants from the earlier *aliyot* (Eisenstadt, 1985; Friedlander and Goldscheider, 1979; Shapiro, 1977; Ben Porat, 1986).

During the period of the British mandate, only 10% of Jewish immigrants came from Asia and Africa, and at the time of Independence Jews of Middle Eastern origin made up from 10% to 15% of the total Jewish population of 630,000. This demographic ratio began to change radically with the mass immigration that started on the eve of Independence and continued for four years. Nearly 700,000 immigrants arrived in Israel in the first three and a half years (1948–51) following statehood, half from Europe (the majority continued to come from eastern Europe), and half from Asia and Africa. The yearly number of immigrants never again came close to the immediate post-Independence years, but after a lull from 1952 to 1954 there was a renewal of mass immigration; in 1955 to 1957 (over 160,000 mostly from Morocco, Tunisia, and Poland), and again from 1961 to 1964 (215,000, especially from Morocco and Rumania).

Today, Jews of North African and Asian origins constitute about half of the 3,695,000 Jewish population in Israel.

The fact that Jewish immigrants from the Middle East entered a society that was dominated, demographically and socially, by Jews of European origins suggests that Gordon's (1964) terminology of acculturation and assimilation of immigrants or minorities to a "host" society may be applicable to the Israeli case. However, some observers have objected to a framework in which "Oriental" immigrants are described as acculturating and assimilating to a western society. They point out that the majority of European immigrants came from eastern Europe, and that many immigrants from North Africa and Asia had been influenced by the cultures of western colonial powers, especially France and Britain. Nevertheless, it cannot be denied that there were important differences in cultural background between the two broad categories of immigrants, especially with respect to the relative importance of religion. Although prior to the Holocaust and the Communist takeovers eastern Europe was the center of traditionalist Judaism in Europe, the process of secularization was well advanced among most of the European immigrants before they arrived in Palestine or Israel. The rebellion against traditional religion, which had been common among the immigrants of the second and third *aliyot*, was not important among later immigrants from Europe, but most eastern European survivors of the Holocaust who arrived after the establishment of the state came from countries whose communist regimes and socio-economic changes contributed to the further decline of Jewish religious life. In comparison, there were some communities from North Africa and Asia whose traditional religious life remained substantially intact prior to their immigration. Among other communities, secularization had made some inroads, but it was minor in comparison with the European communities.

Israeli sociologists differ somewhat over their evaluations of the extent to which cultural differences among groups of origin have persisted, but they appear to agree that the acculturation of Middle Eastern Jews to the dominant culture of European Jews has been more extensive than their assimilation. In the terminology of pluralism, cultural pluralism is less today than social pluralism. The dominant Israeli culture was developed by eastern European Jews, and although it may differ in a number of important respects from western culture (Lotan, 1983), the influence of western, especially American, cultural styles has far exceeded those of the Middle East (Benski, 1988). The adoption of Middle Eastern Jewish culture by European Israelis has been confined mainly to some kinds of food, a partly Sephardic pronunciation of Hebrew, some styles of jewelry and embroidery, and some musical influence (Smooha, 1978: 185).

The cultural dominance of European Israelis takes mainly secular forms, but it is also expressed in the religious sphere. Differences in religious services among the *edot* and between Ashkenazim and Sephardim are recognized as legitimate, but a standardized prayer style that was required for state institutions and public ceremonies was adopted. The form of prayer commonly used in Israeli public institutions such as the army and the religious state schools was influenced by Kabbalists of mainly Sephardi extraction living in Palestine in the sixteenth century, but it was adopted and developed in the eighteenth century among the Hasidim of eastern Europe, and it became common among Ashkenazi communities. It differs considerably from the styles of prayer of most communities from Asia and North Africa which are preserved, with some modification, in the ethnic synagogues (Stahl, 1976).

Middle Eastern Israeli groups have varied considerably in their levels of acculturation. Some Yemenite groups, for example, have retained highly distinctive cultural features, and certain practices, such as Yemenite music and dance, have become more popular among them in recent years (Loeb, 1985; H. Lewis, 1984). Nevertheless, most Middle Eastern groups have acculturated extensively to western culture, and this is particularly evident in the changes in family structures and size. The patriarchal extended family has been replaced by the nuclear type; a large proportion of Middle Eastern women has entered the job market, and the average number of children has declined from twice that of European women in the 1950s to only one-tenth more in 1980 (Smooha 1978: 113–14; Hartman, 1980; Nahon, 1984b). The average level of religious observance among Middle Eastern Israelis continues to be higher than among European Israelis and there are continuing subcultural differences in religious customs, but acculturation has meant secularization and the level of synagogue attendance and religious observance in the home has declined dramatically from the first generation to the second (Deshen, 1980; Shokeid, 1985; Goldscheider and Friedlander, 1983).

In recent years some Middle Easterners have emphasized the right of each *edah* to retain its own culture, but there has been little conscious attempt to reinforce or cultivate a separate cultural style. Ethnic pride has been expressed in ethnic festivals, such as the *mimuna* of the Moroccans, and in pilgrimages to the tombs of saints (Goldberg, 1978; Deshen and Shokeid, 1974). The rise in the popularity of these occasions over the last decade or so has been interpreted as a demonstration of the rise in social status of these groups, and their feelings of security after becoming part of the dominant Israeli culture. The erosion of distinctive ethnic cultures does not necessarily mean that Israeli culture is becoming entirely homogeneous. Weingrod (1979) has suggested that there has been a development of a working-class culture that encompasses both blue-collar and the lower ranks of white-collar workers. The majority of the working class are Middle Easterners, but Weingrod sees the emergent working-class culture cutting across ethnic lines. The culture, which includes a focus of the males on soccer, certain types of popular songs, and distinctive clothing styles, is emerging in working-class neighborhoods where there is a continuity of generations; kin live nearby, and the young have had similar experiences in schools, the army, and work contexts.

Turning to social pluralism, there is no formal or secondary pluralism of Jews of different origins in the economy, the national and local government bureaucracies and agencies, the labor unions, the educational system, and the army. The political system is also, for the most part, non-pluralist, but provisions were made in the past by the major parties for sections based on the *edot*. Until the appearance of Shas in the 1980s, ethnic lists and parties were unsuccessful or short-lived (Herzog, 1984). Institutional integration is legitimized by the ideology of *mizug ha'galuyot* (fusion of the exiles), an amalgamation of all Jewish communities from the different countries of the diaspora. The single institutional area where ethnically based pluralism has been legitimized and widely accepted is religion; there are legal provisions for a dual Rabbinate, Ashkenazi and Sephardi, and many religious congregations are largely homogeneous in either their country or continental origins.

Although there is little institutional social pluralism, there is considerable social distance between large proportions of Europeans and Middle Easterners with respect to their residential distribution and primary relationships. Middle Easterners are not concentrated in a single contiguous area, but ethnic concentrations in a number of areas and towns were created by the implementation, in the 1950s and early 1960s, of a state policy that was intended to meet security demands and avoid congestion of the labor market by dispersing immigrants to small and medium-sized "development" towns and settlements in the peripheral and frontier regions of the country (Spilerman and Habib, 1976).

The ecological concentration of immigrant and ethnic groups is a common phenomenon and occurred in Israel among both European and Middle Eastern groups. After 1948, Polish, Rumanian, and other eastern European groups established ethnic neighborhoods in the cities, but these dissolved in the early 1960s with the move of Israeli Jews of mainly

European origins to the new suburbs. In comparison, a number of Middle Eastern groups, such as the Yemenites and Kurds, have remained ecologically distinct. Apart from these country of origin concentrations, there are differences between the two broad categories, European and Middle Eastern, in their residential distributions. The most prosperous neighborhoods, which include both inner-city zones and higher status suburbs, are predominantly European; the areas of lower socio-economic status where Middle Easterners make up the great majority are located, as a result of public housing policy, on the periphery of the cities. There are a number of "intermediate zones," built in areas between the older parts of the cities and the public housing areas, where there is considerable ethnic heterogeneity (Gonen, 1985).

Community and residential separation leads to *de facto* separation in schools, especially at the primary school level. Secondary schools draw from larger areas, and in a number of cases, where new garden suburbs with European majorities are located close to the older estates with Middle Eastern majorities, secondary schools are ethnically heterogeneous. A few studies have shown, however, that closer ethnic contact in schools and neighborhoods has not resulted in extensive interaction at the primary group level. Ethnic preferences continue and ethnic boundaries remain with respect to the more intimate relationships (Smooha, 1978: 126–30). Extensive interethnic contacts occur within the framework of the army, but these rarely become permanent (Roumani, 1979).

A common observation made in Israel is that the rising percentage of marriages between Middle Easterners and Europeans is clear evidence of a trend toward social integration. Marriages between the two broad categories increased, as a percentage of all marriages, from 9% in 1957 to 24% in 1985, but the increase has been slow over the last decade. Taking grooms of the first and second generation from North Africa or Asia who married wives of the first and second generation between 1975 and 1979, 16% married wives of European or American origins. The proportion increased to 19% in 1980–4, and was 17% in 1986. Of first and second generation grooms of European or American origins, 24% married wives of African or Asian origins in 1975–9. The proportion increased to 29% in 1980–4 and 34% in 1986 (Central Bureau of Statistics, 1988). We see here an example of the common phenomenon of a greater intermarriage rate between grooms from high-status ethnic groups and spouses from low-status ethnic groups than between low-status grooms and high-status spouses. It should be borne in mind that the proportion of potential marriage partners from each broad ethnic category is now about half of the total, so that the current intermarriage rate is approaching half of the figure whereby ethnic origin would be irrelevant in the choice of marriage partners.

The extent of social pluralism with respect to such dimensions as residential distribution and primary group relations is closely related to the socio-economic stratification of ethnic categories. In the Israeli-Jewish context, a decline in socio-economic inequality would be expected to increase ethnic assimilation or integration. There have been many studies of ethnic inequality in Israel, but the implications of the findings for ethnicity and ethnic relationships are by no means clear-cut and have been subject to divergent interpretations.

The general picture is one of socio-economic progress and mobility of all Jewish groups of origin, but with respect to most dimensions of inequality, little change in the overall gap between the broad European and Middle Eastern categories. There has been a decline in inequality in average income. The average income of Middle Eastern families as a percentage of the average income of European families increased from 65% in 1956–8 to 80% in 1978–80. There has been little change since the late 1970s; the figure in 1985 for Middle Easterners was 80.7%. Within the category of Israelis who immigrated to Israel between the years 1955 to 1964, the average income in 1985 of those from Europe and America was 97.3% of the base, and those from Africa and Asia, 77.1%. Per capita the inequality is somewhat greater because the average size of Middle Eastern families is still larger, but the decline of family size has meant greater equality as measured by the number of persons per room: while there was an average of 4.5 persons per room in Middle Eastern households in 1956 (compared with 2.7 for European households), the figure in 1987 was 1.2, much closer to the European 0.8. Inequality is still very evident when the top and lowest income levels are examined; the proportion of Europeans in the highest income decimile is four times that of Middle Easterners, and the ratio is reversed in the lowest income decimile (Central Bureau of Statistics, 1988).

Studies of occupational distribution and mobility have shown that there has been pronounced intergenerational mobility within the Middle Eastern category, but that the index of dissimilarity or overall differences in occupational status between the two broad categories has not narrowed. In both categories there has been mobility from blue-collar to white-collar work, but in the European category there has been far greater mobility into the higher white-collar ranks (Matras, 1985; Nahon, 1984). The top occupational category of "professionals, academics, and technologists" has expanded from nearly 10% of all employees in 1961 to nearly 20% today, but whereas a third of employees whose fathers were born in Europe or America are found in this category, only about 12% of employees whose fathers were born in Africa or Asia are in this category. A similar gap is found in the "administrators and managers" category. These gaps are wider within the second generation than within the first. And whereas only a fifth of employees with fathers from Europe or America are blue-collar workers, nearly half the employees with fathers from Asia or Africa are blue-collar workers. Again, the gap is wider in the second generation than in the first. In the clerical and sales occupations, there is no significant difference between the ethnic categories, either in the first or the second generation (Central Bureau of Statistics, 1988). It has been suggested that the self-employment and employer sectors of the labor market have provided an alternative mobility track for Middle Eastern Israelis (Yuchtman-Yaar, 1986), and occupational dissimilarity between the two ethnic categories is less for independents than it is for employees, but even among independents the gap in the second generation is greater than in the first (Nahon, 1984).

More than a third of Israelis from the Middle East may now be judged to be part of the middle class, but the index of occupational dissimilarity between the two broad categories has remained stable since 1960, and this remains true after age is controlled. Although there has been an increase in the proportion of Middle Easterners in the highest occupational stratum, the ethnic gap in this stratum has grown especially within the second generation (Nahon, 1984). The gap in educational level has narrowed, but it has remained considerable in higher education. In 1961, 61% of those aged fourteen and over with fathers born in Africa and Asia had less than nine years of education; in 1981, the percentage had dropped to 17.5%. The respective figures for those with fathers born in Europe or America were 15.8% in 1961 and 5.2% in 1981 (Ginor, 1983). Middle Easterners have typically been assigned to the vocational tracks rather than the academic tracks in the secondary schools, and this has further reduced the likelihood of them going on into higher education (Shavit, 1984). Those with fathers born in Asia and Africa who had thirteen years or more of education increased from 4.5% in 1961 to 11.6% in 1981; the respective increase for those with fathers born in Europe or America was from 19.7% to 41.8%.

Studies have shown that income, occupational, and educational differences remain between the ethnic categories after controls are made for socio-economic family origins, age, and length of time in Israel (Fishelson *et al.*, 1980; Matras and Weintraub, 1977; Matras and Tyree, 1977; Body, Featherman and Matras, 1980; Hartman and Ayalon, 1975; Nahon, 1984; Semyonov and Tyree, 1981; Rosenstein, 1981; Adler and Hodge, 1983;

Smooha and Kraus, 1985). Discrimination may be a factor here, but the control factors, such as parental background variables, do not account entirely for the differences in achievement within the ethnic categories. There are further attributes which have not been measured in the studies of mobility, such as quality of education and type of experience in the labor market, that may account for the differences between the ethnic categories (Fishelson *et al.*, 1980). Place of residence – especially the difference between the urban center and the urban periphery – has also a strong ethnically differential effect on mobility (Weintraub and Kraus, 1982).

The socio-economic or class distributions of the ethnic categories, whether measured by income, occupation, or education, no doubt account in part for the differences in ethnic status or prestige that are attributed to the ethnic groups. A number of studies, conducted in the 1960s, found that not just Europeans but also Middle Easterners preferred (after their own particular *edah*) the Europeans to Middle Easterners as neighbors or spouses (Peres, 1971, 1976; Shuval, 1962). A recent study of the preferences expressed by a sample of schoolchildren towards vignettes portraying people from European and Middle Eastern origin and of middle and lower socio-economic status found that, once class images were controlled, ethnic preferences disappeared (Rofe and Weller, 1981). However, a much larger study – using a vignette design – of the adult population found that there are prejudicial attitudes specifically related to ethnic origins beyond those that adhere to other factors, such as socio-economic status, recent immigration, and cultural deprivation. Middle Easterners were not found to prefer their own group socially, but Europeans expressed social distance from Middle Easterners even when the socio-economic status of the European and Middle Easterners' vignettes were held constant (Schwartz *et al.*, 1989).

Differences in ethnic status were clearly brought out by a study by Kraus (1982) when respondents were asked to grade a number of origin groups according to their "social standing." The findings pointed to a mainly bimodal hierarchy of ethnic prestige: there was a wide consensus that all groups of European origin have a higher prestige than all groups of North African and Asian origin. Kraus found that, although there were high correlations between the groups' ethnic prestige and their mean levels of education and occupational prestige, there was also a high correlation with the cultural backgrounds of the groups. She concluded that the prestige hierarchy of ethnic groups expresses the broad stereotypes of cultural and socio-economic background.

There has also been striking inequality in the political sphere; Europeans, especially eastern Europeans, have provided the great majority of leaders and top positions in government, the political parties, the Zionist organizations, and the Histadrut. There has been a long-term trend of greater Middle Eastern representation, but up to recent years this was far more evident at the local government levels than at the national level (Yishai, 1984).

Feelings of discrimination and deprivation among Middle Easterners led them to withdraw their electoral support from the "establishment" party of the Labor alignment which had dominated every government until 1977. Interpreting their social plight in terms of ethnic relations ("What the Ashkenazim have done to us") rather than class relations, they did not develop a leftist or "proletarian" consciousness, neither did they, in the main, transfer their support to ethnic parties. Ethnic parties have had some limited success in recent years, but this has been primarily among religious voters. Tami, a split from the National Religious Party, entered the Knesset with three members in the 1981 elections, obtained one seat in 1984, and its representative joined the Likud for the 1988 elections. Shas, a split from the ultra-Orthodox Agudat Yisrael party, won four seats in 1984 and six in 1988. The representatives of these parties constituted only a minority of the Knesset members of Middle Eastern origins. Most Middle Eastern voters have transferred their support from the Ma'arach (Labor Alignment) to the right-wing Likud, a predominantly Ashkenazi party but one that, like the Middle Easterners, had been outside the "establishment" for many years. The result is that the Ma'arach and the Likud have now about equal strength in the Knesset, and both parties have sought the support of the electorate of Middle Eastern origins by increasing their representation on the party lists. The number of Knesset members of Middle Eastern origins increased from fifteen (out of a total of 120) in 1971 to thirty-nine in 1988. The number of Middle Eastern ministers grew from two in the pre-1977 government to eight in 1987. There has also been an increase of Middle Easterners in central positions in the Histadrut, diplomacy, and the civil service. An appeal to the electorate of Middle Eastern origins was evident in the "Project Renewal" that directed resources to poor, predominantly Middle Eastern neighborhoods, and school programs now place greater emphasis on the cultural legacies of Middle Eastern *edot*. However, these politically inspired concessions have had as yet little effect on the socio-economic gaps between European and Middle Eastern Israelis.

3

Theoretical perspectives in Israeli sociology

A major focus of sociology in Israel has been ethnic differences and assimilation within the Israeli-Jewish population. Almost all studies investigating inequality or the class structure have dealt with ethnicity, and the same is true of studies on religiosity. Publications on ethnic differences and ethnicity among Jews (Smooha, 1987) have far outnumbered those on other important research topics such as the Arab minority and religion in Israel. This focus is understandable given the basic assumption among Israeli Jews that Israel is first and foremost a Jewish state, and the dominant ideology of the "ingathering" and "merging" of Jews from different parts of the world. Much of the theoretical debate on ethnicity in Israel has revolved around the question of the distance between the ideology of ethnic amalgamation and the ethnic reality. This has not always been an explicit issue, but it provides an important part of the background of the differences among the theoretical perspectives to be outlined below.

The four general perspectives on ethnicity outlined in the first chapter have had their Israeli representatives, and they have appeared roughly in that order: the perspectives focusing on ethnic adaptation and socio-psychological aspects were followed by a conflictual pluralistic approach, and then by a perspective which emphasized the class basis of ethnic differences. The proponents of the last two perspectives presented them as alternatives, and in opposition to, the former approaches to ethnicity in Israel. The meanings and explanations of ethnic differences among Israeli Jews remain topics of considerable controversy among sociologists. In some cases, proponents of certain perspectives have modified their positions in response to the challenge of other approaches, but this is not always acknowledged.

The first major perspective on Jewish ethnicity in Israel was associated with S. N. Eisenstadt who, together with a number of his colleagues and students, focused on the absorption and modernization of immigrants, especially those from Asia and North Africa. In his book, *Israeli Society* (1967), Eisenstadt wrote that, "it is the encounter between the new immigrants and the institutional structure rooted in the pioneering ideology that constitutes the central theme of our analysis" (p. 6). In Eisenstadt's historical model of the development of Israeli society, the early stage of the New Yishuv is presented as a society with a general value consensus and little socio-economic differentiation or conflict. The historical point of departure for Eisenstadt's analysis is the values and ideologies of the first modern immigrants or pioneers who settled in Palestine at the end of the nineteenth century and the first decades of the twentieth century. The image of the pioneers and their common focus of identity included self-sacrifice for the future of the collectivity, manual work, especially in agriculture, as a major way to rejuvenate the nation, and a renewal of the Hebrew language and culture. The consensus among the pioneers meant that there was less division and tension than in other modernizing societies, and the influence of the pioneering ideology penetrated all the major institutions and groups, such as the educational system and the youth movement.

Adherence to the symbols of pioneering intensified in the early phase of the Israeli state, but with the development of socio-economic differentiation, contradictions began to appear between the pioneering ideology and the specialization and individualism of a more complex and differentiated social structure. Eisenstadt's detailed analysis of the changes in the economic, political, cultural, and educational institutions need not concern us here. What is pertinent is that the mass immigration, especially of Jews from Asia and North Africa, from the late 1940s through the 1950s and early 1960s, is presented as one entering a society that had been greatly influenced by the pioneering ideology and was ruled by a somewhat transformed pioneering elite; this society, however, had become highly differentiated with features typical of western industrial societies (Eisenstadt, 1967, 1970).

Eisenstadt (1955) presented a model of migration in which he distinguished between three stages: the motivation to migrate which includes both "push" factors, such as insecurity and lack of opportunities in the country of origin, and "pull" factors or expectations of the new society; the process of migration which involves a narrowing of the migrants' social participation; and absorption of immigrants within the socio-cultural framework of the new society. In the third stage the immigrant learns a language, norms, and appropriate roles, experiences changes in primary groups, and develops values and aspirations compatible with those of the new society. Immigrants undergo a process of resocialization in which there is a change in their self-definition and identity.

Eisenstadt (1955, 1967, 1970) focused on the third stage, on the

37

"absorption" or "integration" of immigrants, which was related to the process of modernization. The dominant framework was that of the modernization of traditional immigrants within an essentially modern society. Israel was in an almost unique situation because, unlike most cases of modern migration, where the forces of modern economic and political processes were brought by immigrants to the traditional native groups, in Israel it was traditional immigrants who came to a relatively modern society. Eisenstadt wrote that, "the immigrant encountered an economic and social structure which, within its limited range, evinced most of the characteristics of a modern technological economy. It was based on specialization, technical division of labor, general universalistic orientations, and a market economy" (1970: 112). The immigrants, in contrast, had traditional characteristics such as the importance of extended kinship relations, deference to traditional authority, a relatively non-differentiated economic structure, and an ascriptive social hierarchy. The social structures of the immigrant groups from North Africa and Asia varied in their levels of differentiation, but all tended to have traditionalist orientations: particularism, ascription, diffuseness, and a strong collectivity orientation.

The differences between the immigrants and the absorbing society meant that the immigrants had a number of adjustment problems, such as learning new social skills, becoming more future-oriented, and participating in democracy. Some factors in the absorbing structure impeded the process of absorption. These included the allocation of services without consideration of the immigrants' productivity which limited incentive to work, and the dependence of immigrants on bureaucratic agencies which resulted in many cases in passivity and apathy. Other factors facilitated absorption. The social security provided by the absorbing institutions as well as new environments, such as *moshavim* (cooperative agricultural communities) and local workers' committees, enabled many immigrants to acquire new skills and develop new attitudes. Eisenstadt argued that the absorbing organization should be flexible and take into account the characteristics of immigrants, because it was important not to destroy the family and intergenerational relations.

The emphasis on the relationship between absorption and modernization was often accompanied by the argument that there is no pluralistic tendency among the Jewish population in Israel. Joseph Ben-David (1953) wrote that there is no ethnic diversity among Israeli Jews in the sense of different cultural systems. Israeli Jews constituted one society with a common cultural orientation, and only on the margins of the society was there a number of groups which had not yet been absorbed in it. There was a need, therefore, to direct attention to social change and not to ethnic differences.

Rivka Bar-Yosef (1968) wrote that pluralism was relevant to the relations between Jews and non-Jews in Israel but that, "Israeli-Jewish society never in any sense presented a picture of a pluralistic society." Among Israeli Jews there was a feeling of nationwide solidarity, a sense of collective identity, and a consensus of the basic values. With regard to the immigrants from Asia and North Africa, it was impossible to distinguish between the processes of absorption and modernization. She noted that Israel in the early 1950s was not an industrial society comparable to the advanced industrial societies, but from the perspective of the immigrants, Israel was a relatively modern society. Following Eisenstadt, Bar-Yosef described the process of resocialization as well as the problems of adjustment of the immigrants. Bar-Yosef (1970) wrote that the riots of immigrants in the Wadi Salib area of Haifa in 1959 stemmed from the gap between expectations and reality among Jews from Morocco. In Morocco they had been part of a "transitional society" in which some had moved into white-collar work but others had held marginal positions. Many had seen migration to Israel as a solution to their problems, but they had been frustrated by their low status and perceptions of downward mobility. Further adjustment was required, and it was implied in the "absorption through modernization" perspective that this would be achieved.

The socio-psychological approach, which directs attention to prejudice and attitudinal measures of social distance, has not challenged the "absorption through modernization" approach, but has extended the discussion of the cultural orientations that either impede or encourage absorption. Studies in the 1950s and 1960s found that, not only did large proportions of European Jews have reservations about Middle Eastern Jews as neighbors or marriage partners, but Middle Easterners themselves tended also to prefer Europeans over other Middle Eastern groups. Expressions of prejudice among Middle Easterners against other Middle Eastern groups were almost as strong as the prejudice of Europeans against Middle Easterners. At the same time, all groups emphasized the common historical roots of all Jews, and the majority both expected and expressed support for the reduction of ethnic differences (Peres, 1971, 1976; Shuval, 1956, 1962).

The first major challenge to the "absorption through modernization" approach within academic sociology in Israel came from Sammy Smooha whose book, *Israel: Pluralism and Conflict*, appeared in 1978. Smooha made a number of criticisms of the absorption–modernization model, but perhaps his major theoretical criticism was the neglect of considerations of power. In addition, Smooha noted that the tendency had been to study prejudice rather than discrimination, and that the deeper ideological sources of prejudice had been ignored.

Smooha presented the perspective of pluralism as an alternative to the absorption–modernization approach. His pluralist perspective was, however, more a set of loosely linked concepts than a theory or a model that would generate hypotheses or suggest explanations. The concepts of cultural pluralism, social pluralism, socio-historical setting, inequality, cohesion, conflict, and change were applied as a framework to organize a large amount of data on relationships between European and Middle Eastern Jews, between religious and secular Jews, and between Jews and Arabs in Israel. The relationships of Europeans and Middle Easterners were characterized by subcultural rather than core-cultural differences and by significant social separation in personal rather than impersonal frameworks, although residential concentrations also resulted in separation in the school system. Smooha emphasized the socio-economic gaps between Europeans and Middle Easterners, but he noted that power disparities were even more substantial. These differences were seen against the background of an initial group contact in which mainly poor immigrants from underdeveloped countries had come to a country that had an already established European group, but he suggested that the Europeans built on their initial advantages through their control over the distribution of resources and their discriminatory practices.

Smooha presented a "dynamic paternalism–co-optation model" of relations between Europeans and Middle Easterners. The Europeans viewed the Middle Easterners as a backward group who posed a threat to the western culture and political democracy of Israel. The intention behind the policies of absorption and modernization was to prevent "Orientalism" and to promote integration and equality. The occupational system was opened to Middle Easterners mainly at the lower middle and lower levels, and the entrance of the Middle Easterners into the system made possible the upward mobility of the Europeans. Over the years, however, the Europeans have become less fearful of cultural dangers and political instability, the Middle Easterners have increasingly entered the middle class, and there has been some transition to a liberal competitive system in which ethnicity has weakened, relationships between Europeans and Middle Easterners have improved, and class differences which crosscut the ethnic groups have become more prominent.

A more self-consciously radical alternative to absorption through modernization was presented by the class approach to ethnicity of the dependency theorists, and most comprehensively by Shlomo Swirski (1981) in his book on the ethnic division of labor between Middle Easterners and Europeans (see also, Bernstein, 1980, 1981; Bernstein and Swirski, 1982). Swirski wrote that Smooha's pluralist approach was an advance on Eisenstadt in so far as it put great emphasis on power, exploitation, and conflict, but Smooha had not developed an independent theoretical analysis that could account for the formation of, and changes in, the pluralist situation. Smooha had not clarified why he had chosen particular concepts, and in many cases he had simply substituted different terms for concepts from the absorption through modernization approach; for example, the term "educational gap" was substituted by "pluralism of educational institutions." Smooha had emphasized that, despite the conflict between them, the pluralism of relationships of Europeans and Middle Easterners was narrowing, but he had not provided an alternative explanation of the process of integration and absorption. Swirski presented a dependency theory with its emphasis on the ethnic division of labor as a framework that, unlike pluralism, could provide alternative explanations of ethnic inequality and consciousness in Israel.

Swirski argues that the prevalent ideology in Israel of the scattered communities of Jews coming together in unity and brotherhood only serves to mask the true situation of ethnic division. The modernization approach is the sociological counterpart to this ideology, and is based on a number of false assumptions. One such assumption is that the basic essentials of modern society already existed in Israel at the time of the mass immigration from Asia and Africa, and that the immigrants entered the low ranks of a modern occupational structure. The sociologists working within the modernization perspective expected that the social mobility of immigrants and their diffusion throughout the occupational structure would follow their acculturation to western norms and values. In fact, Swirski argues, both the low and upper ranks of the modern occupational structure emerged during the period of immigration and the following years. He admits that economic growth was initiated by Zionist immigrants from Europe and that the development of capitalism was strengthened during the British mandate, but he emphasizes that, prior to the establishment of the state and the mass immigration, there were severe limitations on labor power, markets, and the accumulation of capital. In the first years of the state most industrial plants were small, with antiquated equipment, and there was a general lack of industrial expertise and of scientific and technological knowledge. It was the immigrants from Asia and Africa who made possible the rapid economic development from the middle 1950s; they provided a cheap, manipulable, and geographically mobile labor force.

The low position of Middle Easterners was not the consequence, as the modernization approach would have it, of their traditionalism or the fact that they came from non-industrial societies. A large proportion of European Israelis came from eastern Europe, from the periphery of world capitalism, and they entered the process of industrialization at the same time, or, at the most, one generation earlier than the Middle Easterners. The low rank of Middle Easterners was a consequence of their absorption within the process of rapid economic development, and it was in the same process that Europeans became owners, managers, and professionals.

Middle Easterners were dependent for work, housing, finance, and social services on institutions and organizations dominated by Europeans: private industry, the government, the Histadrut (General Federation of Labor in Israel), and the Jewish Agency. The policies and administration of these institutions served to reinforce the privileged position of Europeans and the inferior position of Middle Easterners. Political institutions played an important part in the ethnic division of labor, not so much because they were manned by Europeans, but because their desire to encourage investment and production led them to aid and support the owners and controllers of capital who were mostly Europeans.

The ethnic division of labor was accompanied by ecological separation, and it is here that Swirski draws upon the perspective of "internal colonialism" and uses the terms "center" and "periphery" to refer respectively to the large cities and the development towns. Of the population of the development towns 70% is of Middle Eastern origin, and in some development towns the percentage of Middle Easterners is 90% or more. A disproportionate number of Middle Eastern immigrants were sent by the state agencies to the development towns, and the majority of those who subsequently left for the urban centers were Europeans. The European managers and senior officers who live in development towns are found in separate neighborhoods, and in most cases they are connected to plants or offices that have their centers in the large cities.

Swirski deals with other aspects of ecological separation, such as the ethnic differences among wealthy and poor neighborhoods in the large cities, but the case of development towns is dealt with in most detail. He argues that the Europeans' center is the major beneficiary of the considerable state investments in development towns. The large corporations of the center own the biggest plants in the development towns; government investments are channeled through them, and their offices take the major decisions on the use of capital in the towns in accord with the interests of the center. The development towns are dependent on the financial and managerial services of the center, and only low level occupations are open to the towns' populations; they receive lower wages than the workers in the center, there are few opportunities for advancement, and the level of services, such as health, education, and cultural activities is low. Economic dependence is compounded by dependence in the political sphere; political institutions are highly centralized and local branches are managed from the outside, in line with the assumptions of the center.

In his discussion of ethnic consciousness, Swirski argues that a common consciousness of Middle Eastern Jews now overshadows the consciousnesses of separate *edot*. He contrasts his approach with the sociologists working within the modernization perspective who saw ethnicity tied to traditionalism and expected a decline in ethnic identity and consciousness among Middle Easterners in Israel. Swirski argues that the subordinate position of Middle Easterners within the ethnic division of labor, their subjection to discrimination, and the "colonialist" orientation of the Europeans have erased the differences among the North African and Asian *edot* and created a common consciousness. There is no equivalent need to investigate European consciousness since its forms and expressions are more readily available in the mass media, literature, and educational programs. Europeans do not tend to express themselves in particularist terms, but rather in terms of "the state" or "the society," as representing the interests of all. The only factor which would force the Europeans to express their ethnic identification in an explicit manner would be the success of a movement or organization of Middle Easterners.

Swirski's discussion of Middle Easterners' consciousness is based on conversations with a hundred activists who, Swirski admits, are not representative of the population of Middle Eastern origin. The prominent features of the activists' consciousness were feelings of deprivation and discrimination, socio-economic and cultural domination by Europeans, and a negative evaluation of Middle Eastern leaders who had "sold themselves" to the European establishment. Swirski admits, however, that even many of the activists indicated an ambiguity concerning their ethnic consciousness. Many did not use the term "Ashkenazim" but would refer to the "establishment," "government," or simply "them."

43

They felt that something should be done to improve the position of Middle Easterners, but they were suspicious of any attempt at a separate political program of Middle Easterners.

Swirski contrasted his approach with cultural approaches, including those cultural approaches that analyze ethnicity as an emergent phenomenon and not simply as an element of cultural heritage or traditionalism. His objection to these approaches is that they view ethnicity as an adaptation to circumstances and do not ask how those circumstances came into being. Swirski tends to assume that an approach which emphasizes the cultural aspects of ethnicity can not be a radical one questioning establishment concepts and assumptions, but this is not necessarily the case. For example, Arnold Lewis (1985), an anthropologist who emphasizes the cultural basis of ethnic identification, analyzes the terms *edot ha'Mizrach* and "Oriental Jews" as examples of phantom ethnicity, and as symbolic vehicles used mainly by Israelis of European origin to explain and justify the lower socio-economic position of North African and Asian Israelis by largely fictitious cultural differences. Lewis argues that these terms rarely delineate existentially meaningful identities; they are not rooted in a cultural tradition or in a tangible ethnohistory.

The anthropologists Shlomo Deshen and Moshe Shokeid state that there has been an overreaction to what they call the "cultural-anthropological" approach, on the part of those who see ethnicity as molded by social circumstances and instrumental motives. They seek to redress the balance by emphasizing the "symbolic estates" and "primordial sentiments" in ethnicity (Shokeid and Deshen, 1982). Their work focuses on symbolic action, particularly within religious and political contexts, that attempts to mediate between the traditional practices of the *edah* and an identification as Israeli citizens.

In general, those who have focused on the *edah* rather than on the Oriental or Mizrachi identification have been anthropologists who approach the subject from a perspective that emphasizes the cultural, primordial, expressive, non-rational components of ethnicity. Those who have focused on the Oriental identification have been sociologists who have emphasized the socio-economic, political, instrumental, rational components of ethnicity. An exception is the sociologist Eliezer Ben-Rafael who, in his book *The Emergence of Ethnicity: Cultural Groups and Social Conflict in Israel* (1982), presented a predominantly cultural analysis of ethnicity in Israel.

Although all of the works by sociologists discussed thus far analyzed ethnicity in Israel, ethnic identity was not their principal focus. Eisenstadt's focus was on the absorption of immigrants, Smooha's on social and cultural pluralism, and Swirski's on ethnic inequality. In comparison, the major focus of Eliezer Ben-Rafael's book is the phenomenon of ethnicity and the particular forms that it takes in Israel.

Ben-Rafael treats ethnicity primarily as a cultural phenomenon, and argues that the form that it has taken in Israel is the consequence of an encounter of the cultures of Jews originating from Europe and from North Africa and Asia. There are two principal socio-cultural categories in Israel, originating from Europe and the Middle East, but only one of these, that from the Middle East, includes groups (*edot*) with an ethnic consciousness. However, ethnic consciousness emerged, in part, because of the encounter with the dominant non-ethnic category.

The cultural orientations of the dominant Ashkenazi category were largely formed by Zionists who immigrated from eastern Europe prior to the establishment of the State of Israel. They had already undergone a process of secularization prior to their migration, and they understood their migration as "a denial of history," as a break from the religiocultural and social features of the Jewish communities of the diaspora. They were committed to a secular notion of nationhood that was justified in terms of the universal right of all nations to autonomy and emancipation. Religion, their "Judaism" and "Jewishness," was but a reflection of the national principle; they felt no enduring commitment to the cultural features of their communities of origin and were prepared to accept cultural change.

The absence of an awareness of kind based on country or community of origin among European immigrants was congruent with the ideology of *mizug ha'galuyot* (fusion of the exiles). In its traditional formulation, the gathering and amalgamation of Jews from different parts of the world referred to the future messianic kingdom, but it was now secularized as part of the modern Zionist ideology. This fusion was to be implemented by the unconditional acceptance of all Jewish immigrants as full citizens of Israel, and immigration was to be encouraged, and the adaptation of immigrants assisted, by economic privileges during their first years in Israel. It was expected that new immigrants would adapt, socially and culturally, to the new society, and that they would be guided in this by "veterans." Although "veteranship" was accorded importance, inequality could only be justified on the basis of individual achievement.

Most immigrants from North Africa and Asia had undergone comparatively little secularization, and they conceived of their immigration as a fulfillment of messianic prophecies or as a means of expressing and continuing their sacred culture. They did not distinguish Judaism from their "parochial" cultural legacy, and were not, therefore, ready to abandon those cultural attributes that they had adhered to in the diaspora. Their contact with secularized Jews in Israel came as shock to many, and their consciousness of the need to defend their primordial attributes led many to strengthen their traditional ways during their first years in the new society. This meeting led to the emergence of the *edot* as distinct socio-cultural entities and distinct identities ("Moroccan," "Yemenite," etc.), even though these identities continued to be bound to the broader identity of Jew. It should be noted that Ben-Rafael denies that the term *edot ha'Mizrach* refers to an ethnic group or identity. It is, like the term "Ashkenazim," a term referring to a "socio-cultural category," and emerged in order to signify the *de facto* pluralism between the two Jewish socio-cultural categories. The term does not denote a major focus of ethnic self-identification because, unlike the *edah* identity, it does not refer to an ascriptive basis or have much meaning within the wider frame of Jewish identity. Ben-Rafael also denies that there is a substantial submelting of Jewish groups from the Middle East. Even when there is marriage of Jews from different *edot*, they tend to retain their *edah* identities with perhaps one side adopting the *edah* of the other.

The ethnicity of the *edah* is a special kind. Israel was a case of a "returning diaspora," of people who, prior to their immigration, felt bound to and part of the nation. The absence of differentiation between Jewishness and the cultural legacy of the community of origin meant not only that the *edot* were concerned to maintain their particular religiocultural expressions, but also that they conceived of themselves as part of a larger whole in which they would amalgamate. They also believed in the fusion of the exiles, but, in comparison with European immigrants, for Middle Easterners there was a tension in the Israeli context between this belief and their emergent ethnic identities. A primordial identity which is defined as temporarily meaningful may be a paradoxical one, but it accounts for many of the features of ethnicity in Israel. Members of the *edot* continue to follow, and in some cases even reinforce, certain traditional customs and rituals, but despite their interpretation in ethnic rather than class terms of their deprivation and low status, they do not politically organize on an ethnic basis. There have been a number of ethnic political lists and parties, but none have achieved sustained success. There is no development from ethnic groups "in themselves" to ethnic groups "for themselves," because this would contradict their support of the ideology of fusion. They do not support ethnic politics because this would institutionalize what is the major object of their criticism – the non-implementation of fusion. Ben-Rafael uses the term "crypto-pluralism" to describe the situation among Jewish groups in Israel; there are considerable socio-economic and cultural differences, but these are not given an unambiguous institutionalization in the polity. This is, perhaps, an unfortunate term because the meaning is not that pluralism is hidden (it is clear from Ben-Rafael's account that it can be very visible), but rather that it has no ideological legitimation, either among the dominant non-ethnic group or among the *edot*.

Ben-Rafael's empirical data are based on his investigation of middle-class Moroccan and Yemenite Jews in Israel, and here he broke new ground by focusing on middle-class rather than lower- or working-class Jews from North Africa and Asia. He argues that the fusion ideology encourages, and the openness of the dominant European category allows, mobile Jews from Middle Eastern origins to assimilate and undergo a process of "de-ethnization." Because their community of origin believes in its future disappearance, it does not retain a strong hold on mobiles, and the culture of the mobiles tends to become an eclectic one, combining, for example, support for democracy with a patrimonial orientation. At the same time, it is the very openness of the European category that contributes to the continuation of cultural distinctiveness in the "ethnoclasses" of the lower strata of Jews from the Middle East. Because the mobiles from the *edot* assimilate into the predominantly European middle class, they distance themselves from their origins and have little cultural influence on the majority who remain in the lower strata. Thus, ethnicity is likely to remain an important feature of the "truncated ethnoclasses" in Israel.

The differences of the approaches discussed above have revolved mainly around two interrelated areas of dispute: the relationship of ethnic groups or categories with inequality, and the nature and causes of ethnic identification and consciousness. With regard to the first area, all interpretations have accepted the *fact* of a considerable overlap between geographical origins and socio-economic distribution in Israel, but the approaches differ in the extent to which they qualify this overlap and their analyses of it. The approach with the heaviest and least qualified focus on the overlap between ethnicity and class is that of Swirski. His description of the emergence and development of an ethnic division of labor provides an important corrective to the modernization approach, but the applicability of the center–periphery and internal colonialism model with respect to relationships of European and Middle Eastern Jews may be questioned. As dependency theorists have recognized, an ethnic division of labor is never fully coterminous with regional divisions; individuals from the core settle in the periphery to direct economic enterprises and administer the region, and there is a migration of people from the periphery to the center. There is a clear difference, however, between the overlap of region and ethnicity in a country such as Britain (Hechter, 1975), and the situation in Israel. The populations in the development towns are predominantly Middle Eastern, but the majority of Middle Easterners live in the urban centers. There is a considerable ethnic division of labor in the major cities, but the terms "center," "periphery," and "internal colonialism" are hardly applicable here. There is more justification in using these terms with regard to the Arabs in Israel (Zureik, 1979).

Swirski presents a dichotomous model of stratification in Israel. He admits that both Europeans and Middle Easterners are internally differentiated by status according to countries of origin, but he states that the economic differences among the Middle Eastern *edot* (Moroccans, Iraqis, etc.) are insignificant compared with their common position within the ethnic division of labor. He does not, however, produce data to support this statement. Statistics on occupational distributions do show considerable differences according to country of origin within both broad categories, and it has been suggested that a middle category of Sephardic, but mostly non-Oriental, groups may be identified (Weiker, 1983).

Swirski presents one hierarchy, with the emphasis on the overlap between ethnicity and economic position. The impression given is that the ethnic categories are homogeneous in terms of class and that nearly all members of disprivileged *edot* have faced similar levels of deprivation and discrimination. It would be foolish to deny the significance of the considerable statistical gaps in income and occupation between Europeans and Middle Easterners, but the considerable number of middle-class Middle Easterners and lower-class Europeans should not be ignored. Despite their differences, Eisenstadt, Smooha, and Ben-Rafael have emphasized the growing importance of middle-class Israelis from North African and Asian origins.

In his more recent writings on ethnicity, Eisenstadt (1983, 1985, 1986) has not responded directly to the criticisms of his earlier work, but he has made some changes in emphases. His general framework remains one of absorption, and he writes that most immigrants have experienced mobility and accepted at least some of the basic symbols and premises of Israeli society. But there is now a greater emphasis on the "negative aspects of absorption": the perpetuation of poverty and apathy in deprived neighborhoods, a growing dependence on the state, and the continuous economic and educational backwardness of many development towns.

The problems of absorption are now related less to the "traditionalism" of the immigrants than to the insensitivity of the absorbing society. Differences among ethnic groups or categories are not so much the consequence of initial cultural differences, but of differences that emerged during the process of absorption. These changes were related to the weakening of the revolutionary pioneering ideology so that cultural differences came to be defined more and more in terms of "western" and "Oriental." Eisenstadt writes that there is a contradiction between, on the one hand, granting political participation and absorbing immigrants into the school system and army, and, on the other hand, "attempting at first at least to direct their political activities through paternalistic, often semi-coercive measures" (1985: 328). It might appear that, at least with respect to some of the terms he now uses, Eisenstadt has included some elements of the more critical perspectives into his own, but although he notes the considerable overlap of class and ethnic divisions, he does not explain ethnic differences by class or economic factors, or by reference to exploitation and discrimination. The lack of development of "development towns" is explained, in part, by their "ecological distance" from the center, but Eisenstadt's explanations remain primarily cultural.

Eisenstadt writes that the problem of absorption was defined by the dominant sectors as one of cultural backwardness of immigrants from Asia and Africa, and they were not inclined to open up the institutions and organizations of the center to this cultural "threat." The central sectors did not find suitable ways of absorbing immigrants beyond "mere bureaucratic procedures" or location in "suitable work frameworks," but Jews from Asia and Africa were not satisfied with this limited absorption, and it was the very success of the most basic economic aspects of absorption that made them demand full acceptance and incorporation. The more mobile elements play a leading role in the demands for inclusion since socio-economic advancement enhanced their sense of deprivation and alienation. Although the majority of leaders of the Likud political party are of European origin, it obtained the support of the majority of Jews of Middle Eastern origins because it was seen by them as providing an opening and full acceptance into the center.

Although Smooha remains very critical of what he calls "the cultural establishment approach" in a recent paper (1987) comparing the cultural, class, and pluralist approaches, he presents the pluralist approach as one that incorporates many concepts and arguments from the two other approaches. He writes that the pluralist approach combines a discussion of the process of assimilation with the crystallization of ethnic stratification. He agrees with the cultural approach that ethnic pluralism in

Israel is not institutionalized or legitimate, and with the class approach that ethnic stratification is extensive, with the majority of Middle Easterners situated in the working or lower class. The emergence of ethnic stratification in Israel is explained by a combination of the "weaknesses" of the immigrants (less secular education, less training and experience in relevant occupations, the absence of strong organization and leadership, etc.), and their manipulation and exploitation by the establishment. However, Smooha emphasizes that there has been an erosion of European dominance with the penetration of Middle Easterners into the leadership of important institutions, and that the Middle Eastern Jewish population has become increasingly divided by class.

In an attempt at self-criticism, Smooha writes that the chief weakness of the pluralist approach "is in being eclectic, synthesizing, and compromising." He asks: "Is not pluralist analysis so neutral, factual, conventional, and inconsequential that the advocates of both the cultural and class approaches will be ready in principle to accept it (if not all its details)?" (p. 56). The answer to this might be that the other approaches would not accept it because it is so factual and inconsequential. The pluralist approach may include elements from the other approaches, but it is questionable whether it is a true synthesis and not just a list of points and arguments. It accepts both instrumental and cultural approaches to ethnicity, but these are added to each other rather than analyzed in terms of a process of dynamic interrelationship.

Smooha's modifications to his pluralist framework have reduced his differences with the cultural perspective over the question of ethnic inequality to a matter of emphasis. Perhaps a wider disagreement remains over the question of the nature and causes of ethnic identification in Israel. In a critical essay on Ben-Rafael's book, Smooha (1985) questions the argument that ethnicity within the Israeli-Jewish population is asymmetrical, and largely confined to Jews from North Africa and Asia. He writes that by attaching the tag of ethnicity only to Israelis from the Middle East, Ben-Rafael stigmatizes them and blames them for their lack of absorption and mobility, whereas the dominant culture or center is seen as the focus of the crystallization of consensus. This ignores the discrimination against, and exploitation of, Middle Easterners, and the ethnic conflict that this generates. Smooha argues that the Europeans have developed an ethnic consciousness as a consequence of their dominant position and the challenge of *edot ha'Mizrach* to this dominance. Ashkenazi consciousness is expressed in their talk of "two cultures," and the ideology of fusion is an ideological mask which hides separateness and inequality.

In his reply to Smooha, Ben-Rafael (1985) writes that he does not analyze ethnicity in a negative fashion or in terms of "whose guilty." Middle Easterners as well as Europeans encourage assimilation, and the amount of mobility or lack of it is a consequence of the "structure of opportunities." He emphasizes that not all groups with common cultural elements become ethnic groups, and that there is no reason why ethnic groups cannot be in conflict with a non-ethnic group, which is in fact the case in Israel. The conflict, however, is over questions of definitions and contents of Jewishness in Israeli society.

Ben-Rafael rejected Smooha's contention that he was part of the "establishment formulation" of ethnic relations in Israel, but he hardly dealt explicitly with the differences between his approach and the absorption through modernization approach. Smooha's criticism is based on the false assumption that Ben-Rafael was asking the same question as that of Eisenstadt and his colleagues: what are the factors that encourage or hinder absorption? In fact, Ben-Rafael's question was: what accounts for the emergence and dynamics of ethnicity in Israel? It is true that economic conflict, discrimination, and exploitation are marginal factors in Ben-Rafael's account, but although these may be prevalent, they are not viewed as the principal determinants of ethnicity which in Israel are primarily cultural. It is not assumed, however, that the absence of these cultural factors or of ethnicity would mean that the subordinate cultural category would demonstrate higher levels of mobility or assimilate more successfully. Ethnicity may prevent acculturation to the dominant culture, but acculturation is not necessarily followed by assimilation. Ben-Rafael was not, therefore, giving an updated cultural explanation of the causes of ethnic inequality in Israel since this was not the problematic of his book. He was not attempting to blame inequality on the cultural features of ethnics, but was attempting to explain why those Jews from North Africa and Asia who, for whatever reasons, remain in the lower strata will remain ethnics.

Once it is understood that Ben-Rafael's problematic stands somewhat outside the disputes regarding the causes of inequality among "ethnic" or "socio-cultural" categories in Israel, the differences between Ben-Rafael's approach and that of Smooha become clearer. Their approaches certainly differ in their emphases, but they are not always necessarily in conflict with each other. With respect to the orientations of the dominant Europeans, Ben-Rafael's statements that they emphasize "guidance" and absorb mobiles from the *edot* do not appear essentially different from Smooha's "paternalism–co-optation" model. It is possible, moreover, to reconcile Smooha's emphasis, which he shares with Swirski, that discrimination is an important factor in the emergence and continuation of inequality in Israel with Ben-Rafael's emphasis that the Europeans' openness to mobiles from the *edot* results in the continuation of the ethnoclasses. Ben-Rafael wrote that mobiles are accepted if they have the appropriate educational and cultural characteristics, but it is quite possible that discriminatory practices limit the number who are able to achieve these characteristics.

This is not to minimize important differences between the approaches. One important difference is their very understanding of the meaning of ethnicity. Smooha argues that the Ashkenazim have become an ethnic group by virtue of their material interests and the differentiation that they make between their cultural characteristics and those of *edot ha'Mizrach*, but these are not sufficient criteria of ethnicity for Ben-Rafael. A mere consciousness of socio-economic and cultural differences is not the essential criterion of ethnicity. A particular type of consciousness is required: a primordial orientation that attributes sacredness to the group's cultural legacy. The Europeans value their western culture and may derogate the Oriental culture of *edot ha'Mizrach*, but theirs is not a culture which defines them as a separate group (as, say, in comparison with non-Jewish westerners) or one, which by reason of its sacredness, they are not prepared to change. The Europeans are, however, part of an ethnic group in Israel *vis-à-vis* the Arab population.

Another difference is with respect to the ideology of fusion of the exiles. Smooha and Swirski argue that it is a mask for exploitation and inequality, but Ben-Rafael's point is not that the ideology is an accurate reflection of reality (it is clear from his discussion of the "objective" features of the ethnic situation that he sees the ideology as far from the reality). The ideology cannot be reduced, however, to a device for manipulation; it is believed in both by the non-ethnics and by the *edot*, and it has important effects on the dynamics of ethnicity in Israel. Myths can have a powerful impact.

Smooha argues that part of Ben-Rafael's argument is that Jews from North Africa and Asia are less prepared to change than Ashkenazim. In fact, Ben-Rafael emphasizes that mobiles from the *edot* do change, and it is here perhaps that Ben-Rafael's thesis raises a question. It is clearer why lower-class Jews remain ethnics than why middle-class mobiles lose their ethnicity. Ben-Rafael's explanation is linked to what he sees as the paradoxical nature of the ethnicity of the *edah*. It is the temporary definition of primordialism that allows the mobiles to de-ethnicize, but it is not spelled out why the fact of mobility should necessarily lead to the activation of this temporariness. The fact that the mobiles are now found in a socio-economic stratum where the majority are not ethnically minded is clearly important, but this could hardly be a sufficient explanation. Since Ben-Rafael emphasizes the link of religion to Jewish ethnicity, perhaps the major factor in the de-ethnization of mobiles is their secularization. It may be hypothesized that socio-economic mobility is accompanied by secularization (this is partly because of the greater interaction of mobiles with secularized Europeans), and this in turn dilutes primordialism and enables the ideology of absorption to be put into practice. On the other hand, it may be that Ben-Rafael has overemphasized the de-ethnization of mobiles. In order to answer these questions, a systematic comparison of lower- and middle-class subjects from the same ethnic groups and categories is required. Ben-Rafael was not able to do this in his book because his sample was restricted to the middle class, and he tended to rely on information on the lower class from his middle-class respondents. The sample of the present work allows for more systematic comparisons.

The theoretical perspectives on Jewish ethnicity in Israel that were reviewed in this chapter were based on, or referred to, empirical studies, but these studies were limited in terms of their samples and the questions that were asked. The focus of most empirical studies in this area has been on social distance and inequality among ethnic groups, and comparatively little attention has been given to ethnic identity and the cognitive images and affective and evaluative components of ethnicity. Nor has there been much attention to the relationship of ethnic consciousness with class consciousness or its relationship with religiosity and religious identity. These are the major topics of our empirical study. They will be analyzed within a framework which will draw on the theories discussed above, and which will attempt to remain sensitive to both cultural and instrumental components of social action.

In more general terms the concern of this study is with the nature of social boundaries within Israeli society; the extent to which ethnic, religious, and class differences contribute to the crystallization of groups with distinctive patterns of behavior and attitudes. In the probing of the dynamics of a social setting characterized by a number of deep social and cultural cleavages, the scope of this study goes beyond the issues in the debates discussed above. By systematic inquiry into the significance of each of the divisions, as well as their complex interrelationships, the fundamental features of Israeli society should be revealed.

4

The sample, its background, and its setting

Ethnicity, class, and religiosity are investigated in this study, both as cleavages with their own particular characteristics and as cleavages that interact and influence each other. In our analysis of ethnicity, which is the most central topic of this study, we attempt to overcome some of the limitations of previous empirical studies that have made a broad distinction between "Ashkenazim" and "Orientals" and then focused primarily on the latter, especially those in the lower strata. European Israelis and middle-class Middle Easterners have rarely been the object of research. We decided on a sample of four specific groups of origin, two European and two Middle Eastern, that are demographically important and, in terms of their socio-economic profiles and cultural characteristics, are broadly representative of the wide spectrum of Jewish groups of origin in Israel. The socio-economic distribution of the sample was structured to enable us to investigate both the effect of socio-economic status on ethnicity and the importance of classes as a separate hierarchy from that of ethnic groups. The sample was not structured for religiosity, but the means by which lists of respondents were drawn up, from the fathers of children in both secular and religious schools, provided a representative range of levels of religiosity among Israeli Jews.

Interviews were conducted in 1982/3 with a disproportionate stratified sample of 826 male residents of Beer Sheva, the largest town in southern Israel. The sample is composed of four groups of origin: two "Mizrachi" or Middle Eastern groups from Morocco and Iraq, and two "Ashkenazi" or European groups from Poland and Rumania. These groups are among the five largest in the Israeli-Jewish population: the largest is the Moroccan group who make up 13.4% (first and second generations together) of the population, followed by the Russians (8%), Poles (7.9%), Rumanians (7.5%), and Iraqis (7.2%). The four groups were chosen for the sample, not mainly because of their size, but because their differences in socio-economic profiles and ethnic status cover almost the entire distributive range of Israeli-Jewish groups: within the broad Middle Eastern category, the socio-economic profile and ethnic status of Moroccans are low compared with the Iraqis; within the broad European category, the socio-economic profile and ethnic status of Rumanians are low compared with the Poles. This sampling allowed a more sophisticated analysis than the crude division between Jews from Europe–America and Jews from Africa–Asia that has been the basis of most statistical comparisons in Israel. The sample was further stratified to obtain a similar distribution of socio-economic status in each group of origin and this enabled us to analyze categories that have largely been ignored in Israeli sociological studies: middle-class Israelis from Asia and North Africa and working-class Israelis from Europe.

Lists of appropriate respondents were made up from primary and secondary school records, supplemented in some schools by questionnaires administered to children, that gave the country of origin, years of education, and occupation of fathers. Thus, a further parameter of the sample was that all respondents were fathers of school-age children. If the fathers were born in Israel, inquiries were made by telephone to discover the countries of origin. Only a minority of respondents were born in Israel; the majority migrated to Israel in their childhood, youth, or young adulthood. All the background details of respondents, including origins, education, and occupation, were checked when the questionnaires were administered by our interviewers. (Further details on the sample are given in appendix A.)

In this chapter we present the background of the four groups of origin in the diaspora, their demographic and socio-economic profiles in Israel and in Beer Sheva, the setting of this study.

In the diaspora

Morocco

Muslim-Jewish relations in precolonial Morocco were governed by the classical Islamic notion of the *dhimmis*, a subject, non-Islamic people of the Book who paid tribute to the Muslim sovereign in return for their protection. Within the broad contours of this arrangement, Jews in Morocco lived in a wide range of political, ecological, and social circumstances. A large proportion lived in the major cities; they mostly resided in their own quarter, the *mellah*, paid annual tribute to the Sultan, and were subject to a number of restrictive laws. However, the Jewish communities were widely distributed throughout the country, and those that lived in the smaller mountain and oases communities depended on the protection of local Muslim patrons.

Throughout Morocco Jews were small traders, artisans, and craftsmen, but in rural areas they were sometimes farmers and shepherds. In the urban centers there was a small wealthy elite, most of whom were engaged in international commerce, and there was also a large poor stratum eking out a marginal living in the premodern urban economy (Meyers, 1982). As *dhimmis* Jews had a large measure of religious liberty, and the important institutions of the community included the synagogue, the *kuttab* (elementary school), and, in the larger communities, the *yeshivah* (advanced religious school). Important elements in Moroccan Judaism included the study of the mystical text, the Zohar, pilgrimages to the tombs of saints, and many popular "magical" practices.

The French Protectorate was established over most of Morocco in 1912, and French colonialism began to transform Moroccan Jewry. The French revoked many of the discriminatory laws, allowed Jews to settle outside the *mellah*, promoted French-speaking schools in which Jewish children learnt secular as well as Jewish subjects, created new economic opportunities, and opened up their administrative ranks to Jewish clerks. Jews came to be far more concentrated in the cities (80% by 1953), especially in Casablanca where their number reached 80,000 in 1948. The Jewish population in Morocco totaled 225,000 in 1951, more than 2% of the whole. A Jewish bourgeoisie developed with a strong orientation toward French culture, and a large proportion of Jewish workers became wage-earners, but there remained a large poor and uneducated stratum of Jews who continued in the more traditional occupations as peddlers and artisans.

The changes under the French gave rise to much higher economic and social expectations among Moroccan Jews, but these were generally not fulfilled and the restrictions and conflicting pressures on Moroccan Jews gave rise to feelings of insecurity (Chouraqui, 1952; Confino, 1953). Many Moroccan Jews interpreted the creation of the State of Israel as the beginning of their redemption, but the mass Jewish emigration from Morocco began only after the surge of Moroccan nationalism in 1954 and intensified after Morocco achieved independence in 1956. Approximately two-thirds of the Jewish emigrants from Morocco migrated to Israel; most of the other third, including a large proportion of the educated middle class, migrated to France.

Iraq

After the Islamic conquest, the position of the Jews in Iraq varied considerably according to the particular ruler in power. The establishment of Ottoman rule in 1534 brought a long period of relative stability, and up to World War I Jews in Iraq were recognized as a religious minority, living in their own quarters, and governed in part by their own leaders. Jews spoke Arabic but with their own dialect, and separation from Muslims was further signaled by some differences in dress.

During the nineteenth century Jewish communities were dispersed throughout the country, but the number of Jews in Baghdad increased from about 3,000 in 1848 to between 30,000 and 40,000 at the end of the century. In 1919, 66% of the 86,000 Jews in Iraq lived in the cities of Baghdad and Basra; in 1947, 74% of the 125,000 Iraqi Jews lived in those two cities, 22.5% in other cities, and 3.5% in rural areas (H. Cohen, 1973: 74). Up to World War I most Iraqi Jews were small traders, hawkers, and artisans; there were very few merchants, clerks, or professionals. After the opening of the Suez Canal, a few Iraqi Jews became wealthy international merchants, but the vast majority were poor.

Under the British occupation and mandate the situation of Iraqi Jews changed considerably. A sizeable Jewish middle class developed; Jews played an important part in the development of trade and commerce, and there was a considerable increase in the number of Jewish clerks and professionals. Many Jews left the traditional Jewish quarters, but they continued to concentrate in their own neighborhoods or streets.

Iraq had not been a center of Jewish religious learning for many centuries, but up to the end of the nineteenth century the majority of children received a traditional Jewish education in the *heder* (religious school), and there was strict observance of the religious law. In the second half of the nineteenth century, schools teaching secular subjects were opened in Baghdad, and toward the end of the century some Iraqi Jews completed secondary education; a few attended universities outside Iraq. After World War I the majority of children attended at least elementary schools, and an increasing number received a modern education. These developments in modern education contributed to some decline in the traditional way of life, especially from the 1920s when a significant proportion of young Jews received all their education in non-Jewish schools. Many of the Jewish civil servants worked on the Sabbath and even on the religious holidays, but the majority continued to maintain the dietary regulations and other important religious practices. This period also witnessed the penetration of organized Zionism in Iraq. The first Zionist Association was founded in Baghdad in 1921 and was followed by the organization of Zionist youth movements. The Muslim nationalists succeeded in 1929 in outlawing the Zionist organizations which then went underground.

Iraq obtained its independence in 1932 and this was followed by disturbances and discrimination against the Jews, a consequence in large part of events in Palestine. A pogrom occurred in Baghdad in 1941, and oppressive measures were passed against Jews from 1945 to 1950. In 1950–1, after a law was passed giving Jews the right to emigration, 90% of all Iraqi Jews (about 120,000) left for Israel. Only a few thousand went to other countries. At the end of 1951 approximately 6,000 remained in Iraq, but most of these left after the 1967 war (H. Cohen, 1973: 73; Patai, 1971).

Poland

A Jewish community of substantial size began to emerge in Poland from about the middle of the thirteenth century. At that time Jews in western and central Europe sought to escape persecution and economic restrictions, and they found refuge in Poland where, in the thirteenth and fourteenth centuries, successive kings welcomed Jewish immigrants as a means of developing the country's commerce and industry. The status of the Jews was guaranteed by special charters, and up to the end of the sixteenth century the situation of Polish Jews was better than in other European countries.

The history of Polish Jewry took a dark turn in 1648 when about 40,000 or 50,000 Polish Jews (20% to 25% of the total Polish Jewish population) were massacred in the uprising of Ukrainian peasants and Cossacks (Weinryb, 1972: 181–205). The troubles in Poland continued and the Jews were harshly affected by the deterioration of the Polish economy and the political instability in the seventeenth and eighteenth centuries. After the partitions of Poland at the end of the eighteenth and beginning of the nineteenth century, the majority of Polish Jews, numbering about 900,000, came under Russian rule. There was a mass emigration of Jews from eastern Europe from the 1880s to World War I, but natural growth was high and when Poland obtained its independence after the war Polish Jewry numbered 3 million, about 10% of the country's total population. During the interwar period the number of emigrants was only half of the natural growth, and in 1939 the number of Polish Jews had reached 3.5 million (Marcus, 1983: 3–14, 387–8).

Jews in Poland came to be visibly recognizable, far more so than the Jews in the Middle East, by their clothes, language (Yiddish), and a way of life that was dominated in all its spheres by religion. The social separation between Jews and non-Jews in Poland encompassed legal status, economic activities and occupations, ecological distribution, and political institutions. From the beginnings of their settlement in Poland, the Jews were engaged primarily in trade and crafts, and they occupied an interstitial position between the nobility and the peasant masses. A large proportion lived in the towns and small towns (*shtetls*) where they sometimes constituted the majority of the population. The Jews who lived in the villages did not work on the land but were engaged primarily in leaseholding and trade. The Jewish communities were largely self-governing; the governing body of the *kehillot* collected taxes, supervised the various religious and educational institutions, and negotiated with the non-Jewish authorities. The local *kehillot* joined to form regional associations, and for more than 200 years there existed a nationwide Jewish organization, the Congress of the Four Lands.

The Hasidic movement which emerged in the first half of the eighteenth century was at first opposed by religious scholars who saw its emphasis on mystical prayer as a threat to the centrality of religious scholarship, and its separate religious centers and prayer houses as a threat to the cohesion of the Jewish community. In the long term Hasidism revitalized traditional Judaism in Poland, and the former opponents of the Hasidim joined them in the nineteenth century to fight the penetration of the Haskalah (Enlightenment) movement. The majority of Polish Jews remained traditionally religious up to World War I, but in the last two decades of the nineteenth century the traditional way of life began to be challenged by the Socialist and Zionist movements, especially in the larger towns and cities (Sharot, 1982).

In contrast with Russia where Jewish life was changed radically by the Communist Revolution, the vast majority of Jews in interwar Poland continued to live in a highly separate society; over three-quarters considered Yiddish their first language, and they had their own educational system, communal organizations, youth movements, press, Yiddish theatre and films, and so on. Only a small minority, less than 10%, were assimilationists who adopted Polish culture with enthusiasm, and they suffered considerable psychological strain from the refusal of the Poles to accept them (Heller, 1977). The Polish representatives to the Paris Peace Conference had signed minority clauses giving Jews full equality, but these proved worthless, and Polish Jews continued to suffer from legal and economic discrimination, political anti-Semitism, social rejection, and pogroms. There was some development of capitalism and a Christian bourgeoisie in interwar Poland, but the country remained predominantly agrarian, and despite a loss in their share of trade and commerce, the Polish Jews remained a socially distinct middleman class. In 1931, less than 5% of Polish Jews were in agriculture (compared with 61% of the non-Jewish population), nearly 80% were in trade and manufacturing, and they constituted more than 30% of the population in such towns as Warsaw, Lodz, and Lwow.

In the interwar years Jewish-Polish society was divided further between religious Jews, largely Hasidic, and the secular Zionist and Jewish socialist movements. After World War I Orthodox Jews were still the largest sector of Polish Jewry, and the Hasidim responded to the new opportunities for political expression in the Polish state, and to the threat of the Jewish secular movements, by organizing political parties and by participating in municipal and parliamentary elections. However, Orthodox Polish Jewry sharply declined in the interwar years, perhaps by as much as half; in the 1930s the extent of abandonment of Orthodoxy reached a level unprecedented in eastern Europe (outside Soviet Russia).

The Zionist movement had attracted only a small minority of Polish Jews prior to World War I, but after the war it became the predominant Jewish political sector, appealing to a wide range of Polish Jews who differed in class, religiosity, and political viewpoint. The social and cultural heterogeneity of Polish Zionism accounts for its numerous splits and parties; the religious Zionist party remained small in comparison with the secular Zionist parties that included the centralist "General Zionists," the socialist Zionist parties, and the "right-wing" Revisionists. The socialist Bund party saw the Jewish struggle in Poland as part of the fight for international socialism, and it opposed both the religious sectors and the Zionists (Marcus, 1983; Rabinowicz, 1965; Mendelsohn, 1974).

The majority of Jews who lived in Poland at the outbreak of World War II perished in the Holocaust. Among those who survived and decided to stay in Poland there were some who attempted to rebuild Jewish institutions. The socialist system eliminated the conditions conducive to a distinctive Jewish life and the great majority increasingly adopted Polish culture and abandoned Jewish customs. A study of Polish Jews carried out in 1947–50 found that only 7% of the sample said that they both believed in and practiced Orthodox Judaism. Among the majority even religious holidays such as Hanukkah were no longer observed, and, although the most important Jewish holidays were remembered, they were not observed in a traditional fashion. Zionism continued to attract support regardless of class and degree of assimilation; 74% considered themselves members of the Jewish nation and 38% considered Israel as their homeland (Hurwic-Nowakowska, 1986).

After 1949 Jewish community life was further dissolved as a consequence of the policies of the Communist party and government. Jewish schools, welfare institutions, and the Bund were either destroyed or absorbed by the Communists. Assimilation continued apace, and it was the "anti-Zionist" purges of 1968 that prompted many of the remaining Polish Jews to migrate to Israel or the west. Thus, Polish Jewry declined further from 88,000 in 1948 to between 6,000 and 15,000 today (Meyer *et al.*, 1953; Hundert and Bacon, 1984).

Rumania

There is evidence of Jews living in the area of Rumania from the early second century C.E. Over the centuries the Jewish population grew slowly as a consequence of in-migration, and included Hungarian Jews in the late fourteenth century, Sephardim in the sixteenth century, and Polish Jews from the middle of the seventeenth century. The Jews from Poland and Russia came to be the dominant element in Rumania, and, even though the country was under Ottoman rule, Jewish religious and cultural traditions were very similar to those of other eastern European communities. Rumanian Jews spoke Yiddish, their teachers and rabbis came from Poland and Russia, and Hasidism became important, especially in Moldavia where, up to the twentieth century, a large proportion of Jews lived in traditionalist *shtetls* (Baron, 1930; Sternberg, 1984).

Rumania gained independence from the Turks in 1877 and the Kingdom of Rumania was proclaimed in 1881. A census in 1899 counted nearly 267,000 Jews, 4.5% of the total population. About 80% of Rumanian Jews lived in cities and towns, making up 32% of the urban population, and in some towns of Moldavia the majority of artisans and merchants were Jews. As in Poland, the small towns remained largely traditionalist, but secularization began to make inroads in the urban centers and the Zionist movement grew in an environment of anti-Semitism and of discrimination in education and the professions. Emigration increased and the Jewish population fell to about 240,000 (3.3% of the population) in 1912 (*Encyclopaedia Judaica*, vol. XIV, 1972).

After World War I "Greater Rumania" gained territories from Austro-Hungary, Russia, and Bulgaria, and in 1924 the Jewish population of the enlarged country numbered 796,000 (5% of the population). The 1919 Versailles Peace Settlement compelled the Rumanian government to grant citizenship to its Jewish subjects but economic and educational restrictions continued. The anti-Semitism that had been the official policy of both Liberal and Conservative political parties in Rumania prior to World War I continued after it, developing into more vicious forms, as, for example, in the Iron Guard movement. Only in certain intellectual circles did Jews gain social acceptance, but by the mid-1930s the assimilationist position appeared hopeless (Fischer-Galati, 1981).

Even though they were anti-Semitic and in alliance with Nazi Germany, the Rumanian political leaders ceased in 1943 to co-operate in the extermination of the Jews, and half of Rumanian Jewry was saved from the Holocaust (Lavi, 1974). From 1944 to 1947 there was a large Jewish emigration, including 24,000 "illegal" immigrants to Palestine, and in 1947 just over 428,000 remained in the country. Further emigration reduced the number still further to 144,000 in 1956 and no more than 100,000 at the end of the 1960s (*Encyclopaedia Judaica*, vol. XIV, 1972).

After the Communists came to power Rumanian Jewry came to be divided between the Zionists, who were the majority, and the Communists and other left-wing groups who made up a strong minority. In contrast to Poland, the Rumanian Communist leadership did not attempt to destroy Jewish communal life. Instead it attempted to change Jewish attitudes through Jewish political front organizations and its support for Communist propaganda in Yiddish. Jews were encouraged to consider themselves Rumanians and distance themselves from other Jews, but Yiddish cultural activity was encouraged under semi-official party guidance, and in the eastern European context there was a comparatively tolerant approach toward Zionist organizations (Vago, 1981).

The groups in Israel

The period of immigration has to be taken into account when comparing Moroccans, Iraqis, Poles, and Rumanians in Israel. If a substantial proportion of a group from a particular country immigrated at a relatively early date, not only did the earlier arrivals have a head start, but later arrivals from the same group had the advantage of contacts with their landsmen in such matters as obtaining jobs and housing. The period of immigration influenced the geographical distribution of the group in Israel, and this in turn affected opportunities for mobility.

Table 4.1 shows that the Poles made up a large proportion of the earlier waves of immigrants. During the period of the British mandate, the Poles were by far the largest group of immigrants. In 1920–31 the Poles constituted 41% of all immigrants followed by Jews from Soviet Russia (29%); in 1932–41, the Poles constituted 42% of all immigrants, followed by Jews from Germany and Austria (22%). Throughout the 1940s the Poles continued to be one of the largest immigrant groups. From 1951 the number of Polish immigrants dwindled greatly, and apart from the years 1955–7, when they constituted 18% of immigrants, their number remained at a low level. The number of Rumanian immigrants increased during the 1940s and continued into the early 1950s; they represented

Table 4.1. *Immigrants: percentages according to continents and four countries of origin*

	1919–48	1949–51	1952–60	1961–4	1965–71	1972–9	1980–5
Asia	8	35	13	9	18	7	9
Africa	1	14	49	51	24	7	23
Europe	88	48	36	35	41	68	41
America and Oceania	2	1	2	5	16	17	27
Morocco	—	4	33	44	15	3	3
Iraq	—	18	1	—	—	—	—
Poland	35	15	13	2	5	2	2
Rumania	8	17	11	28	1	7	9
Total number of immigrants (in thousands)	483	690	294	228	198	268	94

Source: Central Bureau of Statistics, 1988.
Percentages may not add up to 100 due to rounding.

28% of all immigrants in 1950 and 23% in 1951. They were by far the largest immigrant group from Europe during the late 1950s and the 1960s until the Six Day War.

The Iraqi immigration was concentrated in the years 1950–1; they were 19% of all immigrants in 1950 and 51% in 1951. The Moroccans, in comparison, began to arrive in large numbers from 1952; in 1952–4 they were 30% of all immigrants; 43% in 1955–7, and 34% in 1958–67. After 1967 the origins of immigrants changed considerably. A small flow continued from Rumania, but none of the four groups studied here stood out any longer; the largest groups now came from Russia, and from North and South America (Friedlander and Goldscheider, 1979). In the 1980s immigration as a whole dwindled to a small trickle, but in 1990 there are clear indications that a large new immigration from Russia has begun.

The geographical distribution of the groups in Israel is related to their peak periods of migration. Of particular importance was the fact that the Moroccan immigration peaked at the time of the government policy to direct immigrants away from the urban center of the country and settle them in new towns and rural settlements in the northern and southern periphery. This had an accumulative effect since many later Moroccan immigrants chose to settle in those communities where there was already a Moroccan concentration. In 1961, a relatively large proportion of Moroccans lived in rural communities (although not in *kibbutzim*) (Klaff, 1977). By 1972 the proportion in rural communities had dwindled considerably, but there was little change in the distribution of Moroccans between the old and new towns. The earlier immigration of the Iraqis meant that they were far less affected by this policy, and they tended to settle in the urban center of the country. Immigrants from Europe, such as the Rumanians, were also encouraged to settle in the periphery, but they were able to use their greater independent resources and contacts to exercise their choice to settle in the center. Some initially went to the new towns but later left, so that Jews from North Africa became by far the dominant population in the "development towns." Thus, in 1972, 47% of the Moroccans lived in the new urban settlements compared with 17% of the Iraqis and Rumanians and only 6% of the Poles. In contrast, only 46% of the Moroccans lived in the old established urban centers compared with 77% of the Iraqis, 78% of the Rumanians, and 84% of the Poles (Central Bureau of Statistics, 1972).

The 1983 census shows little change in the overall pattern (the following figures include first and second generation). In the city of Tel Aviv the Poles constitute 16.7% of the population compared with 7.5%

Rumanians, 7.5% Iraqis, and 4.5% Moroccans. In the wealthy suburb of Ramat Ha'sharon outside of Tel Aviv the proportions of Poles (13.7%) and Iraqis (13.4%) are almost identical; Rumanians constitute 6.2% and Moroccans 4.9%. The Rumanians are the largest of the four groups in Haifa and in some other smaller towns, such as Rehovot. Jerusalem is an exception among the older cities; Moroccans constitute 12.3%, Iraqis 9.9%, Poles 6.0%, and Rumanians 4.3%. A clear contrast is obvious, however, when we turn to the new towns in the periphery: in the northern town of Qiryat Shemona, the Moroccans constitute 52.3% of the population, the Iraqis 7%, the Rumanians 4.0%, and the Poles 1.7%; in the southern town of Dimona, the Moroccans constitute 50.6%, the Rumanians 5.9%, the Poles 1.1%, and the Iraqis 0.8% (Central Bureau of Statistics, 1984).

Weiker (1983) has provided indexes of residential concentration of groups of origin (first and second generation) in the three largest towns from the 1961 and 1972 census data. There was a decline in residential concentration during the decade for all four groups, but in all cases the Rumanians were the least likely to concentrate and the Moroccans the most likely; for example, in Tel Aviv in 1972, the index of residential concentration was .173 for Rumanians and .526 for Moroccans. The Iraqis were the second most likely group to concentrate in Jerusalem and Haifa, but in Tel Aviv the Poles were somewhat more concentrated than the Iraqis.

A further measure of in-group and out-group tendencies is the "attraction index," a measure of those marrying persons from the same country of origin (or whose fathers were from the same country), that takes into account the overall available "marriage pool" for each country. In 1962, the indexes were: Iraqis .92, Moroccans (grouped with Algerians and Tunisians) .74, Rumanians .58, and Poles .48. By 1979 the indexes had fallen considerably but the placing of the groups was the same: Iraqis .37, Moroccans .34, Rumanians .32, and Poles .28.

The greater concentration of Moroccans, both in the development towns and in particular neighborhoods in the large cities, has meant that they have retained, and in some respects even developed, a higher degree of cultural distinctiveness than the other groups. In this respect they display greater similarity to Yemenites than to Iraqis. Cultural change is evident in the sharp decline in family size and religious practice, but Moroccan groups still study the Zohar, ethnic festivals and celebrations are very popular, and pilgrimages to the tombs of saints have increased considerably in recent years. Ethnic music continues to appeal to the young.

Turning to occupational distribution, the data on the first generation from the three censuses (table 4.2) indicate both considerable mobility in all four groups and a continuation of inequality among the groups. Again, the Poles and the Moroccans are at the two extremes. The white-collar category increased in the Polish group from 44% in 1961 to 58% in 1981, and in the Moroccan group from 12% in 1961 to 28% in 1981. In the Moroccan group there was a considerable drop in the proportion in agriculture, but in contrast with the Poles and Rumanians there was no decline in the proportion in blue-collar work. The proportion of Iraqis in lower ranking white-collar jobs and trade is now about the same as among the European groups, but in the highest occupational categories of professionals and managers the major difference is between the European groups on the one hand and the Middle Eastern groups on the other: 29% of the Poles and Rumanians are in this category compared with 15% of the Iraqis and 10% of the Moroccans.

Indexes of dissimilarity in occupation among the four groups show that, in 1961 and 1971, the distance of Iraqis from Moroccans was greater than from Rumanians and Poles. However, by 1981 the distance of Iraqis from the Europeans had increased and they were now about equal distance from the Rumanians on the one side and the Moroccans on the other (Nahon, 1984a). The mean occupational prestige scores of the four groups in 1974, based on a National Mobility Study, also revealed substantial inequality between the European and Middle Eastern groups; the scores for males aged twenty-five to sixty-four who were born in Israel or who immigrated before age fourteen were Poles 50, Rumanians 40, Iraqis 25, and Moroccans 23 (Matras and Tyree, 1977). An even greater dichotomization was found by Kraus in her study of prestige attributed to groups of origin. On a nine-point scale, the score for Poles was 7.7, for Rumanians 7.5, for Iraqis .6, and for Moroccans .2 (Kraus, 1985).

Intergenerational advance in all groups, together with the continuation of the social gap, are shown in data on education. A comparison of the education of males born abroad aged sixty to sixty-four with males and females aged thirty to thirty-four in 1983 shows that the proportion of those with only primary education has declined dramatically in all four groups, although about a quarter of the younger age cohort of Moroccans and Iraqis is still in this category. At the level of higher education there is a wide difference between the Middle Easterners and Europeans: in the young cohort 15% of the Moroccans and 18% of the Iraqis have thirteen or more years of education compared with 51% of the Rumanians and 58% of the Poles (Nahon, 1987).

The combination of veteranship in the country, demographic promi-

Table 4.2. *Occupational distribution of country of origin groups, 1961, 1972, and 1981 percentages*

Occupational categories	Poles 1961	1972	1981	Rumanians 1961	1972	1981	Moroccans 1961	1972	1981	Iraqis 1961	1972	1981
Professionals and managers	44<	22	29	37<	19	29	12<	7	10	32<	12	15
Clerks and traders		29	29		26	25	12	15	18	9	25	26
Services	6	6	4	8	8	7		15	12		8	9
Agriculture	6	5	4	9	4	2	25	8	6	12	5	5
Blue-collar workers	44	40	35	46	42	37	51	55	54	37	47	49

Source: Nahon, 1984a.
Percentages may not add up to 100 due to rounding.

nence, and a high socio-economic profile has made the Poles an important element in the political sphere. One indicator, among others, is that the last three prime ministers (Begin, Peres, and Shamir) are of Polish origin. Rumanians have not had the benefit of veteran organizations and networks, and they are much less prominent than the Poles in politics.

The expectations of many Moroccan Jews that what they had not attained in Morocco because of discrimination they would attain in Israel were not fulfilled, and they have been prominent in protest demonstrations and movements, such as in the riots that broke out in the Haifa slum of Wadi Salib in 1959, and in the Black Panther movement that emerged in the Musrara quarter of Jerusalem in 1970 (Bar-Yosef, 1970; Bernstein, 1984; E. Cohen, 1972). They have been among the major supporters of the ethnic political parties, Tami and Shas, but the reaction of most Moroccans to the political establishment of the Ma'arach was expressed by supporting the nationalist right-wing. In recent years politicians of Moroccan origin have made gains: fifteen of the thirty-one non-Ashkenazi members of the Knesset in 1984 were Moroccans, making their representation in parliament (13%) almost equal to their proportion in the population (14%). The number of ministers of Moroccan origin increased from none before 1977 to three in 1987. Moroccans have been elected as mayors in a number of towns such as Ashdod, Ashkelon, Sderot, and Yavneh.

The Zionist background of many Iraqi Jews enabled them to become prominent among the non-Ashkenazi politicians and public servants of the new state, and every Israeli government has had at least one minister of Iraqi origin. From 1984 to 1988 there were three ministers of Iraqi origin. Unlike some Moroccan leaders, the Iraqi politicians are rarely ethnoclass leaders or trade-union militants; they are generally successful businessmen or lawyers.

The setting: Beer Sheva

Beer Sheva has a population of 110,000 and is the commercial center for the urban and rural settlements in the southern part of the country. Its development as a modern city began after the War of Independence in 1948, and its population grew rapidly in the 1950s and 1960s. Between 1960 and 1965 the population of the city grew by 66%, between 1975 and 1980 by 11%, and today there is a negative migration balance as some residents move to independent suburban communities close to the city or to the center of the country (Efrat, 1987). Most of the residents of Beer

Sheva who are in the work-force are employed in the city. Of all Jewish employees in the Beer Sheva region in 1983, nearly 20% were employed in industry, 17% in trade and finance, and 42% in public services.

All but 1,000 people in Beer Sheva are Jews, about a third of European or American origin and two-thirds of African or Asian origin. Nearly half of the population was born abroad, and the other half is mainly second generation. The proportion of European-Americans and of third and subsequent generations are underrepresented in Beer Sheva and the North Africans are overrepresented. However, the proportion of North Africans in Beer Sheva is far less than in the smaller "development towns." In fact, with respect to its Moroccan and Polish population, the demographic composition in Beer Sheva falls between the urban center on the one hand and the urban periphery on the other. The proportions of Rumanians and Iraqis in Beer Sheva are similar to many other cities and towns in the country. This ethnic heterogeneity makes the town a most suitable setting for a study of ethnicity in Israel.

The Moroccan group is the largest in Beer Sheva; together with Jews from Tangier, its first and second generations constitute 28% of the first and second generation population of the city. The Algerians–Tunisians (14%), and the Russians (12%) come next. Following them are the Rumanians (10%), the Iraqis (7%), and the Poles (4%). If data were available on third and subsequent generations, we would no doubt find that the Polish group would be several percentage points larger. The many other groups of origin in Beer Sheva (German, Czech, Bulgarian, Egyptian, Libyan, Indian, etc.) are smaller.

From the earliest years of its modern development new immigrants made up the majority of settlers in Beer Sheva, but through the 1950s it was the minority of "veterans" of European origin who occupied the major positions in the principal institutions of the city: the town hall, local Histadrut council, and local Labour Party branch. The veterans co-opted some of the immigrants who later gained control. This was especially true of the Iraqis, most of whom came to Beer Sheva in 1950–1. The higher status immigrants among the Iraqis tended to settle in the center of the country, and those that came to Beer Sheva were mainly from the lower strata. The concentrated in-migration of Iraqis to Beer Sheva meant that there were strong family and landsmen links among them in the town, and they established ethnic organizations which provided a springboard for members of the *edah* to gain important positions in the town. In 1962, a mayor of Iraqi origins was elected.

The first wave of Rumanian immigrants in Beer Sheva came in 1950–2, at the same time as the Iraqis. Another wave came in 1956–7, and others arrived in the 1960s. They established an organization of the *edah* in the town, as did the Polish immigrants, many of whom came in two waves, in 1949–50 and 1957–60. The Polish immigrants in Beer Sheva were mainly artisans, small merchants, and clerks with a minority of professionals and academics, but the group as a whole was absorbed comparatively easily, finding as they did a common language with, and cultural closeness to, the veterans.

Immigrants from Morocco started to come to Beer Sheva in large numbers in 1953, and a large wave came in 1957 at the same time as the Poles. The North Africans perceived that the Polish immigrants received better treatment than themselves and this created much bitterness among them. Partly as a consequence of the fact that, unlike the Iraqis, the Moroccans did not arrive in Beer Sheva all at once but in a number of waves, they failed to organize as effectively as the Iraqis; a strong leadership did not emerge, and they were less successful in obtaining good housing and jobs (Zamir, 1966; Gradus and Stern, 1979).

A study of Jews of Moroccan origin in Beer Sheva, carried out in the 1970s, pointed to important differences among them with respect to their exposure to western (French) culture, prior to their immigration (Amilianer, 1979). The sample of 250 was divided into three groups. The first, least westernized group (17% of the sample), had spoken mainly Arabic in Morocco and continued to speak Arabic among themselves in Beer Sheva. Of this category 40% had been born in villages in Morocco, but most of these had migrated to the Moroccan coastal cities (47% lived in Casablanca prior to their migration). None had lived in the French areas in Morocco; 62% had lived in mixed Arab-Jewish neighborhoods, and the rest in the *mellah*. The largest group (62% of the sample) had been born in traditional communities where Muslims were the dominant group, but they had been exposed to French culture in the French-Jewish schools. Half of this category had lived in the *mellah* and half in mixed Jewish-Arabic neighborhoods. The third category (22%) was born to parents who were already acculturated to French culture. French was their mother tongue, they were more educated and less religiously observant than the other two categories, and they were educated in French-Jewish schools or in general French language schools. This group still spoke French within the family and among friends in Beer Sheva.

The socio-economic heterogeneity of the Moroccans in Beer Sheva is indicated by the 1983 census material that shows both the ethnic composition and socio-economic characteristics of neighborhoods in Beer Sheva. If we take the proportion of Moroccans in Beer Sheva as a whole as a bench mark, they are overrepresented (39%) in the poorest neighborhood (D), but they are only slightly underrepresented (21%) in the major middle-class neighborhood (H). The Poles represent a reverse picture: they are underrepresented in D and overrepresented in H. The Rumanians and Iraqis are underrepresented in both the poorest and in the middle-class neighborhoods; they are found in greater proportions in some of the neighborhoods that have intermediate socio-economic profiles (Central Bureau of Statistics, 1984). This distribution attests to Beer Sheva as a suitable setting in which to investigate the independent effects and interrelationships of ethnicity and socio-economic status in the four groups of origin.

II

Social patterns and behavior

Part II focuses on what might be called the more objective dimensions of ethnicity, religion, and class: their institutional and behavioral expressions. In chapter 5 two neighborhoods, one predominantly working-class and the other predominantly middle-class, are compared by investigating the cultural forms and social activities of their synagogues and neighborhood committees. The methods used to gather the information discussed in this chapter, such as participant observation and open-ended interviews, complemented the survey that provided the data analyzed in the other chapters. Whereas chapter 5 analyzes religious behavior at the community and congregational level, chapter 6 focuses on religious observance at the individual and family level. In both cases the relationships between religion and ethnic origin and between religion and class are emphasized. From the focus in chapter 6 on a cultural factor, religion, the study moves on in chapter 7 to an analysis of the social structure of ethnicity and class as reflected in the friendship networks of respondents.

5

Neighborhoods: synagogues and neighborhood committees

In the 1950s Middle Eastern and European groups of origin in Beer Sheva founded ethnic organizations which provided both contexts of sociability and material help, such as small loans, for their members. Over time these organizations lost their instrumental functions to state, municipal, and other public agencies, and as contexts for social interaction, they held little appeal for the younger generation who grew up in Israel. Ethnic organizations or *Landsmannschaften* are far less important today, but the ethnic synagogue has remained important among Middle Easterners.

As in other countries of immigration, such as the United States, the ethnic religious congregations provided a medium for the continuation of traditional religious practices and a center for the social interaction of members whose common origins, native language or dialect, and common cultural and social patterns provided important bases for the comforting and familiar patterns of communication and community. However, in the United States most ethnic churches and synagogues did not last beyond the first generation, and the second generation tended to reject the traditional ethnic culture of their parents and to join interethnic congregations along denominational lines (Herberg, 1960). Since more than half the adult population of Israel was born or socialized in the country, it is now possible to investigate whether a similar process of de-ethnization of religion is occurring in Israel.

Tabory and Lazerwitz (1983) write that, whereas in the United States ethnic pluralism has historically been discouraged and religious plural-ism encouraged, the opposite is the case in Israel: an Orthodox estab-lishment has guarded its monopoly of religious authority in official realms against Conservative and Reform Judaism, but it has not opposed the formation of ethnic congregations. As long as religious differentiation is in accord with the basic patterns of Orthodoxy, particular ethnic religious customs have been acceptable. But, although there is no ideology in Israel that calls for the erosion of local religious *minhagim* (customs), there are a number of reasons to expect that ethnic synagogues based on origins from particular localities and countries will continue to be more common among Jews from North Africa and Asia than among Jews from Europe.

Firstly, in recent times there was greater local differentiation of *minhagim* among Jewish communities in North Africa and Asia. The Jewish prayer book has never been uniform and local *minhag* (custom) has always been important, but improved communication and more extensive and widespread use of the printing press in Europe led to greater standardization and consolidation in the religious rite in Europe than in the Middle East. With some exceptions, such as the Yemenite communities, there was some standardization of the Sephardi rite among Middle Eastern communities, but this was not as extensive as the consolidation of the Ashkenazi rite among most European communities.

Secondly, religion among Middle Eastern Jews tended to be less differentiated from the family and the local community than among European Jews. The importance of genealogical lines and the related territorial belongingness deepened the importance of the family and the local community among Jews in Islamic countries. In contrast to European immigrants who came to Israel as individuals or small families, large numbers of Jews from North Africa and Asia came as whole communities, and, despite their geographical distribution and cultural adaptation in Israel, they have not broken their contacts with the family and the community. As long as religious observance remains anchored in strong familial and community ties, the ethnic synagogue is likely to continue (Shokeid, 1984).

Thirdly, whereas religious Orthodox Jews from Europe tended to be non-Zionist or anti-Zionist and most Zionist Ashkenazim were not religious at all, many Middle Eastern Jews saw Zionism and the establishment of the Jewish state as affirmations of the tradition that they had upheld in their countries of origin. The tradition may have contained many parochial elements found in their locality of origin, but their concern to continue that tradition was an expression of their strong identification as Jews in the Jewish state (Ben-Rafael, 1982: 39–40, 50–4).

Fourthly, a greater tolerance with respect to levels of religious observance among Middle Eastern Jews has reduced internal division within the ethnic communities. There was less emphasis among Middle Eastern Jews on strict religious norms limiting relationships with non-Jews, and religious traditionalism in North Africa and Asia was not challenged, as it was in Europe, by non-Orthodox movements or by anti-religious secularism (Sharot, 1976, 1982). The concern of religious European Jews with the defense of Orthodoxy continued in Israel and contributed to their polarization from the secular sectors of their communities of origin. Middle Eastern Israelis have abandoned some observances, but their greater religious tolerance has contributed to the emergence of a "partly religious" or *mesorati* (traditional) pattern of observance that enables their communities of origin to retain their cohesion (Shokeid, 1984).

Lastly, ethnic pluralism in Israel is legitimized only in certain spheres such as religion and folklore, and immigrants, especially those from Asia and Africa, were subject to pressures to discard a large part of their traditional cultures and adopt the dominant westernized Israeli culture. One response of many Middle Eastern Israelis to the absorption policies of the veteran, mainly European Israelis, was to compartmentalize their traditions within the enclosed contexts of their families and ethnic synagogues (Stahl, 1976). Later, the improvement in the socio-economic position of Middle Eastern Israelis and their substantial acculturation to western culture provided a basis for a more self-confident assertion of their own cultural heritages (Weingrod, 1979).

In contrast with religious congregations, public organizations at both national and local levels are expected to function in a non-pluralist fashion. We felt, therefore, that it would be instructive not only to study the patterns of ethnically based religious pluralism, but also to compare and investigate the interplay of this pluralism with organizations that are intended to serve the population according to universalistic principles. Since religious congregations draw their affiliates on neighborhood as well as ethnic lines, it was decided to include a study of neighborhood committees in the same areas. Neighborhood committees are expected to mediate between individual residents or groups and city or national agencies, to provide or contribute to various services, such as the condition of the streets, civil defense, social assistance, activities for the youth and the elderly, and the integration of immigrants. In order to investigate these institutions, our survey was complemented by neighborhood research employing the methods of participant observation, interviews with leaders, activists, and samples of members in the organizations, and a review of documents such as organizational rules and protocols of meetings.

Two neighborhoods, G and H, were selected for special study. H is the largest middle-class neighborhood of the city and G, although by no means the poorest or most deprived neighborhood, is predominantly working class. The residents of H are divided about equally between European and Middle Eastern origins. In G, two-thirds of the residents are of Middle Eastern origin and a third of European origin (Central Bureau of Statistics, 1984). However, each neighborhood has a subsection which differs from the predominant socio-economic and ethnic profiles; H has a poorer subsection ("old H") where the population is predominantly Middle Eastern, and G includes a middle-class area where more than half the population is European.

The working-class neighborhood

In G the synagogues represent the clearest expression of ethnic pluralism. The area contains seven Moroccan synagogues, three Tunisian, one Iraqi, one Algerian, one Georgian, one Rumanian, and one synagogue with Ashkenazi members from various origins. Observations and interviews were conducted in three of these synagogues; two *edah* synagogues, Moroccan and Rumanian, and the Ashkenazi synagogue. A comparison of the two ethnic synagogues demonstrates a difference between European and Middle Eastern religious Israelis that can be observed widely in Israel: whereas European congregations based on country of origin are declining, among Middle Easterners the synagogue based on country of origin remains the prevailing type.

Both the Moroccan and Rumanian synagogues are located in the poorer parts of G. The Rumanian synagogue was established more than thirty years ago and now has forty worshipers; the majority were manual workers but are now mostly pensioners over sixty years of age. The state of the congregation illustrates the typical process of Ashkenazi synagogues based on country of origin; it is a first generation phenomenon that gradually declines as its original members grow older and die out.

The Moroccan synagogue is located in a section where there are many Jews from North Africa who came to Israel in the early 1960s. The congregation started in an old, decaying building, but it is now situated in a modern building with about 100 seats. With the exception of one Tunisian, all members are of Moroccan origin, and, with three exceptions, the members are wage-earners with a low socio-economic status. The congregation includes a number of young members, but the majority are in their forties. The synagogue is governed in a patrimonial fashion by a prosperous independent businessman and is named after his father who was among its founders and contributed considerably to the expenses of the building. The *rosh* (head) governs with the help of a treasurer and synagogue secretary, and he deals with such matters as the issuing of loans to members with sons who wish to marry. He is accorded great honor, and his entrance in the synagogue signals a focus for the gathering of members.

In addition to the regular services, some members are engaged in other traditional activities. A small group of the more elderly members visits houses of deceased, participates in memorial prayers, and reads the Zohar, the major cabbalistic treatise, on Saturday evenings. Apart from these activities, members seldom meet for social occasions outside the synagogue.

Interviews with members showed that they saw the synagogue as an important medium for the continuation of the *edah* and its religious traditions. Most members maintained a high level of observance of the *mitzvot* (commandments); about a third indicated that they observed fewer *mitzvot* than their fathers and a half defined themselves as "traditional," meaning partly religious, rather than religious (*datiim*). Very few perceived important cultural differences between Moroccan Jews and other *edot ha'Mizrach*, but the majority emphasized that there were wide cultural differences between themselves and Ashkenazim, including religious Ashkenazim. The differences between religious *edot ha'Mizrach* and religious Ashkenazim that were mentioned included *minhagim*, especially those on the religious holidays, the more tolerant attitude of *edot ha'Mizrach* toward religious observance, and, more generally, completely different patterns of behavior.

In answer to questions on the reasons for their affiliation to the particular synagogue and the importance of the synagogue in the neighborhood, members mentioned such reasons as their fathers had worshiped there, the style of prayer, and the importance of the *edah* and its traditions. Thus, although many members emphasized their cultural commonality with other *edot ha'Mizrach* and about half put their identity as part of *edot ha'Mizrach* before their identity as Moroccan Jews, in the sphere of religion the *edah* identity and allegiance to its traditions remain of considerable importance. Among the Middle Easterners, the *edah* synagogue would appear to have a future that goes beyond the first generation.

The members of the Ashkenazi synagogue stem from a number of countries (Poland, Hungary, Rumania, and Russia). The synagogue, an attractive building with about eighty seats, is situated in the middle-class section of G, and its members include bank managers, hotel and other property owners, and academics. The congregation began thirty years ago, and although the membership is an ageing one, it does not have the atmosphere of decline of the Rumanian synagogue. Most members are over fifty years of age and their sons have tended to leave the area, but some of the sons return to pray with their fathers on the religious holidays.

Members tend to belong to the Mafdal (National Religious Party), the modern Orthodox political party, and they emphasize their strict observance to the *mitzvot*. Activities in the synagogue focus on prayer and on religious studies directed by the more scholarly members. There is no full time *hazan* (cantor) and members take turns to lead the services. There are also no elections; the leadership rotates in an informal process and leaders are not regarded as having special status or honor. Members do not emphasize ethnic traditions, nor do they look upon the synagogue as a social milieu for Jews from a particular country of origin. The congregation is built on principles of a common Ashkenazi pattern of Orthodox observance and way of life; members distinguish themselves from secular Jews and from what they see as lax observance in many other congregations.

Turning to the neighborhood committee in G, it is clear that it functions in an area where ethnic communities, focused on the synagogue, are still strong. However, its activities are dictated and restricted in large part by the presence of the Project Renewal, a program for disprivileged neighborhoods under the auspices of the Ministry of Housing. The concerns of the Project include the improvement of housing, general cultural activities, such as music and drawing circles, and sports, but it tends to ignore ethnically informed culture, especially religion.

The head of the local Project Renewal committee was a former activist in the neighborhood and he collaborates with the neighborhood committee that includes his personal friends. Many residents make no distinction between the two committees, and since resources are largely distributed by the Project Renewal, the neighborhood committee has little basis for an independent stance. The committee has found a niche in mediating between the bureaucratic apparatus of Project Renewal and the local considerations and needs of the neighborhood. It has intervened, for example, when residents have complained that the Project Renewal committee mistakenly allocated apartments to certain families rather than others.

The concern of members of the neighborhood committee to assert their independence and influence was demonstrated when they opposed the establishment of an additional Moroccan synagogue (there were already seven Moroccan synagogues in G), in favor of the establishment of a synagogue for Georgians who had none and were conducting services in a small yard. In its success in this and other cases, such as providing assistance for especially underprivileged families, the committee acted under the banner of a local particularistic approach as opposed to the general bureaucratic approach of the Project Renewal committee.

It is particularly in the realm of religious needs and activities that the neighborhood committee can show its rapport with the local population. Since the Project Renewal has shown little response to demands for religious services, religious residents have addressed their claims to the neighborhood committee. The members of the latter are similar to the members of the Project Renewal committee in their non-religiousness and in their determination to leave the local rabbis out of decision-making processes, but after many hesitations they supported a demand of young religious couples for a neighborhood *mikveh* (ritual bath). The committee's fight for this request in the relevant ministries and offices was dictated less by the members' conviction for its justification (a *mikveh* existed in an adjoining neighborhood), than by their concern to display the committee's importance and strength *vis-à-vis* the Project Renewal.

The middle-class neighborhood

The retention of ethnic traditions, especially religious ones, continues in the working-class sectors of Middle Easterners, but among many of the middle class there is a greater inclination to abandon their traditions and accept the European patterns. The middle class continues, however, to express pride in their particular *edah* and in *edot ha'Mizrach*, and they are concerned that their cultural traditions will be preserved as part of the cultural whole. Most of those who are affiliated with a synagogue are unwilling to accept "Ashkenization" in the religious sphere, but the establishment of a "non-ethnic" congregation in Beer Sheva reveals that for some the value of amalgamation is so important that they are ready to attempt to implement it even in the religious sphere where ethnic pluralism is legitimate. The history of the non-ethnic congregation demonstrates the problems of Middle Eastern Israelis who seek what they consider would be a true, rather than unidirectional, cultural fusion with Europeans.

The non-ethnic synagogue has a middle-class congregation; the majority of members have academic credentials and work in high-ranking white-collar occupations. The level of religious knowledge among members is high and they do not feel the need of a rabbi as a *halachic* (religious law) authority. The history of the congregation began in 1962 when a number of Jews from both European and Middle Eastern origins formed a prayer group and met for services on the Sabbath and the religious holidays in a religious school. This arrangement continued for four years; there were few worshipers and they were able to agree on a service that included both European and Middle Eastern styles of prayer. With the declared aim of bringing the *edot* closer together, the participants decided to establish a non-ethnic synagogue. A modern style synagogue was built with about 150 seats; it was financed in part by the founders and in part by a number of organizations, including the Ministry of Religion. During its first years new members maintained the composition of about half from Europe and half from North Africa and Asia.

Although the regulations of the synagogue included provision for experimentation and the introduction of different forms of prayer, the European style was, from the beginning, the dominant one with only a few isolated customs and prayers according to Middle Eastern styles. Some Middle Eastern members attempted, without success, to introduce additional prayers of *edot ha'Mizrach*, such as a prayer said on the Sabbath before Purim and hymns during the Yamim Noraim (Days of Awe). After European members opposed the introduction of expressions and symbols according to Middle Eastern customs in the prayers on Rosh Hashanah (New Year), a number of Middle Eastern members began to conduct a separate service in a room of the synagogue.

In 1972 a committee was elected to examine possible changes in the prayers on the high holidays. Some changes were introduced, but the opposition of European members led to their omission a year later. Many of the Middle Eastern members subsequently resigned their membership and established their own synagogue on the same street with services based on Sephardi customs. The proportion of members from Middle Eastern origins in the non-ethnic synagogue fell to about a fifth and has remained at that level.

The structure of the service has remained basically European with only occasional Middle Eastern modifications. The European style is obvious in the reading of the Torah, the associated customs of religious honors, the central prayers on the Sabbath and the religious holidays, and in the arrangement of the synagogue hall; the rows of seats face the Ark rather than surround it as is common in the synagogues of Middle Easterners. The few customs of Middle Easterners that were introduced include hoisting the Sefer Torah (Scroll of the Law) before it is read (in addition to the European custom of hoisting it after it is read), and a prayer on Sabbath eve reminding worshipers of the lighting of candles in place of a similar prayer according to Ashkenazi custom.

Interviews revealed that, although Middle Eastern members were more likely to stress a cultural distance between *edot ha'Mizrach* and Ashkenazim, they indicated a greater readiness to accept other religious customs; half of the Middle Eastern members and a third of the European members said that they were willing to pray according to every form of

Jewish prayer. By any objective measure Middle Eastern members had given up a larger part of their traditional style of worshiping, but the feeling of having given up religious customs was expressed in about equal measure by European and Middle Eastern members.

The failure of the interethnic congregation in its attempt to amalgamate European and Middle Eastern Jews demonstrates that, although middle-class Israelis from the Middle East tend to acculturate to, and associate with, the dominant European sector in their class, these processes are not likely to extend to religion in the near future. In a largely unconscious fashion the Europeans tend to regard cultural amalgamation as unidirectional; the norms and styles of European Jews are taken for granted, and non-Europeans are expected to behave in conformity with them. In most non-religious or secularized cultural spheres a considerable degree of acculturation to the "western" patterns has occurred among Middle Easterners. But although Middle Easterners have also displayed considerable adaptability in the religious sphere, the refusal of religious European Israelis to make more than minor modifications is likely to lead to a continued separation of religious congregations.

In H synagogue members are divided between Ashkenazim and North African or Asian congregations, but most residents are not affiliated with a synagogue and the local neighborhood committee is less likely to confront, and act as a broker for, ethnically based religious congregations. The predominantly middle-class profile of the neighborhood has marginalized its committee which is located in a small apartment in a modest building. On paper the neighborhood is divided into ten sections and each section is supposed to elect a representative to the committee, but in practice this body is run by a handful of volunteers, and the chairman has held his position for so many years that he has become identified with it. With one or two exceptions, the committee's administration of neighborhood services is sparse and sporadic. Complaints about the lack or level of services in the area, such as the absence of a building for a youth club or the neglect of traffic lights, are deflected by committee members who claim that the image of a well-established, middle-class neighborhood results in its neglect by the city agencies which expect the "wealthy" inhabitants to take care of their problems by themselves.

The achievements of the committee in recent years, such as preventing the closure of a club for working women and persuading the police to increase its patrols, have been modest and demonstrate the minor importance of the committee in the public life of the neighborhood. The more important achievement in the neighborhood, such as the expansion of the local school and the establishment of a large synagogue, have been organized by local inhabitants without any link to the committee.

H is not, however, homogeneously middle class, and the committee has had, on occasion, to deal with ethnic differences and social divisions. The gathering of lower-class residents from the Georgian *edah* to drink and play cards in the local park led to tensions with other residents who complained to the local authorities. The committee sided with the well-established part of the neighborhood and supported action that returned the park to its previous calm. As "compensation" the chairman of the committee sponsored a report describing the social plight of the Georgians and calling for mutual understanding. He also proposed a modest sum to support a small Georgian folklore band that could take part in future cultural events. Thus, the committee sought to improve relations between a particular *edah* and others by promoting ethnic cultural activities under its institutional auspices.

The resources of the committee were not adequate to deal with the much larger problems of the working-class section of the neighborhood. In 1982–3, in response to the absence of aid and action on the part of the committee, a group from "old H" proclaimed their independence and, with the help of a local social worker, established an independent committee. It succeeded in obtaining finance from diverse agencies, including the Ministry of Welfare and the municipality, and it now organizes various activities for that section of the neighborhood. The initiative was an expression of the estrangement between the "old" and the "new" H, and it showed that lower-class areas are able to obtain resources from local and central institutions through independent mobilization.

Comparisons

We have noted that the only significant institutional area of legitimate ethnic pluralism within the Israeli-Jewish population is religion, and that Jews from the Middle East are more inclined to support an ethnic synagogue. Although Judaism may be considered the most important historical focus of Jewish unity, in Israeli society it reinforces ethnic heterogeneity among Jewish groups of origin. Religion is associated with ethnic divisions at two levels; at the level of the individual *edah*, especially among Middle Easterners, and at the level of the more general distinction between Ashkenazim and *edot ha'Mizrach* or Sephardim. There is little formal pluralism in other institutional areas, but there is considerable inequality in the socio-economic distribution of the groups of origin. The administration by neighborhood committees is premised on non-pluralist principles; they are expected to service all the ethnic groups in the area and its activities reflect the class composition of the neighborhoods. However, the combination of ethnically based religious pluralism and ethnic stratification leads the committees to concern themselves with, and even strengthen, ethnic pluralism.

In the working-class district ethnic congregations continue to be strong among Middle Easterners, but they are in decline among religious European Jews who tend to establish Ashkenazi synagogues. The neighborhood committee is a non-ethnic agency, but it maintains its independence in the face of the bureaucratic apparatus of a national project by responding to the parochial needs of groups which are organized around the ethnic synagogues. The competition of non-ethnic brokers and their distribution of resources in response to the ethnic groups' demands tend to strengthen the ethnic divisions within the neighborhood.

Religiosity and identifications with the *edah* and with the broader category (*edot ha'Mizrach* or Ashkenazim) are much stronger among Middle Easterners than among Europeans, but socio-economically mobile Middle Easterners tend to be both less religious and less ethnic than the majority from their groups of origin. There are, however, some economically successful individuals, such as the head of the Moroccan synagogue in G, who retain strong ties with their *edah* and become "notables" or "patrons" in the ethnic congregations of the predominantly working-class milieu. This is more likely to be the case among independent businessmen than among other sectors of the middle class; the self-employed tend to have fewer years of education and more homogeneous ethnic friendship networks than middle-class employees.

In H the middle-class Middle Easterners display greater tendencies to acculturate to the dominant secular culture, but among those for whom religion is a focal point of identity "Ashkenization" does not normally extend to the religious sphere, and an attempt at religious amalgamation in a non-ethnic synagogue was largely unsuccessful. The history of the non-ethnic congregation shows that the major orientation among Europeans is not one of ethnic exclusion of Middle Easterners; religious as well as secular European groups are open to mobile individuals from Middle Eastern origins, but it is assumed that the mobiles will conform to the dominant European patterns. Religious pluralism based on ethnic origins is legitimate, but, when religious amalgamation is attempted, it is the Middle Easterners who are required to make the major concessions.

After unsuccessful attempts to introduce changes in the services, the majority of Middle Eastern members seceded from the "non-ethnic" synagogue. It is significant, however, that the seceders did not return to separate *edah* synagogues but established a new congregation whose services are according to Nusach Yerushalmi (the Jerusalem Version). This form of service is that of the prestigious Sephardi veterans and differs considerably from the services of most of the immigrants from the Middle East who migrated to Israel in the 1950s and 1960s. The Sephardi synagogue in H has grown in size and contains new members from many Middle Eastern *edot*. Thus, among Middle Eastern mobiles who have disaffiliated from the *edah* congregations but who do not feel comfortable in the Ashkenazi congregations, a solution has been found in a Sephardi congregation. Whereas at the working-class level the *edah* synagogue remains strong among Middle Easterners, at the middle-class level there is a tendency for religious Jews to separate, at least for religious services, into two broad categories, Ashkenazim and Sephardim.

Many Middle Easterners from the middle class continue to affiliate with an ethnic Sephardi synagogue, but the synagogue is less a center of an ethnic community as it is among the working class, and they do not make demands as ethnic groups on the neighborhood committee. The predominantly middle-class character of H has not only marginalized the committee, but has also led to the neglect of the social problems of the working-class sector. The latter reacted by establishing their independent committee and mobilized resources for their own needs. Although social, economic, and political forms of ethnic pluralism are rarely legitimized, the response of national and city agencies to the requests of deprived sectors can lead to local organizational divisions between a predominantly European middle class and a predominantly Middle Eastern working class.

6

Religiosity and secularization

Secularization and its limits

Our investigations of neighborhoods and ethnic synagogues have pointed to the important relationship between religion and ethnicity. If religiosity in Israel is an important basis of ethnicity, secularization would necessarily lead to a decline in ethnicity. In this chapter, we present the findings from our survey that relate to the question of secularization among the four groups of origin, Moroccans, Iraqis, Poles, and Rumanians.

Secularization, "the process by which religious institutions, actions, and consciousness lose their social significance,"[1] has commonly been viewed either as a dimension or as a consequence of modernization; industrialization, urbanization, the growth of science and technology, the spread of education, the development of the mass media, and the participation of the masses into political society have been seen as contributing factors in the decline of religion (Wilson, 1966, 1982; Berger, 1967). Secularization is not, however, an inevitable consequence of the many developments that have often been grouped together under the term "modernization," and the relationships of these two multidimensional processes vary considerably depending on the religious, cultural, and social contexts. In many Islamic societies developments such as urbanization and expansion of higher education appear to have contributed to the contemporary resurgence of Islam (Arjomand, 1986). Even in the western Christian context a decline in religiosity or religious practice did not always follow industrialization and urbanization, and there is substantial variation in the degrees and forms of secularization both among and within western nations (Martin, 1978; Mol, 1972).

Whatever its limitations in other contexts, the modernization–secularization perspective appears to work well in the case of western Jews. The precipitating factor in the decline of religiosity among Jews in central and western Europe was their movement out of what had been semi-autonomous and highly boundaried communities. The transition into the wider society involved concentration in large urban centers, diffusion into the modern sectors of education, commerce, and industry, and participation in the political institutions of their respective nations. Increased social interaction with non-Jews and participation in modernizing societies were accompanied or followed by a sharp decline in Jewish religious practice (Sharot, 1976).

Since Jews in traditional communities followed highly detailed religious prescriptions and proscriptions in their daily life, secularization was particularly obvious in the behavioral sphere. Changes in beliefs may have been no less drastic, but the emphasis of Judaism on the performance of numerous *mitzvot* made the decline in religious practice far more apparent. Few secularized Jews went as far as to abandon Judaism, and attachment to the religious heritage continued to be expressed through a few selected rituals rather than beliefs.[2] The particular rituals that have been retained include family celebrations and observances that symbolize the historical continuity and integration of the Jewish nation, but they do not prevent involvement in modern society.

It would appear that there are limits to the decline of religion in even the most secular of societies. One reason for the continuation of at least minimal levels of practice and belief in many societies is the historical interpenetration of religion with ethnic or national identity. Although nationalism has in many instances involved a secularization of beliefs, societies whose historical identity has been anchored in religion have rarely adopted a modern national identity totally emptied of traditional religious content. There are few cases where the relationship between a "people" and a religion has been so close as among the Jews, and in the diaspora, where Jewish identity and the community's survival are perceived to be threatened by assimilation, Jewish religious practice has often been interpreted as a "mask" for ethnicity. In Israel, Jews are more likely to take their Jewish identity for granted and intermarriage with non-Jews is rare, but for a variety of reasons, including the legitimation of their presence and an independent state in the area, most Israeli Jews are concerned to perpetuate their Jewishness. They do so by means of religious symbols and participation in at least a few religious rites (cf. Liebman and Don-Yehiya, 1983; Weissbrod, 1983).

From the last decades of the nineteenth century the process of secularization was accelerated for many Jews by their migration from the undeveloped societies of eastern Europe, where participation in non-Jewish society was highly restricted, to the rapidly industrializing and relatively open societies of western Europe and the United States. A small minority of eastern European Jewish emigrants went to Palestine and established the New Yishuv (Settlement) whose secular features clashed with the Old Yishuv of religious Jews. In Palestine it was the ideology of Zionist-Socialists and not entrance into a non-Jewish society that molded the secular character of the New Yishuv and Israeli state. Rapid industrialization began in Israel in the 1950s, but the new waves of immigrants that came in that period confronted a society whose veteran population and major institutional features were already highly secularized. This posed few problems for most immigrants from Europe, many of whom came from Communist societies in the 1950s, but it did entail cultural shock and difficult adaptation among immigrants from the Jewish communities of the Middle East.

In accord with the modernization–secularization perspective, it would be expected that the sharpest declines in religiosity are found in those communities which pass, possibly because of migration, from "traditional" to "modern" societies. Many immigrants attempt to retain their traditional life-styles in the new milieu, but the younger immigrants and the second generation are likely to pull away considerably from their parents' level of religious practice. Subsequent generations may continue the decline in religious practice, but where religion is tied to ethnicity or nationalism, the decline will diminish or come to a halt. Studies tracing religious observance over several generations of American Jews reveal an overall decline in religiosity with advancing generations, but this decline also lessens with each generation: the distance between the first and second generations is substantial, the difference between the second and third generations is much less, and in the more advanced generations there is a process of stabilization at a minimal level of ritual observance (Sklare and Greenblum, 1979; Goldstein and Goldscheider, 1968; S. Cohen, 1983).

The possibilities of conducting similar intergenerational comparisons in Israel are limited: nearly half of the population was born in the diaspora, and the great majority of adults born in Israel are second generation. However, since Israelis migrated from communities of origin that varied in their degrees of traditionalism and secularization, it is possible to test the diminishing decline thesis by comparing the differences between the religiosity of adults socialized in Israel and their parents from a number of communities. Thus, we asked our respondents not only questions on their own religious practice, but also questions on their fathers' religious practice.

Prior to World War II a large proportion of Jews in Poland and Rumania retained very high levels of traditional religious practice. Nevertheless, the penetration of secular beliefs and ideologies, especially socialism and

Zionism, into the traditional communities began much earlier and influenced far more Jews in eastern Europe, especially in the interwar period, than in most Middle Eastern Jewish communities. The great majority of our respondents from Rumania and Poland immigrated to Israel after the war following the destruction of the traditional communities and the considerable secularizing effects of Communist regimes on those Jews who survived the Holocaust. Secularization was less advanced in Rumania where a large proportion of Jews survived the Holocaust and the post-war regime was more tolerant of Jewish cultural particularism and institutions than other Communist regimes.

The process of secularization began among Middle Eastern communities, such as those from Yemen and Kurdistan, only after they had immigrated to Israel. Of the two Middle Eastern groups in our sample, the Iraqis had been more influenced by western trends prior to their immigration; a decline in religious practice was evident among a minority of Iraqi Jews even before World War I, and the British occupation and the entrance of some Jewish children into state schools from the 1920s were important secular influences on many Iraqi Jews. There was considerable differentiation among Jews in Morocco in terms of their closeness to the Arabic or French cultures, but a large proportion who migrated to Israel came from the least westernized, lower strata of Moroccan Jewry. Thus, our four groups can be differentiated in terms of their level of secularization prior to their immigration; the least secularized were the Moroccan Jews, followed by the Iraqis, Rumanians, and lastly, the most secularized, the Poles.

The modernization perspective would expect that the process of secularization, as measured by intergenerational decline in religious observance, is occurring among the majority of Israeli Jews, but that the decline is sharper among the Middle Eastern communities whose origins are closer to the traditional religious society. However, in addition to the level of religious observance prior to immigration, there are a number of other differences between Middle Eastern and European Jewish communities that are likely to affect their patterns of religious observance and secularization in Israel. One difference is that religion among Middle Easterners is less differentiated from family and local community than among Europeans, and, where family and community of origin retain their strength, many religious observances will remain widely practiced. The greater tolerance with respect to different levels of religious observance and the absence of a militant defense of "Orthodoxy" have also contributed to the emergence of a partly religious, or what is called in Israel, "traditional" pattern of observance.[3] Some observances have been widely abandoned but others are retained, and Middle Eastern Israelis see themselves as continuing in the tradition of their fathers. In comparison, European Israelis are more polarized between a secular majority and a strictly Orthodox minority who sees little value in the traditional pattern (Shokeid, 1985). The socio-economic distribution of Jews of Middle Eastern origin in Israeli society might also limit a secular trend. In addition to limiting social interaction with European Israelis, the subordinate socio-economic and political position of Middle Easterners might also reinforce their religious practice indirectly by preserving their family and community patterns and their religiously informed identity.

Religiosity, generation, and socio-economic status

Respondents were asked if they practiced five specific *mitzvot*, and they were asked also if their fathers practiced or, if deceased, had practiced, the same *mitzvot*. The five *mitzvot* were: donning *tephillin* (phylacteries) every day; not traveling on the Sabbath; using separate utensils for milk and meat (*kashrut*); reciting the *kiddush* (sanctification) over the wine before the Sabbath meal; and fasting on Yom Kippur (the Day of Atonement). These were chosen to range from an observance (donning *tephillin*) which is kept by only a minority who practice all or most Jewish observances, to an observance (fasting on Yom Kippur) that is practiced by most Israeli Jews, including those who practice few other observances.[4] The five *mitzvot* were found to meet the requirements of a Guttman scale; for respondents the coefficient of reproducibility was .93 and the coefficient of scalability .77; for respondents' fathers the coefficients were .93 and .79 respectively. Levels of observance were computed according to the number of *mitzvot* that were practiced, ranging from five to zero.

Three interrelated hypotheses, derived from the modified modernization or diminishing decline perspective, were tested. The first was that the predominant intergenerational trend in religious practice would be one of decline in all four groups of origin. Although respondents of the four groups of origin came from societies that varied in their levels of modernization, with the exception of the later Polish and Rumanian immigrants, the majority did not come from a predominantly secular community, and it was expected that respondents' experiences of the largely secular Israeli society would result in a lower level of religious practice than their fathers.

The second hypothesis was that, the higher the level of religious observance of the fathers, the greater the distance would be in religiosity between respondents and fathers. This hypothesis was based on the argument that the pace of secularization between generations is greater where there is a wide distance between the comparatively traditional societies in which the older generation was socialized and the comparatively secularized societies in which the younger generation was socialized.

The third hypothesis was that, in addition to fathers' religiosity, the relative importance of the independent variables influencing respondents' religiosity would depend on the level of traditionalism or secularization in the communities of origin. In addition to the fathers' religiosity and country of origin, the other independent variables examined were: two components of the respondents' socio-economic status (education and occupational prestige), fathers' occupational prestige, respondents' year of immigration, age, and their wives' continents of origin (Europe–America or Asia–Africa).

In analyzing the effects of status components on Jewish religiosity most previous studies have focused on education rather than on occupations. S. Cohen (1983: 80–3), who found an inverse relationship between religious observance and education among Boston Jews, writes that higher education imports values such as cosmopolitanism, cultural relativism, toleration, and individualism that undermine traditional religious commitment and practice. Education is most likely to affect the religiosity of those who are closer to the traditional base, and this was found to be the case by Goldstein and Goldscheider (1968: 198–9) in their study of the Jewish community of Providence, Rhode Island; there was a significant inverse relationship between the number of school years and religiosity only among the foreign born, and among the third generation, respondents with a post-college education had a slightly higher religious observance than those with only a high-school education. In their study of religiosity in Israel, Goldscheider and Friedlander (1983) found that the relationship between religion and education was not linear; the highest levels of religiosity were found among those with less than eight years of schooling, but there was an upturn of religiosity among those with twelve or more years of education.[5] The effects of education have generally been presented without controlling for occupation,[6] but in Israel, in particular, it is important to measure the relative independent effects of education and occupation; the study of the Bible and the Talmud is a compulsory part of the curriculum in all schools, and a significant minority attend religious schools in the state system or under the auspices of a religious movement.

It is expected that occupation will have a greater influence on levels of religiosity in the Middle Eastern groups, because those in the more prestigious occupations are likely to be more closely associated with Israelis of European origin who make up the majority in these occupations and have an overall lower level of observance. The number of years lived in Israel will also affect a greater decline in religiosity in the Middle Eastern groups, since the longer life experience in the more secular Israeli context will remove respondents further from the traditional base of their families' countries of origin.

The relationship between age and religiosity in Israel is likely to be a function of other factors such as generation and the number of years lived in Israel. In the United States age has been found to have an independent effect; the concern of parents to transmit a Jewish identity to their children produces a rise in their observance as their children reach school age and continues until the children are of *bar mitzvah* age (Sklare and Greenblum, 1979: 73–8, 181–98; Sharot, 1973; S. Cohen, 1983: 124–6). The transmission of Jewish identity is less problematic in Israel and there are many alternative agencies other than religious observance and affiliation.

It is expected that the level of observance in the spouses' family of origin will influence the husbands' pattern. Data were not collected on the religiosity of respondents' in-laws, but it is evident that the average level of religiosity of in-laws from North Africa and Asia will be higher than that of in-laws from Europe. Thus, a negative correlation can be expected between respondents' religiosity and European spouses, and a positive correlation with Asian–African spouses. The spouses' origins will not, in most cases, reverse the respondents' pull away from their parents, but is it likely to influence the level of decline that occurs. The spouses' origins have been found to be an important factor in the United States where comparisons are made between central and eastern European origins (Sklare and Greenblum, 1979: 71–3; Himmelfarb, 1980), but in Israel, where the dominant form of Orthodoxy differentiates clearly between male and female religious roles, their effect is likely to be less.

The diminishing decline of religiosity

The data presented in tables 6.1 and 6.2 support the hypotheses that there is a general intergenerational decline in religiosity, that the sharpest declines are found in those groups from the most religious backgrounds, and that at the lowest levels of observance there is intergenerational stabilization.

The backgrounds of the two Middle Eastern groups are more religious than those of the two European groups, but there are important differ-

Table 6.1. *Religiosity of respondents and fathers, averages ($\bar{x}$), standard deviations (σ), and coefficients of variability (v)*

| | Respondents' religiosity | | | Fathers' religiosity | | | |
	$\bar{x}$	σ	v	$\bar{x}$	σ	v	N
Moroccans	3.23	1.24	.38	4.44	.75	.16	202
Iraqis	2.18	1.21	.56	3.52	1.45	.41	204
Poles	1.11	1.30	1.17	1.83	1.84	1.01	179
Rumanians	1.69	1.32	.78	2.39	1.74	.73	203

Table 6.2. *Specific religious observances among fathers and respondents*

	Respondents %	Fathers %	Difference between respondents and fathers %	Respondents fathers' practice %	N	Respondents not practiced by fathers %	N
Don *tephillin*							
Total	12.3	48.5	36.2	23.6	(90)	1.7	(7)
Moroccans	25.5	84.5	59.0	29.6	(50)	3.2	(1)
Iraqis	7.8	54.4	46.6	11.7	(13)	3.2	(3)
Poles	5.0	20.5	15.5	18.9	(7)	1.4	(2)
Rumanians	10.3	32.0	21.7	30.8	(20)	0.7	(1)
Not travel Sabbath							
Total	20.4	49.8	29.4	33.5	(133)	7.5	(30)
Moroccans	39.1	87.0	47.9	40.0	(72)	33.3	(9)
Iraqis	18.1	52.9	34.8	23.0	(25)	12.0	(12)
Poles	9.9	27.5	17.6	30.0	(15)	2.2	(3)
Rumanians	13.2	28.9	15.7	35.6	(21)	4.1	(6)
Separate meat/milk dishes (*kashrut*)							
Total	42.8	59.8	17.0	66.2	(315)	8.1	(26)
Moroccans	75.7	95.6	19.9	78.7	(155)	11.1	(1)
Iraqis	46.1	67.6	21.5	63.0	(87)	10.6	(7)
Poles	16.6	30.9	14.3	39.3	(22)	6.4	(8)
Rumanians	29.8	41.5	11.7	60.0	(51)	8.3	(10)
Kiddush							
Total	52.8	66.4	13.6	71.4	(375)	16.2	(43)
Moroccans	89.8	98.0	8.2	90.0	(181)	75.0	(3)
Iraqis	55.9	78.2	22.3	63.9	(101)	27.3	(12)
Poles	28.3	40.0	11.7	52.8	(38)	12.0	(13)
Rumanians	34.3	46.1	11.8	58.5	(55)	13.6	(15)
Fast Yom Kippur							
Total	80.4	87.8	7.4	87.6	(607)	29.2	(28)
Moroccans	93.8	99.0	5.2	94.7	(196)	0	(0)
Iraqis	90.1	97.5	7.4	90.9	(179)	60.0	(3)
Poles	52.8	63.5	10.7	71.7	(81)	20.0	(13)
Rumanians	85.2	88.2	3.0	84.4	(151)	50.0	(12)

ences among Middle Eastern groups, and it would be a mistake to counterpoise two homogeneous religiocultural blocs of "western" non-religious Jews and "eastern" religious Jews. The high level of observance of the great majority of Moroccan fathers is obvious; more than 80% practiced all the rituals and about a third more Moroccans than Iraqis practiced the first three rituals. In comparison there is little difference between the Rumanians and Poles except at the level of the fifth ritual – fasting on Yom Kippur. Here the high level of secularity of the Polish fathers is obvious; more than a third did not observe any of the practices.

Turning to the respondents' patterns, the effect of Israeli society would appear to blur any overall distinction in religiosity between Middle Eastern and European Jews. At the "strictly religious" end of the scale (donning *tephillin*) there is a clear difference between the Moroccans and the Iraqis, but there is not a significant difference between the Iraqis and the two European groups. The difference between the Moroccans on the one hand and the three other groups on the other is clear also in avoiding traveling on the Sabbath. Moroccans continue to demonstrate a higher pattern of observance than Iraqis with respect to the third and fourth *mitzvot*, but here there are also significant differences between the Iraqis and the Europeans. At the end of the scale, fasting on Yom Kippur is observed by similar percentages of Moroccans, Iraqis, and Rumanians, and it is the Poles who provide the more secular exception.

There are significant declines in intergenerational religiosity in all four groups. Among the Europeans the difference between the generations varies little regarding the different *mitzvot*, but among the Moroccans and Iraqis the intergenerational falls in observance are particularly sharp at the level of the first two "stricter" *mitzvot*. On the measure of *kashrut* or dietary laws, there are similar intergenerational differences in the Moroccan and Iraqi groups, but on the fourth observance (*kiddush*) the Iraqis continue the pattern of intergenerational discontinuity, whereas between the two Moroccan generations there is little difference. The small intergenerational differences among all groups with respect to fasting on Yom Kippur suggests that once a low level of observance is reached a process of stabilization occurs.

In most cases, the higher the level of the fathers' religiosity and the "stricter" the *mitzvah*, the greater the intergenerational discontinuity. However, there is considerable continuity in the observance of the last three *mitzvot* among Middle Eastern Israelis, especially the Moroccans. The high level of observance among Moroccan respondents of both the dietary laws and *kiddush* suggests that they are unlikely to approach the low observance pattern of European Israelis in the foreseeable future.

Table 6.3. *Correlation matrix of religiosity and independent variables*

	Poles	Rumanians	Iraqis	Moroccans	Total sample
Fathers' religiosity	.53	.59	.24	.34	.61
Occupational prestige	−.09	−.08	−.36	−.19	−.29
Years of schooling	−.09	.00	−.23	−.07	−.20
Wives' continent of birth (Europe-America)	−.04	−.18	−.28	−.17	−.41
Year of migration	−.12	−.13	.00	.22	.04
Age	.13	.01	.14	.11	.01
Fathers' occupational prestige	−.15	−.02	−.15	−.11	−.15

The probability of a respondent observing the *mitzvot* is greatly increased if they were practiced by his father, but this probability decreases on moving from the "popular" to the "stricter" *mitzvot* (column 4 in table 6.2). A comparison of the coefficients of variability of the two generations (table 6.1) indicates that there has been some increase in polarization between "religious" and "secular" Jews, but this stems, in the most part, from the fact that some respondents pulled more sharply away from their fathers than others. The last column in table 6.2 shows that few respondents perform rituals that were neglected by their parents; this is true for all groups with only minor variations among the *mitzvot*.

The correlation matrix and the regression analyses (tables 6.3 and 6.4) demonstrate that the relative importance of influences on religiosity varies according to the level of religious observance of each group. The correlation matrix shows the important influence of fathers' religiosity on respondents' religiosity, especially among Poles and Rumanians. Most of the correlations with the other variables are lower, but they are all in the expected direction; there are negative correlations with respondents' occupational prestige, years of education, wives born in Europe–America, and fathers' occupational prestige. These negative correlations are especially prominent among the Moroccans and Iraqis. The only positive correlation for all groups is with age; older respondents tend to have higher levels of religiosity. Among Moroccans, the earlier the year of immigration, the lower the religiosity; among Poles and Rumanians, the later the year of immigration, the lower the religiosity.

The correlations between many of the independent variables and their differential impact in the four groups indicate the need for regression analysis. The regression analysis (table 6.4) of the entire sample shows

Table 6.4. *Influences on religiosity: regression coefficients metric (b) and beta (β)*

Independent variables	Moroccans		Iraqis		Poles		Rumanians		Total sample
	b	β	b	β	b	β	b	β	β
Fathers' religiosity	.42*	.25*	.22*	.26*	.43*	.61*	.44*	.59*	.46*
Year of migration	.05*	.23*	−.01	−.01	.02	.13	−.01	−.06	−.04
Fathers' occupational prestige[1]	−.01	−.12	−.01	−.11	−.01*	−.17*	.00	.06	−.06
Age	.03*	.15*	.02	.09	.00	.02	.00	−.02	.04
Occupational prestige[1]	−.01	−.16*	−.02*	−.28*	−.01	−.14	−.01	−.06	−.16*
Wives' continent of birth[2]	−.54	−.12	−.38	−.12	−.10	−.03	−.64*	−.18*	−.16*
Years of schooling	.03	.07	.02	.05	.05	.15	.06*	.18*	.09*
Iraqi[3]									−.07
Polish[4]									−.11*
Moroccan[5]									.07
R^2	.20		.24		.33		.41		.45
a	2.04		2.16		.53		2.40		

*Coefficient is more than twice its standard error.
1 According to Hartman's (1975) occupational prestige scale for Israel.
2 Dummy variable: "1" wives of European-American origin. "0" wives of Asian-African origin.
3 Dummy variable: "1" Iraqi. "0" non-Iraqi.
4 Dummy variable: "1" Pole. "0" non-Pole.
5 Dummy variable: "1" Moroccan. "0" non-Moroccan.

that the most important influence over respondents' religiosity is fathers' religiosity; this factor mediates almost completely the link between country of origin and religiosity.[7] The other variables that reach statistical significance for the entire sample are less important substantively. Both higher occupational prestige and wife of European or American origin reduce religiosity; the net contribution of these variables to the variance of religiosity beyond that of fathers' religiosity is -8%.

The separate regression analysis for the four groups of origin reveals different patterns. There is a greater distance in religiosity between respondents and fathers in the Moroccan group than in the European groups, but there is little difference between them in the extent to which fathers' religiosity explains variance in religiosity among respondents; the metric coefficient between respondents' and fathers' religiosity in the Moroccan group is almost identical to that of the Poles and the Rumanians. The Iraqi respondents are the exception here; there is clear divergence among them in the extent to which they moved away from their fathers' base.

The divergence in religiosity among both Moroccan and Iraqi respondents can be explained, in part, by the variables that relate to the degrees of contact and involvement with the relatively secularized Israeli society. In the Moroccan group we find significant effects of year of migration and age on religiosity; younger Moroccans who have lived in Israel for a longer time tend to be less religious. (In table 6.4, due to control for year of immigration, "age" refers to age of immigration.) Higher occupational prestige also reduces religiosity in the Moroccan group, but its effect among the Iraqis, most of whom migrated to Israel at the same time, is more prominent.

The stronger influence of fathers' religiosity and the weaker influence of socio-economic status in accounting for the variance in religiosity among Moroccans compared with the Iraqis may reflect the stronger intergenerational familial and community ties of that group. Evidence of the latter is provided by data which were collected from respondents on their three best friends (see the following chapter). Moroccan respondents were more likely to have best friends from their own country of origin than Iraqis, and Iraqis were more likely to have friends of European origin, especially among higher socio-economic status respondents. It is a reasonable assumption that the assimilation of a larger proportion of Iraqi Jews in European circles both reduces their religiosity and increases the variance in religiosity within the group.

Starting at lower levels of religiosity reduces the effects on Polish and Rumanian respondents of their differential involvement in secular society. Among Poles only higher occupational prestige of fathers reduces respondents' religiosity. Significant influences on the religiosity of Rumanians are wives' continent of origin and years of schooling. Rumanians married to wives of Asian-African origin tend to be more religious. There is a positive correlation between years of schooling and religiosity in the Rumanian group; the correlation is marginal in magnitude, but it should be noted that when occupational prestige and other variables are held constant there is no negative correlation between education and religiosity in any group.[8] It may be suggested that more years in school in Israel effect a decline in religiosity since more educated youth move into higher status occupations where the influences of modernity are greater, but since education in Israel is not unequivocally secular it has little, if any, independent effect on religiosity after occupation is controlled.

Conclusions

The hypotheses derived from the diminishing decline framework have, for the most part, been supported: an intergenerational erosion of religious observance occurred in all four groups of origin, but the distance between the generations was greater in the Middle Eastern groups who were closer to the traditional base and whose members' religiosity was affected more by factors that strengthened the effects of the comparatively modern milieu (socio-economic status and number of years in Israel). It is clear, however, that the process of secularization does not follow a fixed pattern in line with modernization regardless of cultural and social structural differences among groups. Israelis of Moroccan origin may have drawn further away from their fathers than European Israelis, but they have retained a comparatively high level of observance. The difference between the Moroccans and the European groups remains substantial and is unlikely to disappear in the near future. Among Moroccans, at the present rate of intergenerational erosion, it would take another three generations before they drop to the current Polish level of observance of the dietary laws, and another six generations before they reach the current Polish level of observance of *kiddush*. If the Moroccans conform to the pattern of diminishing decline, their movement toward the minimal Polish practice would take even longer.

The comparatively high level of Moroccan religious observance has been attributed to its anchorage in strong familial and community ties and to the importance of religion in the identity of Moroccan Jews. These factors may have been reinforced by the concentration of Moroccans in the lower strata and their experience of relative deprivation and social rejection in Israel. If this is the case, only a considerable weakening of ethnic stratification is likely to accelerate the intergenerational erosion in religious practice among Moroccan Israelis and produce a temporary exception to the diminishing decline of religiosity.

7

Friendship networks

Friendships: theoretical models

In his well-known delineation of the dimensions of assimilation, Milton Gordon noted that structural assimilation was "the keystone of the arch of assimilation." A minority's interaction with the majority at the primary group level was bound to be accompanied or followed by its assimilation in other dimensions (cultural, marital, identificational, etc.), and this would lead to its disappearance as a separate entity (Gordon, 1964: 80–1). Recent studies of ethnicity have tended to move away from the implicit one-directional emphasis of assimilation and have reconceptualized interethnic relations in terms of boundaries, but the importance of extensive interethnic friendships and intermarriage in the weakening or dissolution of ethnic groups has been reiterated.

Intermarriage is a clear indicator of a change in ethnic boundaries, and in the United States the increase and extensiveness of intermarriage among most white ethnic groups probably signals the "twilight of their ethnicity" (Alba, 1985). In Israel, a large proportion of marriages now cuts across countries of origin, but the proportion that crosses the broad European and Middle Eastern categories has increased only marginally in recent years. The Moroccan respondents in our sample had the highest proportion of in-marriage: 71% were married to spouses of Moroccan origin, and only 8% were married to spouses of European origin. The Polish respondents had the highest proportion of out-marriage: 38% were married to spouses of Polish origin and 19% were married to spouses of North African or Asian origin. The Iraqi pattern was closer to the Poles: 45% married to spouses of Iraqi origin and 18% married to spouses of European origin. The Rumanian pattern fell between the Iraqis and the Moroccans: 56% married to spouses of Rumanian origin and 15% married to spouses of North African or Asian origin. In a society where the vast majority of the adult population is first or second generation, friendship networks may provide a better indicator of the permeability and future of groups boundaries, and it is on these that we focus.[1]

We have noted the disagreement among Israeli sociologists over the relative importance of boundaries based on the many communities of origin ("Moroccans," "Yemenites," "Poles," etc.) or on a broad dichotomy between Ashkenazim and *edot ha'Mizrach*. Sociologists supporting perspectives emphasizing economic inequality rather than cultural factors have argued that the differences among *edot* from the Middle East have declined considerably, and that there is now only one major ethnic division of Israeli Jews between Ashkenazim and *edot ha'Mizrach*. Smooha (1978) argues that, although cultural pluralism among Israeli Jews has narrowed substantially, there remain clear social or structural divisions, especially in the more intimate areas of social interaction. The most radical formulation of a single ethnic division is presented by Swirski (1981) who argues that the subordinate position of Middle Easterners in the ethnic division of labor, and their subjection to discrimination by Europeans, have erased their differences and produced a new social entity. Friendships will be confined, therefore, not so much to country of origin but to continent of origin (Europe/America) or Africa/Asia). Weimann (1983) used the small world method to trace acquaintance networks and concluded that they were dichotomized between Europeans and Middle Easterners. It is reasonable to assume that if acquaintances are dominated by the ethnic factor, intimate friends will be even more so.

Weimann noted the inequality between Europeans and Middle Easterners, but he did not ask (and his data would not enable him to answer) the question of the extent to which the ethnic homogeneity of acquaintances is a consequence of ethnic self-selection or a function of the socio-economic distribution of the categories. Since broad geographical origins and class overlap but are far from identical, it is possible to investigate the relative importance of class and broad geographical origins on friendship networks. In addition to the question of the relative importance of countries of origin and the broad distinction between Ashkenazim and *edot ha'Mizrach*, it is possible to pose two further questions. Firstly, are friendships more homogeneous in terms of the broad ethnic distribution or in terms of class? Secondly, what is the relative importance of broad ethnic origin and class in the choice of friends?

A number of possible combinations of the relative homogeneity/heterogeneity of class and ethnic friendship networks may be distinguished. Different perspectives in sociology, and in Israeli sociology in particular, generate conflicting expectations of these possibilities. The first possibility, where friends are heterogeneous in both class and ethnic origin, is a melting-pot, and is close to the position of the "absorption through modernization" perspective in Israeli sociology, especially in the 1950s and 1960s (Eisenstadt, 1955, 1969). The second possibility, homogeneous class networks with heterogeneous ethnic networks, is in accord with a classical Marxist perspective: common economic or class interests unite and amalgamate groups who come to see the irrelevance of differences in ethnic origins. This is not a position found among Israeli sociologists, but it is possible that, as the native born replace the immigrant generation, class is becoming a more important basis of culture and primary association (cf. Weingrod, 1979). The third possibility, heterogeneous class networks with homogeneous ethnic networks, conforms to a pluralist model: the "vertical" ethnic distinctions cut through the "horizontal" divisions of class. Smooha (1978), the major exponent of the pluralist model in Israel, does not ignore class, but his emphasis is on inequality between the ethnic categories. The tendency to conflate ethnic and class divisions is found in a more radical form in Swirski's (1981) emphasis on the ethnic division of labor and relations of dependence. An expectation with respect to social networks would logically conform here to the fourth position: friends are homogeneous in both ethnic origins and class.

Ethnic groups are rarely coterminous with classes and many ethclasses may develop if people choose their friends on the basis of both ethnicity and class (Gordon, 1964). Another possibility is that one class is a melting-pot of ethnic groups while another is divided ethnically. This is likely in immigrant societies when new immigrants wish to retain their traditional culture in ethnic associations and are concentrated in the lower strata and less modernized sectors of the society where ascriptive rather than achievement criteria remain important. The more socially mobile immigrants and their children may have greater opportunities to move into social circles where the veteran population is numerically dominant. A relationship between socio-economic status and de-ethnization has been taken as evidence to support a melting-pot portrayal of the society (cf. S. Cohen, 1977), but if ethnic groups continue to be disproportionately concentrated in different classes, it is possible that amalgamation will be restricted to the middle class and that ethclasses will remain the rule in the lower stratum.[2]

In Israel the relative opportunities for making friends from the same class and broad ethnic group are greater for some ethclass categories than for others. The general data on Israeli society show that Middle Eastern Israelis in white-collar occupations and European Israelis in blue-collar occupations are demographic minorities in both their class, where the other broad ethnic category is in the majority, and in their broad ethnic groups, where the other class is in the majority. It may be assumed, therefore, that they have fewer opportunities than white-collar Europeans and blue-collar Middle Easterners to have friends similar in both class and broad ethnic origin.

In brief, the socio-economic distribution of the ethnic categories has to be considered when dealing with the relative importance of class and ethnic origins in the choice of friends. If middle-class Middle Easterners and working-class Europeans are found to have more heterogeneous ethnic networks, this would indicate that the levels of ethnic homogeneity are in part a function of the class distribution of the ethnic categories. If, despite their fewer opportunities to find ethnic members in their class, their class networks are no more heterogeneous than the categories in a majority, this would be a further indication that the level of intraethnic friendship is a function of class distributions, rather than intraclass friendships being a function of ethnic distribution.

Our sample was deliberately taken in a city and in neighborhoods which are relatively heterogeneous with respect to both countries and continents of birth. Thus, the make-up of the population allowed for a possible wide choice of friends in terms of their origins. A third of the best friends of our sample lived in the same neighborhood as respondents and over 80% lived in Beer Sheva. There were no differences among the four groups of origin nor between blue- and white-collar workers with respect to the proportions of friends who lived in Beer Sheva or the same neighborhoods as the respondents.

Respondents were asked to name three men, not including relatives, whom they considered their three best friends and then to provide information about their friends' countries of origin and occupations. If a friend was born in Israel, his father's country of birth was noted. Based on this information the relative homogeneity or heterogeneity of friendship networks was analyzed in terms of three dimensions: country of origin, a dichotomous ethnic categorization of Europeans and Middle Easterners, and a dichotomous class classification of blue collar and white collar.

We are relying on respondents' own labeling of best friends, and this may risk inappropriate comparisons either among groups of origin or between blue- and white-collar workers. In Britain, for example, it has been argued (Allan, 1977) that the notion of "friend" has different meanings for the middle and working classes. The working class in Britain are likely to define a "friend" or "mate" as someone with whom they interact in a particular context or situation, and they are less likely

Table 7.1. *Respondents who meet best friends frequently at work, at home, in the synagogue, and for leisure activities outside the home (%)*

Percentage meeting first best friend	Poles		Rumanians		Moroccans		Iraqis	
	blue	white collar	blue	white collar	blue	white collar	blue	white collar
At work	32	36	33	37	45	46	49	53
At home	93	95	81	92	93	85	83	90
In synagogue	4	4	4	6	25	19	7	8
For leisure activities	82	81	81	79	79	86	67	77
N	83	96	91	119	128	71	141	52

Note: These distributions relate to the first best friend mentioned by respondents, but the distributions for the other two best friends were very similar.

than the middle class to entertain non-kin in their homes. Such differences do not appear to prevail in Israel. We asked respondents whether they met their friends frequently at work, in their homes, for leisure activities outside the home, and in the synagogue. With respect to the relative importance of these different contexts, no important differences were found between blue- and white-collar workers in any group of origin. Neither were there important differences among the groups of origin (table 7.1). Moroccans and Iraqis were somewhat more likely to meet their friends at work, and the Moroccan groups included a larger minority who met their friends at the synagogue. But Middle Easterners were just as likely as Europeans to invite friends to their homes and to join them in leisure activities.

Friendships and ethnic origins

The following analysis compares the relative homogeneity/heterogeneity of friendship networks according to country of origin, the dichotomous ethnic categorization, and class. We then examine whether intraethnic friendships (within the European and Middle Eastern categories) are a consequence of the class distribution of the ethnic categories, or whether intraclass friendships (within the blue-collar and white-collar categories) are a consequence of the ethnic distribution of the class categories.

Logit analysis (Goodman, 1972; Knoke and Burcke, 1980; Swafford, 1980) was adopted to estimate the main effects and interaction effects of country of origin (four categories) and social class (a dichotomous variable) on the odds of having at least one out of three best friends from

Table 7.2. *Multiplicative (τ) parameters for the effects of country of origin (A) and class (B) on the odds of ethnically heterogeneous and class heterogeneous networks (C)*

	According to friend's country of origin (N = 720)[1]	According to friend's continent of origin (N = 720)[1]	According to friend's social class (N = 573)[1]
General odds	7.23	1.52	1.18
Country of origin			
Morocco	.50*	.54*	1.49*
Iraq	2.14*	1.20	.76
Poland	1.23	1.17	.80
Rumania	.75	1.31*	1.11
Social class			
White-collar workers	—	1.22*	.70*
Interaction of social class and country of origin			
White-collar workers			
Moroccans	—	1.25	—
Iraqis	—	1.75*	—
Poles	—	.73*	—
Rumanians	—	.63*	—
Blue-collar workers			
Moroccans	—	.80	—
Iraqis	—	.57*	—
Poles	—	1.78*	—
Rumanians	—	1.23	—
Type of model	saturated	[AB][AC]	[AB][AC][BC]

*Significant ($\alpha \leq .05$).
1 Reduction of N is due to missing data (lack of information about respondents' friends).

a different country of origin, the other broad category, and the other class. The first line of table 7.2 shows the relative openness in all three network dimensions; the general odds of having at least one close friend from another group are greater than the odds of not having one. However, the general odds of having at least one close friend from a different country of origin are considerably greater than the odds of having at least one close friend from the other broad ethnic category or from the other class.

All four categories of origin tend to form networks outside the *edah* (column 1),[3] but Moroccans reveal a somewhat greater tendency toward closure. Moroccan origin reduces the general odds from 7.23 to 3.62. A general distinction between "ethnic" *edot* from the Middle East and "non-ethnics" from Europe is not, however, substantiated; the Iraqis reveal the greatest tendency to form networks outside the *edah*, and the Poles and Rumanians fall between the two Middle Eastern groups in this respect. The relative homogeneity of *edah* networks among Moroccans may be attributed in part to the greater number of Moroccans in Beer Sheva, but the greater heterogeneity of the Iraqi networks cannot be explained by population size; the Iraqi networks are more heterogeneous than the two European groups even after the relative proportions in the population are considered.[4]

Social class has neither main effect nor interaction effects on the heterogeneity of networks according to country of origin. It would appear that in many groups, including some from the Middle East, the overall importance of country of origin in friendships has declined to such an extent that there is no longer any relationship between *edah* association and class. The cultural heritage of the *edah* may be "carried" by the family and *edah* synagogue, but only among a small minority is it likely to be reinforced by best friends.

There is the further question of whether the Israeli-Jewish population is amalgamating in a melting-pot of all groups of origin, dividing into two melting-pots of Europeans and Middle Easterners, or, a third possibility, becoming a melting-pot in the middle class and remaining divided ethnically in the working class. In fact, the reality is more complex than any of these three models (column 2 in table 7.2). Moroccans are the most homogeneous group according to the broad ethnic categorization and Rumanians are the most heterogeneous. However, as with the country of origin pattern, there is not a general division between Middle Easterners and Europeans; Poles and Iraqis are both intermediate groups and very similar in the levels of their networks' heterogeneity.[5]

The correlations between "mixed marriages" and heterogeneous networks (in the broad ethnic sense) were not high: Iraqis .33, Moroccans .38, Poles .39, and Rumanians .23. Wife's origin had no main effect on the heterogeneity of networks, but it had an effect interacting with origins of respondents. Among Iraqis and Moroccans marriage to a European wife increased the odds of heterogeneous networks, but among Poles and Rumanians marriage to a wife from Middle Eastern origins decreased the odds. Thus, in both types of "mixed marriages," the tendency was to associate with the Europeans, the most prestigious category.

In contrast to the country of origin pattern, class does have significant effects on the broad ethnic networks: white-collar occupation multiplies the general odds for heterogeneous networks by 1.22. The interaction between class and country of origin reveals, however, that there is no overall distinction, encompassing all groups of origin, between a middle-class melting-pot and an ethnically divided working class. Social class affects differently the relative openness or closure of the two broad ethnic categories. Among Middle Easterners, white-collar occupations increase the tendency to form networks outside the broad ethnic category.[6] Among Europeans the effect of class on the heterogeneity of broad ethnic networks is in the opposite direction: blue-collar occupations increase the tendency of Poles to heterogeneity by 1.78 and of Rumanians by 1.23.

Networks are substantially more homogeneous in terms of the broad ethnic categorization than in terms of *edot*, but only blue-collar Moroccans and Iraqis include more than 50% whose three best friends are all from their broad category. Blue-collar Moroccans, in particular, have homogeneous networks; about two-thirds have all three best friends from Middle Eastern *edot*. Blue-collar Iraqis have slightly less homogeneous networks, but the homogeneity of their broad ethnic networks stands out in comparison with the heterogeneity of their specific ethnic networks; only 7% have homogeneous Iraqi networks. These findings give some support to those perspectives that emphasize the division between Europeans and Middle Easterners, but it should be emphasized that this broad ethnic homogeneity is restricted to blue-collar Middle-Easterners, and that among Europeans blue-collar workers have the most heterogeneous networks. Since Middle Easterners constitute the great majority of blue-collar workers in Israel, the importance of inequality for the broad ethnic division is apparent.

We have emphasized the interrelationships between ethnicity and religiosity and, in order to obtain some idea of the influence of religiosity on friendships, respondents were asked if their best friends were as religious, more religious, or less religious than themselves. The data from this question are somewhat problematic because we are depending on respondents' own evaluations of their friends' religiosity in comparison with their own. Nevertheless, it is of interest to note that, whereas two-thirds of the Polish respondents reported that their friends were at the same level of religiosity as themselves, this was true of only half of the Moroccan respondents. A third of the Moroccans and 15% of the Poles said that their friends were less religious than themselves. There were no significant differences between the Iraqis and Rumanians whose patterns fell between those of the Moroccans and Poles. These findings reinforce the argument that among Middle Eastern groups, whose overall level of religiosity is higher than that of the Europeans, there is greater tolerance with respect to differences in religiosity than among Europeans. Of relevance here is the fact that the majority of *haredim* or ultra-Orthodox are of European origin. In recent years the *haredim*, who have large families, have spread out from ·their old neighborhoods to other neighborhoods in the major cities, especially Jerusalem and into a number of smaller towns, but they continue to be highly segregated from the rest of the population (Shilhav and Friedman, 1985).

Friendships, classes, and ethclasses

Most sociologists who have paid attention to class divisions in Israel have usually done so only in so far as they overlap with the broad ethnic division ("the ethnic gap" or "the ethnic division of labor"). Our data indicate that class should be given greater attention as an independent dimension. For the total sample, the general odds of having one close friend from a different class (1.18) are less than the odds of having one close friend from a different ethnic category (1.52). Social class has a main effect on the odds of heterogeneous class networks (column 3 in table 7.2); white-collar occupation increases the class closure (it reduces the general odds, multiplying it by .70). The absence of significant inter-action effects between class and ethnic origin indicates that the relative closure of white-collar categories is common to all four groups of origin. Moroccans, however, have the most heterogeneous class networks independent of their social class.

Further evidence of the relative importance of ethnic origins and class is shown in table 7.3 which presents the odds in eight categories of respondents (four groups of origin each divided by class) having class and ethnically heterogeneous networks. Blue-collar Moroccans and Iraqis are the only categories whose broad ethnic networks are more homogeneous than their class networks. Among white-collar Moroccans the odds of class heterogeneous networks are about equal to the odds of their ethnically heterogeneous networks, but among the Iraqi, Polish, and Rumanian white-collar categories, the difference in odds is especially great; they tend to combine ethnic openness with class closure.

For most categories the distinction between blue- and white-collar workers is more important than ethnic origins in the composition of friendship networks, but our data do not show the existence of a clear class boundary in social relations between blue- and white-collar workers. The absence of a clear boundary can be demonstrated by

Table 7.3. *Odds of having at least one close friend from the other broad ethnic category, and the other class**

	Different broad ethnic category	Different class
Blue-collar workers		
Moroccans	.54	2.51
Iraqis	.85	1.18
Poles	2.59	1.35
Rumanians	2.00	1.87
White-collar workers		
Moroccans	1.25	1.23
Iraqis	3.89	.62
Poles	1.53	.66
Rumanians	1.58	.92

*The odds (Ω) are computed according to the parameters presented in table 7.2. The formula for column 1 (saturated model) is:

$$\Omega_{1j} = \tau_{i1}{}^* \tau_{j1}{}^* \tau_{ij1}$$

The formula for column 2 ([AB][AC][BC]) is:

$$\Omega_{1j} = \tau_1{}^* \tau_{i1}{}^* \tau_{j1}$$

where: i represents the category of country of origin (A: ranges from 1 to 4); j represents the category of class (B: dichotomous); 1 represents the category of the dependent variable which pertains to heterogeneous network.

showing the effects on friendship networks of class measures that cut across the blue/white-collar distinction. Table 7.4 shows, in addition to the blue/white-collar distinction, the effects of years of schooling, authority in the work place, and the distinction between independents and wage-earners. Both the education and authority variables were dichotomized: between secondary education (up to twelve years of schooling) and post-secondary or "higher" education (thirteen or more years of schooling); and between having or not having authority over at least one worker.[7] Ethnic origin was included only as a control variable; all possible relationships with the class measures were included, but we omit here the net effects or interaction effects of ethnic origin on friendship networks across the blue/white-collar line.

The combination of four dichotomous class measures constitute sixteen profiles. The main factor that determines the degree of openness is the level of education. Among the less educated white-collar workers, the odds of having blue-collar friends are very high, whereas the more educated are far more "closed" to such relations regardless of their other characteristics (ownership or authority). Education is also the main

Table 7.4. *Odds of having at least one close friend from the other class according to various class measures*

Authority	Ownership	Schooling	Odds	N
Blue-collar workers				
None	Salaried	0–12	.92	115
Over at least one worker	Salaried	0–12	1.24	68
None	Owner	0–12	1.07	32
Over at least one worker	Owner	0–12	1.00	20
None	Salaried	13+	.74	8
Over at least one worker	Salaried	13+	1.84	14
None	Owner	13+	1.46	4
Over at least one worker	Owner	13+	3.66	5
White-collar workers				
None	Salaried	0–12	5.31	71
Over at least one worker	Salaried	0–12	1.73	107
None	Owner	0–12	2.35	19
Over at least one worker	Owner	0–12	2.39	40
None	Salaried	13+	.56	72
Over at least one worker	Salaried	13+	.67	186
None	Owner	13+	.67	5
Over at least one worker	Owner	13+	.80	15

differentiating factor among blue-collar workers, but it lacks a similar degree of discriminating power, and, as would be expected, there are very few blue-collar workers with higher education.

Besides the centrality of education, the table indicates interaction effects among the various class measures. The odds are very high that the most "privileged" blue collars (namely, educated owners with authority) and the "lowest" white collars (salaried workers with no authority and with less than twelve years of schooling) will have friends that cut across the blue/white-collar line. For these profiles, it may be said that the blue/white-collar distinction is irrelevant. It should be noted, however, that there are far fewer blue-collar workers in the higher profiles of the blue-collar category than there are white-collar workers in the lower profiles of the white-collar category.

Differences among groups in the heterogeneity of their networks may be a consequence of the size of their populations (Blau, 1977), and the relative sizes of the ethclass categories must be taken into account when considering the relative determinants of class and ethnic origins in the choice of friends. In accord with their fewer opportunities to find friends from their ethnic category in their class, the odds of white-collar Middle Easterners and blue-collar Europeans having at least one friend from the other ethnic category are greater than those of the other class categories in their respective ethnic groups. Comparisons of the ethnic networks within the class categories also indicate the relative importance of class; the ethnic networks of blue-collar Europeans are much more heterogeneous than those of the blue-collar Middle Easterners, and those of white-collar Iraqis are considerably more heterogeneous than those of white-collar Europeans. White-collar Moroccans have the least heterogeneous ethnic networks of the white-collar categories indicating the greater importance of ethnicity for Moroccans.

Despite the fact that white-collar Moroccans and Iraqis have fewer opportunities to find Middle Easterners in their class, their class networks are less heterogeneous than blue-collar Moroccans and Iraqis. There is also little difference between the levels of class heterogeneity of white-collar Iraqis and white-collar Poles and Rumanians, but the slightly more heterogeneous class networks of white-collar Moroccans are a further indication that the high level of intraethnic friendships among Moroccans cannot be reduced to their class distribution. The ethnic factor may also account for the finding that the fewer opportunities of blue-collar Europeans to find European friends in their class are reflected in the greater heterogeneity of their class networks compared with white-collar Europeans. There is, however, no significant difference between the class networks of blue-collar Rumanians and blue-collar Iraqis, and the class networks of blue-collar Moroccans are clearly the most heterogeneous.

A further test of the relative importance of class and ethnicity in the choice of friends can be made by comparing the percentage of respondents in each category, who have networks that are homogeneous in class but heterogeneous in ethnic origin, with those that are heterogeneous in class but homogeneous in ethnic origin (table 7.5).

We have noted that blue-collar Europeans and white-collar Middle Easterners have fewer opportunities to find friends who are the same as them in both broad ethnic origin and class. This is reflected in the networks of the categories: 14.3% of white-collar Middle Easterners and 5.5% of blue-collar Europeans have networks that are homogeneous in both class and broad ethnic origin compared with 25.4% of blue-collar Middle Easterners and 30.2% of white-collar Europeans. The question is whether friends that are not from the respondents' ethclass are chosen more on the basis of ethnicity or class.

Among blue-collar Europeans and white-collar Middle Easterners the proportional differences between the same class/different ethnic origin and different class/same ethnic origin networks are insignificant. White-

Table 7.5. *Percentage of respondents with networks in homogeneous and heterogeneous categories*

	Same class Same ethnic category	Same class Different ethnic category	Different class Same ethnic category	Different class Different ethnic category	N
Moroccans and Iraqis					
Blue-collar workers	25.4	14.0	35.2	25.4	
	(49)	(27)	(68)	(49)	193
White-collar workers	14.3	30.8	22.0	33.0	
	(13)	(28)	(20)	(30)	91
Poles and Rumanians					
Blue-collar workers	5.5	28.3	25.2	40.9	
	(7)	(36)	(32)	(52)	127
White-collar workers	30.2	29.0	11.1	29.6	
	(49)	(47)	(18)	(48)	162

collar Europeans and blue-collar Middle Easterners are almost identical in the proportions with ethclass networks, but when the heterogeneous categories are compared, there is a clear difference between them. Among white-collar Europeans, networks that are homogeneous in class but heterogeneous in ethnic origins are more than twice as great as those that are heterogeneous in class but homogeneous in ethnic origin. Among blue-collar Middle Easterners the opposite is true, and this is especially the case among the Moroccans: whereas nearly half of blue-collar Moroccans have networks that are homogeneous in ethnic origins but heterogeneous in class, only 10% have networks that are homogeneous in class but heterogeneous in ethnic origins.

Conclusions

Our major findings may be summarized as follows:

1 The friendship networks of the total sample are relatively heterogeneous with regard to all three network dimensions upon which we focused (country of origin, broad ethnic categories, and class).
2 In all four groups of origin, only small minorities have homogeneous friendship networks based on country of origin.
3 Networks based on the broad division between Europeans and Middle Easterners are substantially more homogeneous, but, with the excep-

tion of blue-collar Moroccans and Iraqis, networks based on the blue collar/white-collar distinction are the most homogeneous.

4 In all three dimensions, there is no overall distinction between Middle Eastern and European Israelis in their levels of network heterogeneity.

5 White-collar respondents have more homogeneous class networks than blue-collar respondents.

6 Blue-collar Middle Easterners have the most homogeneous broad ethnic networks; blue-collar Europeans and white-collar Iraqis have the most heterogeneous broad ethnic networks.

7 Moroccans, especially blue-collar Moroccans, have the most homogeneous ethnic networks and the most heterogeneous class networks.

8 With the exception of the Moroccans, most of the differences among the eight categories in their levels of broad ethnic heterogeneity can be attributed to the overrepresentation of Middle Easterners in blue-collar work and the overrepresentation of Europeans in white-collar work.

These findings do not give unequivocal support to any one perspective in Israeli sociology; most contain some truth but all have to be substantially modified. Firstly, regarding the importance of the community of origin or *edah*, it is necessary to qualify any general distinction between "ethnic" Middle Easterners and "non-ethnic" Europeans. There are no majorities with homogeneous *edah* networks in any category, and only among Moroccans does the *edah* retain significance as an important basis of association. The broad ethnic division between Europeans and Middle Easterners has by far supplanted the importance of divisions by countries of origin, but substantial qualifications have also to be made to the model of an ethnic dichotomization within the Israeli-Jewish population. Homogeneous broad ethnic networks are found in a majority only in the blue-collar Middle Eastern categories, and these are the only categories with networks that are more homogeneous in terms of broad ethnic origins than in terms of class. The suggestion that the middle class is an ethnic melting-pot is substantiated with the qualification that the assimilation of white-collar Moroccans is less extensive than that of white-collar Iraqis. However, from the perspective of blue-collar Europeans, the working class is also a melting-pot. In fact, the assimilation of blue-collar Poles and Rumanians into the Middle Eastern category is greater than the assimilation of white-collar Moroccans into the European category.

Even though the predominantly European middle class accepts middle-class Middle Easterners and the predominantly Middle Eastern working class accepts working-class Europeans, it would be an exaggeration to describe the whole society as a melting-pot. This is because the substantial degree of ethnic stratification restricts, and is likely to continue to restrict in the foreseeable future, the overall levels of interaction between Europeans and Middle Easterners.

Ethnicity explains little of the pattern of friendship networks; much of the pattern of intraethnic friendships is a function of the class distribution of the ethnic categories, and the pattern of intraclass friendships is largely independent from the ethnic distribution of the class categories. The choice of friends is made more frequently on the basis of class rather than ethnicity, and for Europeans and white-collar Iraqis, ethnicity appears to have little independent influence. Ethnicity remains a significant factor among blue-collar Middle Easterners, especially Moroccans, and, to a lesser extent, among white-collar Moroccans.

The different patterns of Moroccans and Iraqis show the dangers in making generalizations regarding the Middle Eastern *edot*. Iraqis demonstrate a pattern very close to a modified melting-pot model: the middle class assimilates into the predominantly European middle class and emphasizes class rather than ethnic closure, and the working class retains a high level of ethnic separation from Europeans. The Moroccans, white-collar as well as blue-collar, retain a higher degree of ethnic closure, to some extent as an *edah*, but more especially as part of the Middle Eastern category. That they have the most heterogeneous class networks is consistent with their relative ethnic homogeneity.

The differences between Moroccans and Iraqis are likely to be found among other Middle Eastern *edot*; we would expect groups such as those from Turkey, Egypt, Syria, and Lebanon to be closer to the Iraqi pattern, and groups such as those from Tunisia and the Yemen to be closer to the Moroccan pattern. These differences cannot be explained by demographic factors such as relative numbers and years of immigration, and they are not simply the consequence of the socio-economic profiles of the groups; levels of cultural and religious traditionalism are also important.

If the neighborhoods in Beer Sheva, from which our sample was taken, presented a representative picture of Israel as a whole, one might conclude that a modified melting-pot model is closer to the truth than the model of an ethnic dichotomy within the Jewish population. The residential distribution of our sample is not atypical, but it is considerably more heterogeneous than in many other neighborhoods and towns; a significant proportion of Middle Eastern Jews in Israel live in areas such as "development towns" and deprived neighborhoods in the major cities, where they constitute the great majority of the population. The evidence from this study suggests that, within relatively ethnically heterogeneous residential areas, there is little ethnic selection and rejection at the interpersonal level. Ethnic separation would appear, therefore, to be tied to the unbalanced geographical distribution and substantial residential segregation of different groups of origin (Klaff 1977; Gonen, 1985).

Comparing Israel with other societies, neither ethnic nor class boundaries are especially rigid among Israeli Jews; there is considerable "crossing of the lines" in both respects.[8] The absence of clear class boundaries is not difficult to understand; Israel is a new society of immigrants that did not develop out of a feudal or estate system and whose recent industrialization involved high levels of both upward and downward mobility. The absence of rigid ethnic boundaries within the Jewish population is related to the lack of core-cultural differences (although important subcultural differences are present), and to the dominant ideology of "fusion of the exiles." There may be a considerable distance between Israeli ideology and reality, but the majority's unconditional support for the ideology stamps ethnic prejudice or discrimination against other Jews as illegitimate.

There is a rigid ethnonational division in Israel, that between Arabs and Jews, and here Israel demonstrates certain similarities to the United States: a comparatively rigid ethnic line, based in the United States on race and in Israel on religion and national identity, exists together with comparatively permeable ethnic divisions based on origins from many countries and subcultural differences. The black–white boundary in the United States and the Arab–Jewish boundary in Israel are more determinant of friendship than class (on the U.S. see Jackson and Jackson, 1983), but class is more important than the divisions among white ethnic groups in America (Laumann, 1969, 1973) and Jewish groups in Israel. The threefold religious division in the United States of Catholics, Protestants, and Jews, and the broad ethnic division in Israel between Ashkenazim and *edot ha'Mizrach* are comparable in importance but, unlike religious pluralism in America, structural ethnic pluralism in Israel is largely a function of class distribution.

III

Identities and images

Part III focuses on the subjective dimensions of ethnicity, class, and religion: the identifications of respondents, how they perceive the social cleavages, and how they evaluate them. The analysis of ethnic consciousness in chapter 8 is followed by an analysis of class consciousness in chapter 9, and in chapter 10 the relationships of these consciousnesses with religious consciousness are investigated. In all cases, the differences in identifications and images among respondents are related to the objective divisions in ethnic origin, class, and religiosity.

8

Ethnic consciousness

Socio-economic and cultural interpretations

In chapter 3 we compared the socio-economic interpretation which argues that *edot ha'Mizrach* have become the basis of an emergent ethnic identification (Swirski, 1981) and the cultural interpretation that focuses on the *edah*. A prominent example of the cultural approach is that of Deshen (1972, 1976) who presents persistence and change of customs and practices as outcomes of a conflict between an identification with the *edah* and an identification as Israeli citizens. Over some issues, particularly those that encroach upon focal aspects of cultural heritage, a separatist stance is taken, but in most cases compromises are made that allow for the continuation of a separate *edah* identity within the broader compass of the national Israeli identity.

One problem with both the socio-economic and cultural approaches to the ethnicity of Middle Eastern Israelis is that they are difficult to reconcile with the common ideology in Israel of a Jewish melting-pot or "fusion of the exiles." We asked respondents, "What is your attitude toward *mizug hu'guluyot* (fusion of the exiles) and the disappearance of different groups of origin within one people?" The great majority of respondents (90%) of both European and Middle Eastern origins, indicated either "positive" (23%) or "very positive" (67%); very few indicated either a negative or neutral position (for similar findings see Peres, 1969).

The cultural and socio-economic approaches to ethnicity have paid almost no attention to European Israelis, but it is clear that, within their conceptual frameworks, the adherence of Europeans to the value of "fusion of the exiles" is not problematic. The cultural–anthropological perspective finds little interest in European Israelis because they do not emphasize distinctive cultural heritages of their communities of origin. From the socio-economic perspective Swirski argues that there is less need to analyze Ashkenazi consciousness, since this is expressed openly in the mass media, in literature, in the educational system, and by official

119

propaganda. Swirski argues that, although there are clear signs of mutual recognition among Ashkenazim, they do not express their commonality in particularistic terms but by such terms as the "state" or "society."

Swirski emphasizes the distance between the ideology of fusion of the exiles and the reality of socio-economic divisions; he appears to view adherence to the ideology among Middle Eastern Israelis as an expression of false consciousness that is a consequence of Ashkenazi ideological hegemony. Deshen argues that cultural distinctiveness does not necessarily imply social division and that his subjects desire "unity in diversity." He refers to "fusion of the exiles" as a stock phrase used by exponents of a paternalistic model in which the erasure of the cultural heritages of Middle Easterners permits their absorption within the dominant western culture. "Fusion of the exiles" may indeed be a stock phrase, and it may indeed have little relationship to social realities, but within the conceptual frameworks of the perspectives it remains difficult to reconcile the Middle Easterners' support of this value with their concern to retain the cultural heritage of their *edah* or with their consciousness as a distinctive *"edot ha'Mizrach"* social entity.

In order to deal adequately with these apparent contradictions or paradoxes, it is necessary to look more closely at the relationships between the specific (*edah*) and broad (Ashkenazi/*edot ha'Mizrach*) ethnic identifications and the wider ethnonational identifications (Jewish and Israeli). Swirski simply takes the wider identifications for granted, and Deshen proposes that among Middle Eastern Israelis there is a conflict between the *edah* identification and the Israeli identification. As an alternative perspective, we propose that differences in the socio-cultural histories of European and Middle Eastern Jews caused immigrants from those areas to conceive of their Jewish and Israeli identifications in different ways, and that these differences have had important implications for the levels and meanings of their subethnic identifications.

The Zionist pioneers from eastern Europe, and especially those of the second and third *aliyot* (1904–23) regarded their *aliyah* as a revolutionary break from the culture of the Jewish community in their country of birth, and a negative orientation toward cultural elements associated with the diaspora, such as the Yiddish language, became common among secular Jews born in Palestine or Israel. With the foundation of the state and the emergence of an Israeli identification some Israelis signaled their break with the past by claiming a "non-Jewish" Israeli identification (Friedman, 1967). The great majority of immigrants from Europe were not radical secularists, and even among those who were, the negative orientation toward the religious life of the traditional diaspora communities, which were mostly destroyed in the Holocaust, has become muted or has disappeared. The Israeli and Jewish identifications are now closely related. The majority of European Israelis have incorporated a largely secularized Jewishness, expressed in a few selected national-religious festivals, into the secular, national Israeli identification. We would expect little reidentification with the Jewish community of origin since it has become largely divorced from the newly constructed Jewish and Israeli identifications. The Ashkenazi identification is also expected to have little meaning for the majority of European Israelis, but the integration of the European groups in Israel and their perceptions of differences, both cultural and socio-economic, between themselves and *edot ha'Mizrach* may have made the Ashkenazi identification more significant than the more specific *edah* identification.

For most Middle Eastern Jews, Zionism and the establishment of the Israeli state were affirmations of the Jewish tradition that they had upheld in their countries of origin. The identification of Middle Eastern Jews in Israel as "Moroccan," "Yemenite," etc., was a development that occurred after their immigration (in their countries of origin they were simply Jews), but this newly formed identification was not divorced from, or seen to be in conflict with, their continuing identification as Jews. As Jews who came to Israel because of, and not in reaction to, the traditions of their communities, they were hardly likely to reject in the land of the Jews the identification that was now associated with the Jewish way of life that they had adhered to for centuries in the land of the gentiles.

The term "*edot ha'Mizrach*" was not related to a cultural entity that existed prior to immigration, and the Middle Eastern communities varied greatly with respect to their Judeo-Arabic dialects, religious customs, and other cultural features. However, in their confrontation with European Israelis, many Middle Eastern Israelis felt that, despite their differences, they were closer culturally to other *edot ha'Mizrach* than to Ashkenazim. The label "*edot ha'Mizrach*" may have originated as a stereotypical device used by European Israelis, but Middle Easterners appear to have rejected its negative connotations and adopted it as a source of identification. In so far as it is based on a feeling of cultural similarities, we would not expect it to be an alternative to the *edah* identification (as Swirski suggests), but rather to accompany and possibly reinforce it.

In analyzing the subjective dimensions of ethnicity we distinguish cognitive, evaluative, and affective dimensions. The cognitive dimension refers to respondents' perceptions of cultural differences, social distance,

Table 8.1. *Percentages in four groups of origin who perceive important cultural differences, high social distance, and acute conflict (points five and six on six-point scale)*

	Poles	Rumanians	Moroccans	Iraqis
Between own edah *and other* edot *within broad category*				
Cultural	12	17	32	26
Social distance	6	12	17	21
Conflict	2	6	7	5
Between own edah *and* edot *from other broad category*				
Cultural	53	53	67	57
Social distance	26	31	35	29
Conflict	17	24	31	21
Between Ashkenazim and edot ha'Mizrach				
Cultural	53	59	66	61
Social distance	20	30	35	28
Conflict	29	36	34	35
N	188	213	216	209

and conflict among ethnically defined Jewish groups. The evaluative dimension refers to respondents' judgments concerning justice or injustice in the distribution of economic position, social status, and political power of the ethnic groups. And the affective dimension refers to the level of identification with the ethnic groups, as well as the subjectively perceived cultural and political saliency of ethnicity.

Dimensions of ethnic consciousness

Cognitive   Very little difference was found among the four groups of origin with respect to respondents' perceptions of ethnic, social, and cultural differences and the extent of ethnic conflict. Table 8.1 gives the percentages of those who perceived important cultural differences, little amalgamation, and sharp conflict. When asked about differences between their *edah* and other *edot within* their broad ethnic category, the Poles and Rumanians were less likely to perceive cultural differences or social distance between themselves and other Ashkenazi *edot* than the Moroccans and Iraqis were likely to perceive between themselves and other *edot ha'Mizrach*. This finding supports those anthropologists and sociologists who have argued that the very notion of *edah* is far more relevant to *edot ha'Mizrach* than it is to Ashkenazim. But it should be noted that, even among Moroccans, less than a third emphasized the cultural differences, and less than a fifth emphasized social distance.

More than half the respondents in all four groups of origin perceived important cultural differences between their *edah* and *edot* in the other broad ethnic category or between the two broad categories (Ashkenazim and *edot ha'Mizrach*). Fewer, between a quarter and a third, perceived high social distance and social conflict between the two broad categories, and here again the differences among the four groups were minor. It may be noted that, whereas sociologists of Israeli society have argued that acculturation of the *edot* to the dominant culture has been more extensive than social amalgamation among the *edot*, the population appears to perceive the opposite. This finding may be interpreted to support the position that emphasizes the importance of cultural factors (at least as subjectively perceived) in the recognition of ethnic boundaries.

Evaluative   Data on relative deprivation or distributive justice among Jewish groups of origin should be set in the context of the emphasis on the value of equality in Israeli society (Shapiro, 1977). Respondents were asked whether there should be more economic equality than exists today among Israeli citizens, less equality, or no change. More than 80% in all four groups said that there should be more equality, 17% said that no change was required, and less than 3% supported greater inequality. The value of equality, together with the value of ethnic integration among Jews, are likely to lead Israelis to condemn inequality based on ascriptive status. However, individual achievement is also highly valued, and it is not uncommon for people to account for low socio-economic profiles of particular groups in terms of low levels of achievement or "cultural disadvantage" (cf. Lewis, 1979).

In order to measure intergroup relative deprivation or distributive justice, respondents were asked whether their *edah* had received less than it deserved, what it deserved, or more than it deserved in the economic sphere, in social prestige, and in political power. The same questions were asked about the two broad ethnic categories. Here, there was a clear difference between the Moroccans and Iraqis on the one hand, and the Poles and the Rumanians on the other (table 8.2). Whereas about 5% of the Poles and an only slightly higher proportion of Rumanians believed that their *edot* had received less than they deserved, a half of the Moroccans and a third of the Iraqis believed that this was the case for their *edot*. Iraqis were in even greater agreement with Moroccans concerning the injustice done to *edot ha'Mizrach* as a whole; about half said that *edot ha'Mizrach* had received less than they deserved

Table 8.2. *Percentages in four groups of origin who perceive group deprivation and discrimination*

	Poles	Rumanians	Moroccans	Iraqis
Unjust deprivation of own edah				
Economic ally	5	6	41	22
In social status	4	7	53	30
In political power	5	18	56	35
Unjust deprivation of Ashkenazim				
Economically	2	5	1	3
In social status	7	6	4	4
In political power	4	8	2	4
Unjust deprivation of edot ha'Mizrach				
Economically	17	20	50	41
In social status	26	36	56	51
In political power	24	27	58	54
Unjustly advantaged Ashkenazim				
Economically	8	9	32	28
In social status	14	11	48	43
In political power	26	21	57	58
Unjustly advantaged edot ha'Mizrach				
Economically	7	11	2	5
In social status	3	5	3	5
In political power	12	13	4	5
Discrimination				
Against *edot ha'Mizrach*	34	29	61	62
Against Ashkenazim	16	11	2	2
Against Arabs	7	7	2	5
N	188	213	216	209

compared with about a quarter of Poles and Rumanians who were of the same view. The great majority in all groups agreed that Ashkenazim were not unjustly deprived and that *edot ha'Mizrach* were not unjustly advantaged, but there were significant differences with respect to perceiving the Ashkenazim as unjustly advantaged. A third of the Middle Easterners and less than 10% of Europeans believed that Ashkenazim received more than they deserved economically; nearly 60% of the Middle Easterners and about a quarter of the Europeans said that Ashkenazim had received more than they deserved in political power.

Similar findings emerged when respondents were asked if there was discrimination in Israeli society and, if so, against which groups. More Moroccans and Iraqis believed that there was discrimination than

Table 8.3. *Deprivation index: average levels (x̄) and standard deviations (σ) for four groups*

	x̄	σ	N
Poles	2.28	.64	169
Rumanians	2.45	.86	183
Moroccans	4.54	1.78	207
Iraqis	4.21	1.78	197
Total	3.45	1.73	756

Rumanians and Poles, and of those who believed that there was discrimination more than two-thirds of Moroccans and Iraqis and less than a third of Poles and Rumanians believed that it was *edot ha'Mizrach* who were discriminated against. Less than 3% of Moroccans and Iraqis and about 15% of Poles and Rumanians believed that Ashkenazim had been discriminated against. Comparatively few mentioned the Arabs or the "minorities" as being discriminated against.

The differences among the four groups of origin with respect to respondents' evaluations of distributive justice and discrimination are summarized in a "deprivation index" (table 8.3). This shows that the average levels of deprivation for Moroccans and Iraqis were twice those of Poles and Rumanians. (The construction of the index is given in appendix B.)

We did not ask any direct questions, such as, "who is guilty" for ethnic inequality in Israel, but we did ask respondents whether they believed there were any groups whose members "have their noses in the air" and, if so, which groups. Respondents were also asked whether there were any groups who required "cultural treatment" and, if so, which groups. These expressions are heard commonly in Israel; the first may refer to ethnic haughtiness, and the second implies that certain groups should benefit from more investment in their education in order to compensate for their "cultural disadvantages."

The group most frequently singled out as having "their noses in the air" were the Ashkenazim: 26% of Moroccan respondents and 24% of Iraqi respondents believed this to be so compared with 14% of Poles and 12% of Rumanians. The category most frequently singled out as requiring "cultural treatment" was *edot ha'Mizrach*, and, although this may be interpreted as a stigmatization, it was volunteered by more Moroccans (36%) and Iraqis (35%) than Poles (26%) and Rumanians (22%). These data, as well as data from other studies,[1] suggest that, although many

Table 8.4. *Hierarchy of identifications*

	Poles	Rumanians	Moroccans	Iraqis
Percent ranking				
Jewish as first choice	31	32	52	50
Israeli as first choice	67	64	39	44
Specific ethnic category				
third choice	12	18	34	34
Broad ethnic category				
third choice	48	37	32	40
Rejection of				
specific ethnic category	44	44	23	17
Rejection of				
broad ethnic category	43	41	23	18
N	188	213	216	209

Note: Index of dissimilarity among the distributions of the categories: identifications placed as first choice above the diagonal; identifications placed as third choice below the diagonal.

	Poles	Rumanians	Moroccans	Iraqis
Poles	—	2.6	27.1	23.3
Rumanians	8.8	—	24.5	20.8
Moroccans	34.0	25.3	—	4.2
Iraqis	31.7	25.5	9.4	—

Middle Easterners accuse Ashkenazim for the subordinate position of *edot ha'Mizrach*, some also accept what has been called the "culture of poverty" argument.

Affective   In order to tap ethnic identifications two sets of questions were asked. Firstly, respondents were asked to rank four identifications in order of their importance for them: community of origin (*edah*), Ashkenazi or *edot ha'Mizrach*, Jewish, and Israeli (table 8.4). The great majority of respondents placed the Jewish and Israeli identifications in first or second place, but, whereas Moroccan and Iraqi respondents were evenly split in placing Israeli or Jewish identification in first place, two-thirds of the Poles and Rumanians placed the Israeli identification before the Jewish. A divergent pattern between European and Middle Eastern Israelis was also found regarding the ethnic identifications. More than twice as many Poles and Rumanians (over 40% in those groups) refused to accept both the specific and broad ethnic labels as identifications, and

Table 8.5. *High level of pride (points five and six on six-point scale) in each identification (%)*

	Poles	Rumanians	Moroccans	Iraqis
Jewish	68	75	93	83
Israeli	89	89	94	91
Specific ethnic category	30	32	75	71
Broad ethnic category	22	36	79	70
N	188	213	216	209

of those that did rank the labels, the majority placed the *edah* identification in fourth place. Moroccan and Iraqi respondents were split in about equal proportions in placing the specific or broad ethnic identifications in third place. The indexes of dissimilarity indicate that on both the specific and the broad ethnic identifications the distance between the European and Middle Eastern categories is much greater than the distance according to country of origin within those categories.

The second set of questions on ethnic identification asked respondents to indicate their level of pride, if any, in the four identifications. Respondents were presented with a six-point scale, ranging from "no pride whatsoever" to "very proud." Table 8.5 shows the percentage reporting a high level of pride (points 5 and 6 on the scale). On all four identifications the Moroccans and Iraqis indicated greater pride than the Poles and Rumanians, and only on the Israeli identification was there little difference between the categories. Consistent with the data on the hierarchy of identifications, Moroccans and Iraqis did not indicate a clear preference for the Israeli or Jewish identifications, and Poles and Rumanians tended to express greater pride in the Israeli identification. The difference between European and Middle Eastern Israelis is especially prominent in their orientations toward the ethnic identifications: the proportion of Moroccans and Iraqis who expressed pride in both the specific and broad ethnic identifications was considerably greater than that of Poles and Rumanians.

Indexes of the specific and broad ethnic identifications were constructed by combining measures from the two sets of questions (table 8.6). (The construction of the index is given in appendix C.) The distribution of levels of identification and the index of dissimilarity indicate clearly the difference between European and Middle Eastern Israelis with respect to both the specific and the broad ethnic identifications. Poles and Rumanians are concentrated at the first level (minimal or no ethnic

Table 8.6. *Distributions in four groups of the indexes of specific (S) and broad (B) ethnic identifications*

Index of identification		Poles S	B	Rumanians S	B	Moroccans S	B	Iraqis S	B
Lowest	1	45	45	46	42	10	15	15	15
	2	27	36	26	26	15	9	18	17
	3	10	5	8	11	9	11	9	10
	4	14	8	16	14	41	42	38	34
Highest	5	4	6	4	8	25	24	21	24
N		188		213		216		209	

Percentages may not add up to 100 due to rounding.
Note: Index of dissimilarity: specific identification is above the diagonal and broad identification is below the diagonal.

	Poles	Rumanians	Moroccans	Iraqis
Poles	—	3.5	48.2	41.4
Rumanians	12.7	—	46.3	39.3
Moroccans	56.1	44.2	—	7.0
Iraqis	48.3	36.4	13.3	—

identification), and Moroccans and Iraqis are concentrated at levels 4 and 5, the highest levels of ethnic identification. Among Europeans the Ashkenazi identification takes preference over the specific identification, but among Middle Easterners there is no clear preference for either the specific or the broad ethnic identification.

Table 8.7 presents correlation coefficients of all possible identification pairs with respect to levels of pride. A high correlation between the Jewish and Israeli identifications, which has been demonstrated by a number of other studies (Herman, 1977), is replicated here. There is also a strong correlation for all groups, but especially for the Moroccans and Iraqis, between the specific and broad ethnic identifications. However, only the Moroccans and Iraqis demonstrated high correlations between their Israeli-Jewish identifications and their specific and broad ethnic identifications. Among the Poles and Rumanians these relationships are weak or non-existent.

Thus, the most prominent division in the level of ethnic identification among Jews in Israel is between European and Middle Eastern Israelis. In analyzing this division we have pointed to an avenue of investigation that has been neglected not only in Israel, but also in the general

Table 8.7. *Correlations of levels of pride in each pair of identifications*

Identifications	Poles	Rumanians	Moroccans	Iraqis
Jewish/Israeli category	.69	.64	.67	.84
Jewish/specific ethnic category	.24	.28	.64	.62
Jewish/broad ethnic category	.22	.16	.55	.66
Israeli/specific ethnic category	.09	.29	.51	.58
Israeli/broad ethnic category	.00	.08	.52	.63
Specific ethnic/broad ethnic category	.59	.64	.85	.83

Note: Due to the low variance among Moroccans, gamma and not the more popular Pearson's R was used.

literature on ethnic identification: the relationship between ethnic identification and the wider identifications of nationality and citizenship. The finding that the European Israelis were disposed to place their Israeli identification before their Jewish identification is congruent with the view of Zionism and the Israeli state as "revolutions" against the Jewish tradition and way of life in the diaspora. The negative orientations toward the traditional way of life in the diaspora also involved the rejection or the minor placement of the identification associated with the Jewish community of origin. Among Middle Eastern Israelis, Israeliness is a source of great pride but it has not yet overtaken Jewishness as the most encompassing identity, and the wider identifications have not become differentiated from the subethnic identifications of the communities of origin.

The specific and broad ethnic identifications do not appear to have become alternative expressions of identification. If Middle Eastern Israelis are proud to be Moroccan or Iraqi, they are also likely to be proud to be part of *edot ha'Mizrach*. Identification with a socio-economic class would normally exclude simultaneous identification with another, but this is not the case with ethnic identifications; they are not necessarily mutually exclusive, and new labels of ethnic identification do not always emerge at the expense of existing labels.

Cultural and political saliency

The importance of the subethnic identifications among Middle Easterners might not appear to favor integration, but the implications of these identifications for integration are dependent on their relationships to cultural and political ethnicity. A high level of ethnic identification may

Table 8.8. *Distribution in groups of origin according to attitude toward cultural saliency*

Attitude toward cultural saliency	Poles	Rumanians	Moroccans	Iraqis
A	5	6	32	16
B	63	68	64	68
C	32	26	4	16
N	182	210	212	204

Index of dissimilarity	Rumanians	Moroccans	Iraqis
Poles	6.3	28.7	16.8
Rumanians	—	26.3	10.5
Moroccans		—	16.8

Question: What is your view regarding the preservation of the special culture of your group of origin?
A The group should preserve its special culture.
B The group should preserve its culture as part of the general Israeli culture.
C There is no need to preserve the special culture of the group or of other groups.

have little effect on integration-mindedness if it is not accompanied by either cultural or political separatism. In fact, the clear division that we found between Europeans and Middle Easterners with respect to ethnic identification is greatly modified when we move to a consideration of cultural and political ethnicity.

In answer to a question designed to tap the cultural saliency of the specific ethnic identification, numerically similar majorities in all four groups indicated that they wished to preserve the culture of their group of origin as part of Israeli culture (line B in table 8.8). A relatively large minority of the Moroccans (32.5%) agreed without any qualification that they should preserve the special culture of their group of origin (line A in table 8.8), and very few believed that there was no need to preserve it (line C in table 8.8). Most distant from the Moroccans were the Poles; only 4.9% indicated an unqualified cultural ethnicity, and 32.4% rejected it entirely. However, the index of dissimilarity indicates that differences in the cultural component of ethnicity are narrower than the differences in ethnic identification. The index shows also that the Iraqi distribution is closer to that of the Rumanian than to the Moroccan.[2]

The distance of the Moroccans from the other groups was also obvious with respect to political ethnicity; 16.2% of the Moroccans favored political organization on the basis of their group of origin, compared with

3.3% of the Iraqis, 1.4% of the Rumanians, and none of the Poles. When asked if they favored political organization of *edot ha'Mizrach*, 26.7% of the Moroccans answered positively compared with 15.3% of the Iraqis; only .5% of the Rumanians and 1% of the Poles favored political organization on an Ashkenazi basis.

Thus, as would be expected, cultural and political ethnicity were found to be almost totally absent among Poles and Rumanians, the groups with a low ethnic identification, and it was in the Middle Eastern groups that the minority with a high ethnic saliency was found. However, even in the Moroccan and Iraqi groups the majority do not support cultural or political ethnic pluralism. A strong ethnic identification without a concern to preserve cultural distinctiveness or to support political mobilization might appear as an example of "symbolic ethnicity." Gans (1979) argued that acculturation and assimilation of white ethnics in the United States are continuing apace, and that it is just because objective differences are disappearing that many seek to emphasize their ethnic identification. According to Gans, the heightened concern with the remaining symbols of ethnicity in the United States does not denote a desire to maintain the ethnic culture nor a revival of the group in political form. In Israel, however, the term "symbolic ethnicity" would not be an adequate categorization of ethnic identification. The majority do not want cultural or political separation, but neither do they wish to see the disappearance of the cultural features associated with their group of origin; they desire to live in a unified Jewish society that recognizes the contribution of the culture of their group to the whole.

The desire for cultural recognition and political participation was probably expressed, in a more urgent way, by those minorities who supported an unqualified cultural ethnicity or an ethnic political organization. Support for an unqualified cultural ethnicity indicates a pluralist, but not necessarily separatist, orientation; it may reflect a view that the cultural contribution of one's group has not been sufficiently recognized in the wider society, and that it will only be recognized if it is given unequivocal support. Jewish ethnic political parties in Israel have never sought political separation as an end in itself; they have demanded a more equal distribution of resources among groups of different origins, in order to arrive at a more unified and integrated society. Perhaps in Israel, even more than in the United States (Gleason, 1979), the terms "pluralism" and "melting-pot" would give an unfortunate impression of mutually exclusive models.

Effects of deprivation and religiosity on ethnic saliency

Only within the Moroccan category did a significant minority express a cultural and political ethnic saliency, and, as might be expected, it is only in this category that significant statistical correlations were found between cultural and political ethnicity. Even here, however, the correlations were not high: between unqualified preservation of the ethnic culture and a desire for a Moroccan political organization, .34; and between unqualified preservation of the ethnic culture and a desire for political organization of *edot ha'Mizrach*, .19. Among Iraqis, 15.7% expressed an unqualified desire to preserve ethnic culture and 15.3% favored political organization of *edot ha'Mizrach*, but the correlation here was statistically insignificant (.07). Thus, although cultural and political ethnicity cannot be said to be inverted (Deshen, 1974), it is clear that ethnic consciousness may be focused on one or the other. This raises the question of whether cultural and political ethnicity are to be explained by different factors.

It has been shown that the Moroccan group has the highest levels of both religiosity and felt deprivation. It is also the only group with substantial minorities whose ethnicity is culturally and politically salient. We may test, therefore, alternative socio-economic and cultural perspectives by examining whether felt deprivation (as measured by the "deprivation index") or religiosity are associated with ethnic saliency within the Moroccan group. Discriminant analysis is a suitable method to use here since the dependent variables are either dichotomous (support or non-support of ethnic political organization) or trichotomous (attitude toward cultural saliency). Regression analysis with these types of dependent variables is problematic. In addition to religiosity and deprivation, we examine the relationships of the dependent variables with socio-economic status, age, specific ethnic identification, and broad ethnic identification.

Column 1 of table 8.9 shows that strong identification with the *edah* and a high level of religiosity greatly increase the chances of ethnic cultural saliency. Lower socio-economic status also increases the chances of cultural saliency, but the effect of deprivation, although in the expected direction, is less. With respect to political saliency, there is a difference between support for political organization on the basis of the *edah* (column 2) and support for political organization on the basis of *edot ha'Mizrach* (column 3). As with cultural saliency, greater religiosity and lower socio-economic status increase the chances of supporting the political organization of the *edah*. Lower socio-economic status also increases

Table 8.9. *Factors affecting attitudes of Moroccans toward cultural saliency (1), political organization on the basis of the* edah *(2), and political organization on the basis of* edot ha'Mizrach *(3). (Discriminant function analysis)*

Discriminating variables		1	2	3
Deprivation		.23	.35	.71
Religiosity		.53	.56	.26
Socio-economic status		−.46	−.62	−.54
Age		−.03	.35	.32
Specific ethnic identification		.66	.20	−.02
Broad ethnic identification		.16	.03	.22
Wilks Lambda		.93	.81	.77
Canonical correlation		.26	.44	.47
(χ^2 test)		.04	.00	.00
Group centroids	A	.38 negative	−.22	−.32
	B+C	−.20 positive	1.03	.88

the chances of supporting the political organization of *edot ha'Mizrach*, but here it is felt deprivation rather than religiosity that strengthens political saliency.

These findings suggest that, although among Moroccans the *edah* and *edot ha'Mizrach* are by no means contradictory or inconsistent forms of ethnicity, ethnic saliency may be focused on either one or the other. If the focus is the *edah*, it is more likely to be related to religiosity. If the focus is *edot ha'Mizrach*, it is more likely to be related to feelings that both the *edah* and *edot ha'Mizrach* as a whole have been unjustly deprived and discriminated against. It should be stressed that these findings apply only to the Moroccans. Iraqis express nearly as much deprivation as the Moroccans, but far fewer support ethnic political organization. This difference may be explained by the fact that the Moroccans have been the least esteemed and most deprived group of Middle Eastern Israelis. They have certainly been more prominent in movements of ethnic protest and ethnic political parties.

Conclusions

A few ethnic radicals have advocated the overthrow of the Ashkenazi dominated establishment and its replacement by a new social order dominated by Middle Eastern Israelis, but even among Moroccans the common demand is for their acceptance by European Israelis as equal partners in the social, cultural, and political life of the nation. They are not willing to accept the unidirectional form of amalgamation, but they will move toward other groups if those groups will move toward them. In this context, ethnicity is not something which is either retained in a separatist fashion or abandoned through acculturation and assimilation, but a point of bargaining and exchange in the symbolic order.

Both European and Middle Eastern Israelis give their verbal support to "fusion of the exiles," but the meanings of this phrase and its implications for ethnic identification can be very different. Among veteran European Israelis "fusion" meant *klitah* (absorption) or a unidirectional form of amalgamation; it was premised on a paternalism that took for granted the superiority of the dominant culture in Israel, and saw little of value in the traditional culture of Middle Eastern Jews apart from a quaint folklore (Smooha, 1978; Stahl, 1976; E. Cohen, 1983; Shokeid and Deshen, 1982). All immigrants, whatever their origins, were expected to abandon their distinctive culture and embrace "Israeli" culture, but these demands were directed especially toward the Jews from Asia and Africa whose traditional cultures were seen to be most distant from modern Israel. The ideology of absorption through resocialization remains an important one, but since the late 1950s it has lost much of its force, and there is now a far wider acceptance and legitimation of ethnic cultural expression in most parts of the political and social spectrum. But with respect to their ethnic identification, it makes little difference whether Europeans are incorporationists, emphasizing the need for Middle Easterners to accept western culture, or supporters of a more balanced fusion; their support for amalgamation, together with their association with the dominant culture, mean that they have no need to assert an ethnic identification.

For Middle Eastern immigrants "fusion" meant the integration of all Jewish communities into a single nation whose Judaism they had upheld in their communities of origin. The confrontation with a secular Israeli-Jewish culture came as an unexpected shock to many, and in the first stages of their adaptation to Israeli society Middle Eastern immigrants did not feel sufficiently secure to assert their heritages in a conspicuous manner. The major reactions of Middle Easterners to the absorption policies of the veteran, mainly European, Israelis, were either to take an assimilationist stance, accepting the dominant culture and distancing themselves from their traditions, or a pluralist stance, in which they adhered strictly to their traditions within the enclosed contexts of their families and ethnic synagogues (Stahl, 1976). The improvement in the socio-economic position of Middle Easterners and their substantial

134

acculturation to the dominant culture have provided a basis for a more self-confident assertion of their own cultural heritages (Weingrod, 1979). Our data show, however, that care should be taken in evaluating recent signs of a reassertion of ethnicity among Middle Eastern Israelis, and that it is a mistake to blanket all Middle Easterners under one category.

9

Class consciousness

Israel's "exceptionalism"

There are a few studies of the historical development of the class structure in Israel (Rosenfeld and Carmi, 1976; Shapiro, 1977; Ben-Porat, 1986, 1989), but discussions of class consciousness or conflict have rarely been part of the discourse on stratification and inequality in the sociology of Israel (partial exceptions are Yatziv, 1979; Ben-Porat, 1985). Attention has focused on the "ethnic gap" between Ashkenazim and *edot ha'Mizrach* and disputes among Israeli sociologists have mainly revolved around explanations of this gap (Smooha, 1978; Swirski, 1981; Smooha and Peres, 1975; Hartman and Ayalon, 1975). Marxist analyses have made references to class conflict within Israel, but this theme has been subordinated to, or conflated with, ethnic conflict either within the Jewish population or between Jews and Arabs. The relative absence of class consciousness, which is assumed rather than demonstrated, is explained by nationalism, the centrality of ethnicity, and the uniqueness of the Israeli version of capitalism in the form of co-operation between the private sector and the bureaucracy of the Labor sector (Machover and Orr, 1971; Zureik, 1979). The author of a recent neo-Marxist work on class structure in Israel from 1948 to the 1980s states that, although the emerging capitalist system in Israeli society has inevitably produced classes "in themselves," there has been no development of classes "for themselves." The state is seen to have had the major role in the process of the class formation of both the bourgeoisie and the proletariat, but a succession of governments, led for most of the period by the Labor Party, succeeded in neutralizing or preventing the development of class consciousness and struggle (Ben-Porat, 1989).

On those few occasions when non-Marxist or non-radical Israeli sociologists have discussed class and class consciousness, they have also emphasized Israel's "exceptionalism." Eisenstadt (1985), for example, has pointed to the "unique" features of Israeli society in accounting for the assumed absence of class consciousness. He writes that the central theme in the development of the Israeli labor or socialist movement was a pioneering one; the emphasis on the creation of a new Jewish working class had strong national connotations. It was the leadership of the labor movement that attained the center of economic and political power and the "usual European class divisions" between capitalists and workers were largely absent.

Horowitz and Lissak (1989: 83–97) provide the most systematic attempt to account for weak class consciousness in Israeli society. They note that social class served as an important basis of political organization in the pre-state Yishuv, but since the establishment of the state there has been a considerable decline in class consciousness despite an increase in inequality. This decline is evident in the disappearance or loss of the expressive and mobilizing power of symbols of working-class identity, such as the red flag and the International hymn, in the loss of force and meaning of the term "the working class," and in the disconnection between social class and voting patterns. Horowitz and Lissak account for this development by reference to four explanatory categories: economic, political, social, and ideological.

An important economic factor is that the inflow of capital from external sources was far greater than domestic capital formation, and the governmental control over the investment of this capital weakened conceptions of a struggle between owners of capital and a working class. A large part of the imported capital was invested within the framework of public ownership (government and the Histadrut), but even most of the privately owned capital was originally imported and allocated by state agencies. In the emergent multisector economy, in which a large proportion of workers were employed by firms under the public ownership of the state or the Histadrut, the hostility of workers was aimed at the political establishment rather than at private employers.

The import of capital also made possible economic growth and a welfare state which softened class resentment by increasing real income, living standards, and mobility. The expansion of upper rank positions was so rapid that those who filled them have not yet had sufficient time to establish themselves as an exclusive status group. An economic elite of the private sector enjoys high prestige, but its emergence under largely public auspices and its continual interconnections with a variety of political and public-sector groups have not inclined its members to articulate their identity in class or political terms.

The political factor is bound to the economic one: the extensive control over the distribution of economic resources by the political establishment has meant that the economically weaker groups have blamed their deprivation on the Labor Party that headed all governments until 1977. Horowitz and Lissak also distinguish a social factor that relates to what they consider are different conceptions of the social order found in Israel compared with most western societies. In Europe the importance of class images is seen to derive from a history of the struggle of social classes for political rights such as suffrage. The historical linkage of class and political struggles has resulted in the division of classes into distinct subcultures with dichotomous images, whereas the absence of such a linkage in Israel has resulted in a multistrata hierarchy without any clear class boundaries. The weakness of the political appeal of class symbolism in Israel is especially apparent among Jews from North Africa and Asia who are more likely to conceive of social divisions as based on attachments to particularistic groups, such as family, religion, and ethnicity, rather than on socio-economic strata.

With respect to the ideological factor, Horowitz and Lissak write that even in the early period of the Yishuv the Labor movement concentrated on building its own economic sector, rather than on emphasizing a class struggle against private capital. The promotion of national over class-based values was evident after Mapai, the largest party in the Labor movement, attained political dominance in the mid-1930s, and this trend was reinforced after the achievement of statehood. Ben-Gurion, in particular, emphasized the Labor movement's national responsibility as the state's ruling group, and he implemented his "statist" orientation by transferring certain economic and social functions from the Histadrut to the state sector.

Some of the points presented by Horowitz and Lissak, such as economic growth, socio-economic mobility, the expansion of the managerial and professional strata, and the development of the welfare state, are not particular to Israel, and if they had a weakening effect on class consciousness in Israel, they presumably had a similar effect elsewhere. One problem in the discussion of Israel's "exceptionalism" is that class consciousness or the absence of it in Israel is compared with a somewhat ideal-type Marxist image of a dichotomous form of class consciousness in European societies, rather than with the actual findings on class consciousness in countries such as England, France, and Italy. Thus, when Horowitz and Lissak write that the tendency in Israel is to perceive class differences as a multistrata hierarchy and that the non-dichotomous image reflects the Israeli reality, they imply that a dichotomous conception is far more common in those capitalist societies where there is a much clearer distinction between capital and labor. However, many empirical studies have shown that a dichotomous image is a minority one in western capitalist societies, and that a number of complex multiclass or strata images reflect the somewhat fragmented class structure of advanced capitalist societies (see, for example, Roberts *et al.*, 1977).

This is not to deny that the political economy of Israel has some special features that have had effects on class consciousness, but we contend that Israel's "exceptionalism" has been overextended by sociologists, Marxist and non-Marxist alike. One problem here has been the tendency to ignore the multidimensional aspects of class consciousness, and to consider only the presence or absence of its visible manifestations in politicized forms. Where, as in Israel, the politicized facets of class consciousness are weak, it has been concluded prematurely that class consciousness as a whole is weak or absent. We expect that the findings on certain dimensions of class consciousness, such as images of the class structure and feelings of class deprivation, will be similar in Israel to those found in other capitalist societies. This is because the extent and structuration of inequality in Israel are broadly similar to other capitalist nations, and especially to those nations where a large percentage of the labor force is in the public sector.

In many respects class consciousness may be found to differ little from what has been found in many western countries, but it remains hidden because the major political parties are divided principally by positions on issues that are rarely reflections of the divergent economic interests of classes. The division between "left wing" and "right wing" in Israel does not focus now on the distribution of wealth or on the appropriate weight of the private and public sectors of the economy (Ben-Porath, 1983); it focuses on the nation's boundaries, on foreign policies, and on the national-cultural images of the society.

It is indeed the case that a most important factor in accounting for the failure of class consciousness to become politicized in Israel is the long standing political and economic power of the Labor "establishment" made up of the Labor Party, the Histadrut, and their related agencies. The Histadrut is more than a federation of trade unions; it is a vast industrial, commercial, and financial empire which employs nearly a quarter of the total labor force. The Histadrut and the government, sometimes in co-operation, control a large part of the economy, and about two-thirds of all strikes in Israel occur in the public sector.

Israel is exceptional not only in the combination of trade-union and entrepreneurial functions, but also in the extensive control of the trade-union organization by political parties. The centralized system in which trade-union leaders are nominated by the political parties and elected in accordance with the support that the party receives in the union's elections has enabled the Labor Party to combine political and economic control over a large proportion of workers. About 90% of organized workers are members of the Histadrut, and the basic union cells of the organization, the workers' committees in plants and work-shops, are chosen on a political basis. Political support also determines managerial appointments in the industrial and other economic enter-prises of the Histadrut, and most key positions, whether in trade-union or managerial roles, have been filled by members of the Labor Party. Under this system there is considerable inequality in earnings, status, and power, but few workers are likely to perceive the Labor alignment or the Histadrut as organizations that support their class interests against employers or controllers of capital.

Dimensions of class consciousness

In order to explore the extent to which class consciousness in Israel is similar and different from other societies, it is useful to distinguish cognitive from affective and evaluative dimensions of class conscious-ness. Similarities may be found with respect to some dimensions and differences with respect to others. The investigation reported below examines to what extent the dimensions of class consciousness are empirically related to each other, and this is followed by an investigation of the relationships of the class consciousness dimensions to a number of alternative and overlapping class classifications. When class conscious-ness is divided into a number of dimensions, it may be found that, whereas certain dimensions are correlated most clearly with a particular class classification, say one based on ownership or control of productive forces, other dimensions are more significantly related to an alternative classification, such as one based on occupational status.

The sample included sufficient numbers of blue-collar, white-collar, and self-employed workers to allow for a comparison of the connections between a number of class classifications and several dimensions of class consciousness. This framework substantially parallels or overlaps with other dimensional schemes of class consciousness (see, for example, Lopreato and Hazelrigg, 1972; Jackson and Jackson, 1983; Phizacklea and Miles, 1980; Ben-Porat, 1985; and especially Landecker, 1981). Three general dimensions, class structure, identity, and struggle, were divided into cognitive and affective or evaluative aspects. Information on the cognitive aspects of the three dimensions was obtained by the following questions:

1 Respondents were asked how many classes they believed exist in Israel; they were requested to name them and indicate their relative sizes.
2 To obtain self-location, respondents were asked, in an open-choice question, to what class they belonged.
3 Respondents indicated on a six-point scale the level of conflict that they perceived between their class and another class (or other classes); the scale ranged from "no conflict whatsoever" to "especially severe conflict."

Information on the affective/evaluative aspects of the three dimensions was obtained by the following questions:

1 Respondents were asked separate questions on their class's share in the economic area, its social prestige, and its political power. In each area, respondents indicated whether they believed that their class received more, as much, or less than it deserved.
2 Respondents were asked on a six-point scale whether they took pride in their class; the scale ranged from "no pride whatsoever" to "very proud."
3 Respondents were asked whether they believed that there was a need for their class to organize politically.

Possible relationships were investigated between these class consciousness dimensions and a number of classifications of class according to objective measures. The classifications were:

1 The distinction between wage-earners and independents or self-employed.
2 The distinction between those who have authority over other workers and those who do not.
3 The distinction between white- and blue-collar workers.
4 A five-class classification which divided both blue- and white-collar employees into "higher" and "lower" categories (the independents remained a separate category). White-collar workers were divided according to occupational prestige: "higher" white collar were mainly professionals and managers, and "lower" white collar, who were in the middle range of occupational prestige, included many clerks. Blue-collar workers were divided according to whether they had authority over at least one other worker or not.
5 Socio-economic status based on occupation, education, and housing density (number of rooms in house in relation to number living there). Separate calculations were also made with the three variables that made up the socio-economic status (SES) index.[1]

Table 9.1. *SES scores of five class categories; average levels ($\bar{x}$), standard deviations (σ)*

	SES		Occupational status		Years education		Housing density		N
	$\bar{x}$	σ	$\bar{x}$	σ	$\bar{x}$	σ	$\bar{x}$	σ	
Lower blue-collar workers	−1.06	1.07	41.31	14.43	10.13	2.76	1.62	.60	193
Higher blue-collar workers	−.34	.93	50.29	16.11	11.34	2.96	1.37	.42	184
Lower white-collar workers	.50	.59	67.38	6.31	12.95	2.67	1.32	.42	117
Higher white-collar workers	1.88	.66	90.79	7.65	16.68	3.09	1.12	.31	169
Independents	.41	1.16	51.41	18.87	10.65	2.84	1.38	.50	135
Total	.07	1.40	59.49	22.72	12.33	3.78	1.37	.49	798

Note: For the SES distributions according to country of origin see appendix A.

Table 9.2. *Class terminology by number of classes (%)*

Number of classes	Employer–worker	Wealth	Strata	Other	N[1]
2	78.0	10.2	3.1	8.6	255
3	19.8	30.4	30.1	19.8	359
4+	10.1	30.8	18.3	41.3	109

1 Reduction of N is due to missing data.
Percentages may not add up to 100 due to rounding.

The five-class classification was constructed to incorporate as many as possible, within the constrictions of our sample, of the important distinctions among classes made in the stratification literature (Giddens, 1980; Parkin, 1979; Poulantzas, 1975). It is used in table 9.1 to show the SES scores of the class categories.

The overall SES scores and the scores of all three components that make up the index indicate sizeable differences among the four salaried categories. The greatest difference is between the higher white-collar category and the rest. Within the self-employed (independents) category there is considerable differentiation, but overall the scores are relatively low and very close to the higher blue-collar category.

Cognitive Studies in western industrial societies have found that the number of classes most frequently distinguished by respondents is three (Bell and Robinson, 1980; Coleman and Rainwater, 1978: 120; Lopreato and Hazelrigg, 1972: 166; Phizacklea and Miles, 1980: 133; Britten, 1984; Hiller, 1975; Scase, 1974). Israel is not an exception here (table 9.2), but the proportion of respondents who said that there were two classes was somewhat higher than in other countries.

When asked to name the classes, the majority used terms that can be classified into three categories: (1) a work-based terminology of employers and workers (or wage-earners); (2) a terminology based on income and wealth (rich, poor); (3) a strata terminology of high, middle, and low. There were clear relationships between the number of classes given and the terms used to name them (table 9.2). A very large proportion (78%) of those who said that there were two classes used the terms "employer" and "employee" or "independent" and "wage-earner." Those who distinguished three or more classes were far more likely to use terms referring to wealth or a strata terminology. When asked to name the largest and smallest classes (table 9.3), the majority of respondents with a dichotomous image named workers (or wage-earners) as the

Table 9.3. *Largest class named by number of classes reported (%)*

Number of classes	1	2	3	4+
Largest class named				
Employers	0	23.3	5.1	2.0
Workers	25.0	55.3	19.0	21.2
Middle class	12.5	6.0	46.4	34.3
Other	62.5	15.4	29.5	42.5
N[1]	8	215	336	99

1 Reduction of N is due to missing data.

largest class, but a not insignificant 23% named employers as the largest class. Respondents with a trichotomous image in terms of wealth or strata were more likely to name the middle class as the largest.

Whatever their class image, the great majority of respondents identified with the class that they perceived as the largest in the society. In identifying their own class the vast majority of respondents chose one of two terms: "wage-earner" or "middle class." These self-locations were in response to an open question, and neither of the labels appeared anywhere in the questionnaire (13% of respondents did not answer this question or did not identify with any class). Other terms such as "worker," "employer," "upper class," "lower class," "rich," and "poor," were used by respondents when they were asked to name the classes of the society, but very few respondents used these terms to identify themselves. (The questions on class structure were asked prior to the question on self-location.)

A clear link was found between class self-identification and images of the class structure (table 9.4). The two most common class identifications, wage-earner and middle class, corresponded to two images of the class structure. The majority of respondents who identified as wage-earners had a dichotomous image of the class structure, and the majority of middle-class identifiers had a trichotomous image. Some sociologists have suggested that a dichotomous classification is related to a conflictual image of society; when people believe that the interests of their class are diametrically opposed to another, they are likely to perceive a single division (Dahrendorf, 1959: 284; Landecker, 1981: 157–8). Our findings did not support this hypothesis; perception of class conflict was not correlated with self-identity or class images (for lack of support in other societies see Graetz, 1983; Lopreato and Hazelrigg, 1972: 187–9, 523; Jackson and Jackson, 1983: 69). Only a minority of respondents perceived

Table 9.4. *Number of classes perceived by class identification (%)*

	Identification	
	Wage-earner	Middle class
Number of classes perceived		
None or one	1	1
Two	58	14
Three	31	66
Four or more	10	19
N	299	385

an acute form of conflict between their class and another, but in this respect Israel is little different from other western industrial societies. Summarizing the cognitive dimensions, class self-identification and images of the class structure formed an interrelated complex, but neither dimension was found to be related to perceived class conflict.

Affective/evaluative aspects Only about a quarter of the sample perceived a general unfairness in the distribution among the classes of wealth, prestige, and political power, and in this Israel is not different from other industrial societies, such as Britain and the United States (Robinson and Bell, 1978). Those who believed that their class received less than its due in the economic sphere were also likely to believe the same with respect to the prestige (the correlation was .52) and political power (.39) of their class, but the relationships between these measures of class deprivation and class pride and the need for class politics were slight. About half of the respondents indicated a high level of pride in their class, but less than a fifth supported the political organization of their class. Even among those who expressed economic class injustice, only 28% said that there was a need for their class to organize politically.

Turning to the relationships between cognitive and affective/evaluative aspects, respondents who identified as wage-earners and had a dichotomous image were no more likely to express pride in their class, and only slightly higher percentages said that their class received less than what it deserved and supported political organization of their class. Those who perceived acute class conflict were also slightly more likely to believe in class injustice and the need for their class to organize politically. The correlations among these dimensions of consciousness were very low (mostly between .10 and .20).

145

Class consciousness and individual work and mobility evaluations

A third of respondents expressed dissatisfaction regarding their salary and possibilities of promotion, and a fifth of respondents were dissatisfied with the nature of their work (these dissatisfactions were highly correlated), but personal dissatisfaction with their work did not contribute significantly to their class consciousness. Respondents who expressed dissatisfaction with their work, salary, and possibilities to advance were somewhat more likely to perceive class conflict, to say that their class had not received what it deserved, and to support class political organization, but the percentages of respondents who expressed individual economic and work dissatisfaction were considerably larger than those who perceived acute class conflict, expressed distributive injustice among classes, or supported class political organization.

Objective classifications and class consciousness

Table 9.5 shows the differences (in percentages) of five classes on the dimensions of class consciousness. Among blue-collar employees there was a somewhat greater tendency to identify as wage-earner rather than middle class, to perceive a dichotomous structure, to use a class terminology based on worker–employer and wealth distinctions rather than a "strata" terminology, and to perceive more class conflict. The independents were understandably the least likely to identify as wage-earners, but they were as likely as the lower blue-collar category to emphasize wealth in their class terminology. The differences among the class categories were, however, very small. When SES was broken down into its three components, occupational status was found to have the highest correlation with number of classes perceived (.22), and to have the same correlation as housing density with perception of class conflict ($-.21$). The similar correlations of the white-collar/blue-collar and SES classifications with the cognitive dimensions of class consciousness are explained by the considerable overlap of the two classifications.[2]

There are a number of explanations in the literature for the inverse relationship between objective location in the class or socio-economic hierarchy and the number of classes perceived. Our findings do not support the hypothesis that people in the lower strata tend to make dichotomous classifications because they are less educated so that their dichotomous classification of classes is just one manifestation of this general tendency (Landecker, 1981: 187). Nor do our findings support the hypothesis that dichotomous classifications are found among

Table 9.5. *Class consciousness of five class categories* (%)

	Lower blue collar N=193	Higher blue collar N=184	Independents N=135	Lower white collar N=117	Higher white collar N=169
Identity					
Wage-earner	52	52	20	44	38
Middle class	48	48	80	56	62
Number classes					
0 or 1	2	3	2	5	3
2	40	40	34	33	22
3	46	48	52	43	54
4+	12	10	13	19	21
Class terminology					
Workers–employers	43	49	32	32	28
Wealth	30	17	30	17	19
"Strata"	9	19	17	27	28
Others	17	15	22	24	25
Pride					
High level	51	58	60	44	55
Belief class receives less than deserves					
Economically	34	27	22	23	24
Prestige	25	14	18	15	13
Politically	28	23	21	17	26
Perception high level class conflict	26	21	17	13	9
Need for political organization of class	26	16	18	20	13
Individual dissatisfaction					
Work	28	8	30	10	11
Salary	55	41	41	36	31
Possibilities of advance	46	22	33	32	25

Percentages may not add up to 100 due to rounding.

workers who do not exercise authority over others, and that three or more classes are perceived by those who exercise authority and possibly receive it also (Dahrendorf, 1959: 287). Our correlations of class perceptions with both occupational prestige and the blue-collar/white-collar classifications suggest that class images are related primarily to different occupational and work situations. Dichotomous classifications reflect the situation of many blue-collar workers and some white-collar workers in low ranks who perform similar tasks with others in their work place, and among whom there is little status differentiation and few opportunities for mobility. Perceptions of three or more classes reflect the situation of many white-collar workers who perform different tasks from others in their work place, and among whom there is considerable status differentiation and opportunities for mobility.

The differences in work and occupation situations are also associated with variance in the perception of class conflict, but differences in wealth (as measured by housing density) are equally associated with variations in perceptions of class conflict,[3] and, as we have noted, there is little association between dichotomous images of the class structure and perceptions of class conflict.

The relationships of the class categories with the affective/evaluative dimensions of class consciousness are mostly in the expected direction, but they are neither prominent nor monotonic (table 9.5). The lower blue-collar category included the highest percentages who expressed class injustice and supported the need for the political organization of their class, but differences among the other categories did not show a uniform trend. Among the employees, the lower blue-collar category expressed by far the highest levels of dissatisfaction with work, salary, and the possibilities of advancement, but with respect to satisfaction with work and the possibilities of advancement the lower white-collar category demonstrated slightly higher levels of dissatisfaction than the higher blue-collar category.

In order to examine further the issue of class deprivation, we analyzed the relative importance of different class measures on respondents' perceptions of their individual chances for occupational advancement and their feelings of class deprivation. A logit analysis is presented (table 9.6), using the same class measures as those used in chapter 7 where we examined their influences on interclass friendship networks. As in that analysis we have here four dichotomized independent variables: the distinction between blue- and white-collar workers, the distinction between secondary and post-secondary education, the distinction between independents and wage-earners, and

Table 9.6. *Odds of being satisfied with (a) chances of advancement and of (b) class deprivation according to various class measures (logit analysis)*

Authority	Ownership	Schooling	(a)	(b)	N
Blue-collar workers					
None	Salaried	0–12	1.57	.22	115
Over at least one worker	Salaried	0–12	2.74	.07	68
None	Owner	0–12	1.25	.25	32
Over at least one worker	Owner	0–12	2.18	.15	20
None	Salaried	13+	1.16	.44	8
Over at least one worker	Salaried	13+	2.03	.14	14
None	Owner	13+	.88	1.42	4
Over at least one worker	Owner	13+	2.36	.85	5
White-collar workers					
None	Salaried	0–12	.85	.15	71
Over at least one worker	Salaried	0–12	2.87	.05	107
None	Owner	0–12	.82	.17	19
Over at least one worker	Owner	0–12	3.37	.10	40
None	Salaried	13+	.99	.08	72
Over at least one worker	Salaried	13+	4.92	.03	186
None	Owner	13+	1.41	.27	5
Over at least one worker	Owner	13+	5.77	.16	15

the distinction between having and not having authority over at least one worker.

The combination of four dichotomous explanatory variables constitute sixteen profiles, and the figures in table 9.6 represent the odds situated in one category of the dependent variable rather than in its other category. For example, the first figure of 1.57 means that the odds of the first profile (blue-collar salaried workers, who have no authority at the work place and who have less than thirteen years of schooling) being satisfied with chances of advancement are 1.57 times higher than the odds of not being satisfied.

The centrality of the effect of authority on satisfaction with chances for advancement is obvious. Workers with authority at the work place, regardless of their other characteristics, tend to express higher levels of satisfaction with their chances of promotion. Authority interacts significantly with the blue-collar/white-collar distinction: the effect of authority among white-collar workers is much stronger than the parallel effect among blue-collar workers.

The extent respondents believe that their class as a whole has received its proper share or been deprived in the economic sphere, social status, and political power is influenced by all four variables in interaction with each other.[4] The differentiation among the various white-collar profiles is, however, quite modest. The interaction terms operate as follows. Higher education strengthens feelings of deprivation, particularly among blue-collar workers. Authority in the work place moderates feelings of deprivation across all compared profiles, but it is especially evident among the blue-collar workers. Owners express high levels of deprivation relative to salaried workers, especially among the blue-collar workers.

Thus, there is no single socio-economic factor which accounts for class dissatisfaction at either the individual or group level, and in most cases the effects of the class factors are interactive. These findings indicate why class consciousness remains weak; for a great number of workers the effects of the class measures on class deprivation crosscut each other rather than having an accumulative effect. For example, although most categories of blue-collar workers have higher levels of class deprivation than most white-collar categories, the blue-collar workers with authority are likely to feel far less deprived than those without authority. Furthermore, it is the relatively small number of workers who lack class crystallization (those with high education but are blue-collar workers with no authority) who express the highest levels of class deprivation. And, finally, it is clear that dissatisfaction with chances of promotion among those with no authority is not translated into general feelings of class deprivation.

Our major empirical findings may be summarized as follows:

1 There is a significant crystallization of the following cognitive dimensions: class self-identification, number of classes perceived, and class terminology. These dimensions are mainly associated with work-occupational situations: the wage-earner identification, a dichotomous image, and a worker–employer terminology are associated with blue-collar employees and lower occupational status; the middle-class identification, a trichotomous image, and a strata terminology are associated with white-collar employees and higher occupational status.
2 There were no clear breaks in identification of images between or among the classes; neither the blue-collar/white-collar distinction nor the professional–manager/other workers distinction fracture the monotonic association of these dimensions with socio-economic status.
3 Perception of class conflict is inversely related with socio-economic status, but its relationships with the other cognitive dimensions were insignificant.

4 There is little crystallization of the affective/evaluative dimensions (class deprivation, pride in class, and desire for political class organization) either with each other or with the cognitive dimensions. Feelings of class dissatisfaction and support for political class organization are higher among the lower blue-collar category, but none of the affective/evaluative dimensions has a uniform relationship with any class classification.
5 The majority of the lower strata, including those with a dichotomous image of the class structure, do not perceive an acute form of class conflict, nor do they indicate high levels of class deprivation or the need for political organization.
6 Individual dissatisfaction with work, salary, and possibilities of promotion is only weakly associated with class deprivation, and these feelings are not translated by the majority into support for class politics.

These findings suggest that class consciousness is weak in Israel, but in most of the dimensions our findings are similar to those found in other western industrial nations. Israeli images of the class structure differ little from those found in other industrial societies, and Israelis were no less ready to locate themselves within the class structure and make a positive affective identification with their class. The majority of respondents, including blue-collar workers, did not perceive a high level of class conflict or feel that the distribution of material goods, status, and political power was unfair, but the low scores in these dimensions were no lower than the scores reported in other countries; in fact, the proportions of blue-collar workers who produced dichotomous images and expressed class dissatisfaction were closer to the more radical French workers than to the British (see Gallie, 1983, for a comparison of French and British workers).

The political dimension

Where Israel does differ from at least some of the European industrial societies is in its low level of politicized class consciousness. We note that comparisons of levels of class consciousness among western societies have emphasized the importance of unionization and political parties and their strategies in accounting for differences. A comparison of the United States and Britain found little difference in the class perceptions of Americans and British, but it was noted that the class structuring of British politics has produced the belief that there is more class consciousness in Britain (Vanneman, 1980). The more radical (although rarely revolutionary) forms of class consciousness among French and Italian workers have been explained in large part by the influence of the French and Italian left political parties that have sharpened class consciousness and generalized class resentment into political strategies (Gallie, 1983; Parkin, 1972; Mann, 1973).

Support for political parties in Israel has been divided more by ethnic lines than by class or socio-economic status. We examine the relationships between voting and social divisions (ethnic and class) in chapter 11, but at this point it is appropriate to present evidence of respondents' images of the parties since this reflects on the issue of politicized class consciousness, or the lack of it, in Israel. The question here is whether respondents perceive the different political parties as representing class and/or ethnic group interests.

Respondents were asked whether they believed any political party (and, if so, which one) represented the interests of their *edah, edot ha'Mizrach*, Ashkenazim, workers, and the rich. Table 9.7 shows the images of three parties: the two largest parties in Israel, the Ma'arach (Labor Alignment) and the Likud (a coalition of nationalist or "hawkish" parties), and a much smaller party, Tami, a religious party which presented itself as representing *edot ha'Mizrach*. Differences among respondents with respect to their images are categorized according to their country of origin and their support for the two major parties. For example (top of column 1), 63% of those of Moroccan origin and who voted for the Ma'arach believed that the Ma'arach represents the interests of workers.

A large proportion of respondents did not believe that any party represented either ethnic or class interests, but an association between the Ma'arach and "workers" was attested to by more respondents than any other association. In all four groups more than 60% of those who voted for the Ma'arach believed that it represented the interests of workers. Voters of the Likud were far less likely to believe this, and the Moroccans who voted Likud were more likely to perceive the Ma'arach as representing the interests of the Ashkenazim. Among the Moroccans who voted Likud, the number who perceived the Ma'arach as representing the rich was nearly as great as those who saw it as representing the workers.

The great majority of respondents did not perceive the Likud as representing a particular class or ethnic group, but about a quarter of the Moroccans who voted Likud believed that it represented workers, their country of origin, and *edot ha'Mizrach*. The significance of these data

Table 9.7. *Images of parties according to country of origin and support for Ma'arach (M) and Likud (L)*

	Poles		Rumanians		Moroccans		Iraqis	
	M	L	M	L	M	L	M	L
Percentage respondents who say that:								
Ma'arach represents								
Workers	60	21	72	33	63	29	61	42
Rich people	2	13	0	10	4	22	6	14
Respondents' country of origin	11	13	8	6	19	0	9	4
Ashkenazim	6	13	8	14	15	48	15	31
Edot ha'Mizrach	11	0	0	2	4	0	4	0
Likud represents								
Workers	3	21	1	8	0	24	7	11
Rich people	16	8	19	4	7	5	11	1
Respondents' country of origin	0	0	1	2	2	26	6	6
Ashkenazim	0	0	0	2	0	3	4	0
Edot ha'Mizrach	11	11	13	8	11	30	9	5
Tami* represents								
Edot ha'Mizrach	54	37	49	56	33	24	35	27
N	63	38	86	52	27	115	54	81

*Only eleven respondents, all of Moroccan origin, voted for Tami.

becomes clear when we note that blue-collar Moroccans are more likely to vote for the Likud than any other category, and that a relatively large proportion of Moroccan Jews in Israel are blue-collar workers.

Thus, the worker image of the Ma'arach is more common among groups of origin, such as the Poles and Rumanians, who vote for the Ma'arach but are predominantly middle class, than among groups, such as the Moroccans, who tend to vote for the Likud and are predominantly working class. The image of the Ma'arach as representing the Ashkenazim explains, in part, this apparent paradox, but the structure of the political economy is also of great importance. The Histadrut, which has been largely controlled by the Labor Party, includes large industrial and commercial corporations and has been a major employer. The class resentment of a large proportion of low-ranking employees, as well as that of small-scale independents, has been in consequence directed against the "representatives of labor."[5] Within this framework, there was little possibility for the development of political forms of class consciousness. In many countries resentment of class inequality has not necessarily induced opposition to the prevailing structure of the society or support for radical politics. The case of Israel shows that feelings of class deprivation need not even generate support for class political organization.

Conclusions

Our findings have shown the importance of analyzing class consciousness as a multidimensional phenomenon. Politicized class consciousness is weak in Israel, but the data on other dimensions, such as class images and dissatisfactions, are similar to those found in other industrial societies. Superficial comparisons with other countries might have led us to expect that Israeli workers would have a more radical class consciousness; in western societies class consciousness is often associated with unionization of a high proportion of workers and a strong Labor Party (Korpi, 1983), and Israel has both. Many writers, both Marxist and Weberian, have explained variations in class consciousness among societies by differences in the political sphere which is granted a "relative autonomy" from the economy. In Israel, however, there is an interpenetration of the economy not only with the state, but also with the federation of unions and the Labor Party. It is the relative lack of differentiation between the political and economic spheres that has resulted in a somewhat low level of politicized class consciousness.

10

Religious, ethnic, and class divisions: convergent or crosscutting?

A religious-secular division

The Arab-Jewish division is an ubiquitous issue for Israelis, but with respect to divisions within the Jewish population, the focus of public attention appears to have moved in recent years from the ethnic division between Jews of European and African or Asian origins to the division between "religious" and "secular" Jews. The mass media has reported numerous conflicts, some involving violent confrontations, between religious and secular Jews over such issues as public transport on the Sabbath, the opening of cinemas on the Sabbath eve, the burning of bus stations displaying advertisements featuring women in swimming costumes or underwear, the free movement of private transport in areas close to religious neighborhoods on the Sabbath, the freedom of archaeologists to excavate ancient sites which may have included Jewish cemeteries, the legitimacy of conversions to Judaism under non-Orthodox auspices, and the question of "who is a Jew." It is true that it has been *haredim* (ultra-Orthodox) rather than "modern Orthodox" Jews who have been involved in these conflicts, but a number of observers have argued that there is a trend within the religious population toward "*hared*ization" and that the Jewish population is becoming increasingly polarized with respect to religion.

A sociological analysis of the religious-secular division or conflict in Israel should not only examine its extensiveness and intensity, but also its relationships with other divisions, particularly ethnic and class divisions. Sociological discussions of conflict have emphasized that, whereas convergent or overlapping conflicts may lead to acute disruptions of society, crosscutting conflicts may serve to stabilize or integrate society (Simmel, 1955; Coser, 1956). The religious-secular division may be an especially important one in Israeli society, but if it crosscuts other significant divisions, there may be little danger that it will disrupt it. A discussion of this question should focus on the relationships between the religious-secular division and ethnic and class divisions. Other divisions or aspects of stratification, such as gender and age, are less interesting in this respect since, unlike religion, ethnicity, and class, whose basic unit of classification is generally the family, they cut through the family unit.

The relationship of the religious-secular division to ethnic and class divisions among Jews has rarely been investigated within a single theoretical framework in Israel. The pluralist approach (Smooha, 1978) has tended to deal with the division between religious and secular Jews as a separate dimension from the ethnic divisions of Arabs and Jews and of Ashkenazim and *edot ha'Mizrach*. The class or dependency model of ethnicity has emphasized the convergence of ethnic and class divisions in Israel, but has paid very little attention to religion (Swirski, 1981). Religion has been an important focus of the cultural perspective on ethnicity (Deshen and Shokeid, 1974; Shokeid and Deshen, 1982; Ben-Rafael, 1982), but there has been little probing of the relationship between class and religion.

An examination of the relationships among religious, ethnic, and class divisions should look firstly at their relative importance. At the level of objective dimensions, it might be possible to compare, for example, the residential segregation of religious and secular groups with that of ethnic groups and classes. At the subjective level, questions can probe the relative importance of the various identifications; which divisions are seen to be most salient and conflict-ridden, which comparisons induce the most relative deprivation, and on what basis are respondents more likely to support political organization.

Secondly, the extent to which divisions converge or crosscut each other should be investigated. At the objective level, one might ask, for example, if different religious groups (or groups within a single religion with different levels of religiosity) have different ethnic origins and occupy different positions in the class structure. At the subjective level, it is possible to discover whether people have converging identifications, whether they perceive an overlapping of religious, ethnic, and class groups in their cultural differences, social distances, and conflicts, whether deprivations reinforce each other, and whether political support will focus on the basis of one affiliation or a combination of affiliations.

The argument here is that, in order to assess the overall importance of the ethnic, class, and religious divisions in Israeli society, it is necessary not only to compare them, but also to examine their convergence or crosscutting. In general, the distinction between working class and middle class cuts across Middle Easterners more than Europeans, and the distinction between Middle Easterners and Europeans cuts across the middle class more than the working class. The religious-secular differ-

Table 10.1. *Religiosity according to country of origin and socio-economic status: averages ($\bar{x}$), standard deviations (σ), and coefficients of variability (v)*

	$\bar{x}$	σ	v	N[1]
Moroccans				
High SES	2.90	1.30	.44	71
Low SES	3.45	1.42	.41	131
Iraqis				
High SES	1.64	1.01	.62	69
Low SES	2.44	1.21	.50	135
Poles				
High SES	.96	1.21	1.26	117
Low SES	1.45	1.43	.99	60
Rumanians				
High SES	1.61	1.39	.86	131
Low SES	1.86	1.18	.63	72
Total				
High SES	1.65	1.42	.86	388
Low SES	2.52	1.42	.56	398

1 Reduction of N is due to missing data.

ences would appear to crosscut the Europeans more than Middle Easterners, but this may be changing as there are signs of *hared*ization among some religious sectors of the Middle Easterners. The various combinations of the relative importance of divisions, and the ways in which they may converge or crosscut each other are numerous. For example, ethnic differences may crosscut the religious population more than they crosscut the secular population, but this may be of less significance for the religious population because, in comparison with the secular population, their allegiance to their position on religion out-weighs their ethnic allegiance.

Origins, socio-economic status, and religiosity

We showed in chapter 6 that religiosity (as measured by level of observance, ranging from five *mitzvot* to none) is related to both country of origin and socio-economic status. For purposes of the analysis here each group was divided into "lower" and "higher" categories of socio-economic status. SES scores lower than the average of the distribution were defined as "lower status"; scores higher than the average or equal to it were defined as "higher status."

Table 10.1 shows that level of religiosity varies by both country of origin and SES. The Moroccans have the highest level of religiosity, followed by the Iraqis, Rumanians, and Poles. In each group of origin higher socio-economic status is associated with a lower level of religiosity, but SES divisions do not alter the placement of the most religious and least religious origin groups: the most religious of the eight categories is the low SES Moroccans followed by the high SES Moroccans; the least religious is the high SES Poles followed by the low SES Poles. The SES divisions do, however, cut across the differences between Iraqi and Rumanian origins; the third most religious group is the low SES Iraqis followed by the low SES Rumanians; the high SES Iraqis and the high SES Rumanians have almost identical levels of religiosity. The coefficients of variability show that there is greater religious heterogeneity within the European groups of origin, especially in their higher socio-economic stratum.

Non-Orthodox movements (Reform, Conservative) are very small in Israel, and religious differentiation in terms of allegiances to different religious movements is of minor importance among most Israeli Jews. The major differentiation with respect to religion is in accord with levels of religious practice and identifications which roughly correspond to levels of religiosity: *dati* (religious), *mesoriti* (traditional), and *hiloni* (secular). Although surveys of religiosity show that there is a continuum ranging from the most observant to the non-observant with no breaks between clearly identifiable levels of observance (Ben-Meir and Kedem, 1979), it is common for people to categorize themselves and others into two (religious and secular), three (adding traditional), or sometimes four (adding *haredim*) categories.

Respondents were asked to divide up the Jewish population in Israel with regard to positions toward religion, and to identify themselves with one of the positions. The great majority of respondents distinguished either two (religious, non-religious or secular) or three (religious, traditional, secular) groups and identified themselves with one of these. Table 10.2 shows the distribution of the identification of respondents, and the average levels of religiosity of each identification by country of origin. In general these parallel the levels of religiosity by country of origin in table 10.1; whereas the dominant identification among Moroccans and Iraqis is traditional, that of the Poles and Rumanians is non-religious or secular.

It should be noted that when we compare respondents from the four countries of origin with the same identification, the average level of religiosity of the Moroccan group is higher than that of the other groups. The average level of religiosity of the Moroccans who identified them-

Table 10.2. *Religious identities and respective levels of religiosity according to country of origin*

| | Religious | | Traditional | | Non-religious | | |
	%	Level	%	Level	%	Level	N[1]
Moroccans	12	4.28	61	3.23	27	2.58	177
Iraqis	8	3.14	53	2.53	39	1.61	188
Poles	5	1.83	21	2.38	75	.71	155
Rumanians	3	2.00	24	2.67	73	1.16	169
Total	7	3.39	41	2.80	52	1.29	689

1 Reduction of N is due to missing data.
Percentages may not add up to 100 due to rounding.

selves as non-religious is either higher or nearly the same as the average religiosity of respondents in the other three groups who identified themselves as traditional.

The differences in identification between the higher and lower SES categories in each group of origin (not shown in the table) were in the same direction, but not as substantial as the average differences in religiosity shown in table 10.1. Only among the Iraqis was there a clear difference: 34% of the lower SES Iraqis and 52% of the higher SES Iraqis defined themselves as non-religious. In nearly all cases, for each identification, the lower SES had a higher average level of religiosity than the higher SES.

We have shown that religious-secular differences, in terms of both religious observance and identification, converge significantly (although far from absolutely) with both ethnic and class divisions. The class-religious difference crosscuts the ethnic religious differences of Iraqis and Rumanians, but it should be remembered that our sample is disproportionately stratified, and that in the country as a whole there is a considerable overlap of ethnic origin and class. The contrast between Moroccans and Europeans in terms of both socio-economic composition and religiosity is particularly clear. However, the implications of these convergences for divisiveness within the Israeli-Jewish population will depend on peoples' perceptions and evaluations.

Dimensions of religious consciousness

We categorized religious consciousness, like ethnic and class consciousness, into three broad components: cognitive, affective, and evaluative. Table 10.3 summarizes the findings for the cognitive components. We

Table 10.3. Cognitive dimensions: percentages of those who report high levels of cultural differences, social distance, and conflict (the two highest options on a six-point scale)

	Moroccans %	Iraqis %	Poles %	Rumanians %	Total %
Cultural differences					
Own *edah* and other *edot* within broad category	32	26	12	17	22
Own *edah* and *edot* from other broad category	67	57	53	53	58
Edot ha'Mizrach and Ashkenazim	66	61	53	59	60
Own class and other classes	38	35	31	29	33
Religious and non-religious	61	66	62	69	65
Religious from own *edah* and from other broad category	61	42	34	38	42
Religious from own *edah* and other *edot* within broad category	26	23	12	14	19
Social distance					
Among *edot ha'Mizrach*	17	21	25	22	21
Among *edot* Ashkenazim	14	8	6	12	10
Edot ha'Mizrach and Ashkenazim	35	28	20	30	28
Own *edah* and other broad category	35	29	26	31	30
Workers and owners	56	50	50	44	50
Religious and non-religious	43	51	64	48	51
Conflict					
Ashkenazim and *edot ha'Mizrach*	34	35	29	36	33
Affluent and economically weak	38	39	30	31	35
Own class and other classes	25	19	10	16	18
Religious and non-religious	50	56	59	58	56
Own *edah* and other broad category	31	21	17	24	21
Own *edah* and other *edot* within broad category	7	5	2	6	5
N	216	209	188	213	826

focus here on the extent to which respondents perceived cultural differences, social distance, and conflict between religious and secular Jews, between classes, between their *edah* and other *edot*, and between *edot ha'Mizrach* and Ashkenazim. For example, about equal proportions of respondents perceived a high level of cultural difference (five and six on the six-point scale) between religious and secular Jews (65%) and between *edot ha'Mizrach* and Ashkenazim (60%). In comparison, only 33% of respondents perceived a high level of cultural difference between their class and other classes in society. Lower differences were perceived among *edot* within each of the two broad ethnic categories. Comparisons of religious groups from different ethnic categories show that cultural differences within each of the two broad ethnic categories were perceived to be much less than the difference between religious Ashkenazim and religious *edot ha'Mizrach*.

The data on the cognitive aspects indicate that the majority of Israelis perceive substantial cultural differences, social distance, and conflict between religious and secular Jews in Israel. Regarding social distance, the religious-secular division is perceived as great as a sharply defined class division between property owners and workers, and regarding conflict, the religious-secular conflict is perceived as much more acute than the ethnic or class divisions. These patterns were the same for all groups of origin and for both higher and lower SES categories. Thus, most Israelis, whatever their origin or socio-economic status tend to see the religious-secular division as more sharp and divisive than ethnic and class divisions.

The dominant position of the religious-secular division at the cognitive level is not paralleled, among most Israelis, at the affective and evaluative levels. Table 10.4 summarizes the data for the affective or identificational components and the evaluative components. The patterns of the Moroccans and Iraqis differ significantly from those of the Poles and Rumanians in these components. We have shown that the Moroccans and Iraqis have higher levels of religiosity than the Poles and Rumanians, but the pride of Moroccans and Iraqis in their religious position is lower than all their other identifications. The pride of Poles and Rumanians in their religious position is lower than their class pride, but higher than their pride in their communities of origin and as Ashkenazim. These differences are mainly the consequence of the far greater ethnic pride of Moroccans and Iraqis, both as separate *edot* and as part of *edot ha'Mizrach*.

In the evaluative component, far more Moroccans and Iraqis feel deprived as members of *edot ha'Mizrach* than as members of their classes or in their religious positions. (Only the figures of those who believe in

Table 10.4. *Affective and evaluative dimensions: percentages of those with high pride in identifications (the two highest options on a six-point scale), feelings of deprivation in political power, and support for political organization of groups*

	Moroccans %	Iraqis %	Poles %	Rumanians %	Total %
High pride					
Jew	93	82	68	73	79
Israeli	94	91	87	88	90
Broad ethnic category	75	67	28	28	50
Edah	76	68	20	32	50
Class	62	56	45	49	53
Religious position	63	42	38	34	44
Political deprivation					
Edah	57	38	3	20	31
Broad ethnic category	58	54	4	8	32
Class	24	27	20	22	24
Religious position	20	17	20	20	19
Support political organization					
Edah	16	3	0	1	5
Broad ethnic category	26	15	1	1	11
Class	27	17	14	17	19
Religious position	22	13	17	18	18
N	216	209	188	213	826

their groups' political deprivation are included in the table, but the same pattern holds for economic and status deprivation.) Very few Poles and Rumanians feel deprived as Ashkenazim, and about the same proportions as among Moroccans and Iraqis feel deprived as members of a class or in terms of their religious or secular allegiance.

Within the Moroccan and Iraqi groups, about the same proportions support the need for political organization as *edot ha'Mizrach*, as members of their class, or for their religious position, but the proportions are relatively small in all cases. Almost no Poles or Rumanians support political organization on an ethnic basis, and similar small proportions support political organization on a class or religious basis. However, in contrast with the other components, support for political organization on a religious basis differs significantly according to level of religiosity. Of the least religious, who practice none of the five *mitzvot* in our index of religiosity, 17% support this kind of (for them, presumably, secularist) political organization. The proportion declines until it reaches its lowest level (9%) among those who practice three *mitzvot*. The proportion then increases among the more religious and reaches its peak among the most religious who practice all five *mitzvot*; almost 50% of the most religious, who are disproportionately of Moroccan origin, support political organization on a religious basis. This finding is in line with actual political support for the religious political parties in Israel; it has been established that about half of the religious sector of the population vote for the religious parties (Smooha, 1978: 221).

In summary, a comparison of the subjective components of religious, ethnic, and class divisions within the Israeli-Jewish population does not support the frequently made observation that a religious-secular division has come to exceed, or will soon exceed, the divisiveness of ethnic and class differences. It is true that the public *perceives* the religious-secular division as being the most acute, but with regard to the affective investments and proposed action of the majority, ethnicity and class prove to be more important than the religious or secular positions.

Overlapping or crosscutting: a factor analysis

A further question, however, is whether the religious, ethnic, and class divisions overlap or crosscut at the subjective level. We have used factor analysis in order to tap the connections within the cognitive, affective, and evaluative components with regard to religious, ethnic, and class differences. Factor analysis is based on the assumption that some underlying factors are responsible for the covariation among the observed variables. The question here is whether there is a common factor or a number of common factors, which may be considered the cause or causes behind the formation of the subjective dimensions.[1] In the following, the factor analyses are performed separately for Moroccans and Iraqis (hereafter Middle Easterners), on the one hand, and Poles and Rumanians (hereafter Europeans), on the other. Although the data for the groups constituting each pair are by no means identical, they are relatively close to each other. We have made this kind of analysis rather than a separate analysis for each group of origin because it is relatively parsimonious.

1 *Perceptions of cultural differences (table 10.5)* For both Middle Easterners and Europeans, perception of cultural differences between religious and secular Jews does not share any common component with perceptions of differences among the class and ethnic categories. Two factors are

Table 10.5. *Perceptions of cultural differences among categories: factor loadings (based on principal factor with varimax rotation)*

Social categories	Moroccans and Iraqis		Poles and Rumanians		
	Factor 1	Factor 2	Factor 1	Factor 2	Factor 3
Respondents' country of origin vs. broad ethnic category	.23	.33	.20	.54	−.04
Specific ethnic category vs. the opposite broad ethnic category	.84	.15	.86	.05	−.02
Edot ha'Mizrach vs. Ashkenazim	.69	.23	.72	.25	.11
Respondents' socio-economic class vs. other classes	.28	.22	.18	.25	.18
Religious vs. non-religious	.17	.37	.07	.03	.62
Religious people of respondents' country of origin vs. religious people of respondents' broad ethnic category	.04	.71	.01	.68	.10
Religious people of respondents' country of origin vs. religious people of the opposite broad ethnic category	.33	.47	.36	.31	.22
Eigenvalue	2.52	1.07	2.37	1.15	1.01
Percentage of variance	36.0	15.3	33.9	16.5	14.6

necessary for the explanation of the interrelations of variables among Middle Easterners. The first factor represents cultural differences among ethnic groups, and the second factor represents differences among religious people from the ethnic groups. Hence, both factors may be interpreted as "ethnic" factors. Three factors are needed for the explanation of the interrelations of variables among Europeans. The first two factors are quite similar to the Middle Easterners' factors. Only one variable appears to have substantial loading on the third factor – the difference between religious and secular Jews. Thus, it appears that perceptions of cultural differences between religious and non-religious Jews are differentiated from the perceptions of other kinds of cultural differences.

2 *Perceptions of social distances (table 10.6)* Among Middle Easterners, perceptions of social amalgamation or distance between religious and secular are differentiated from the perceptions of distance among ethnic and class categories. Here again we have a two factor solution; the first factor represents the distance between Ashkenazim and *edot ha'Mizrach* as well as between social classes. Since the respondents who perceive substantial social distance between Ashkenazim and *edot ha'Mizrach* are likely to perceive substantial distance between classes, the question arises as to whether these respondents see these as overlapping divisions or as two significant but separate divisions in Israeli society. The answer appears to be that they are seen as overlapping, since when respondents were asked to name the largest class among Ashkenazim and *edot ha'Mizrach*, the largest class among *edot ha'Mizrach* that was named most frequently was "workers" or "wage-earners," and the largest class among Ashkenazim that was named most frequently was "employers," "middle class," or "wealthy."

The second factor among Middle Easterners represents amalgamation among various groups of origin which belong to the same broad ethnic category. Among Europeans, we have three factors. Here again, the first factor represents perceptions of distance between *edot ha'Mizrach* and Ashkenazim. The variables highly loaded on the second factor are religious-secular and social classes. We can only speculate here that many Poles and Rumanians perceive a correspondence between lower class position and greater religiosity. The third factor is similar to the second factor in the Middle Easterners' analysis.

3 *Perceptions of conflict (table 10.7)* One factor suffices to explain the interrelations among the variables for Middle Easterners and Europeans.

Table 10.6. *Perceptions of social distance among categories: factor loadings (based on principal factor with varimax rotation)*

Social categories	Moroccans and Iraqis		Poles and Rumanians		
	Factor 1	Factor 2	Factor 1	Factor 2	Factor 3
Various *edot ha'Mizrach*	.23	.62	.15	.21	.58
Ashkenazim from various countries of origin	−.01	.60	.13	.07	.57
Edot ha'Mizrach and Ashkenazim	.86	.12	.81	.24	.22
Respondents' country of origin and the opposite broad ethnic category	.91	.06	.80	.13	.18
Workers and owners	.60	.10	.27	.61	.20
Religious and non-religious	.35	.19	.06	.56	.09
Eigenvalue	2.65	1.23	2.48	1.03	1.01
Percentage of variance	44.1	20.4	41.4	17.1	16.8

Table 10.7. *Perceptions of conflict among categories: factor loadings (based on principal factor with varimax rotation)*

Social categories	Moroccans and Iraqis Factor 1	Poles and Rumanians Factor 1
Edot ha'Mizrach and Ashkenazim	.66	.54
Affluent and economically weak	.65	.53
Respondents' economic class and other classes	.59	.62
Religious and non-religious	.30	.29
Respondents' country of origin and the opposite broad ethnic category	.65	.71
Respondents' country of origin and broad ethnic category	.42	.56
Eigenvalue	2.53	2.51
Percentage of variance	42.2	41.9

Table 10.8. *Level of pride with identities according to country of origin and level of religiosity: factor loadings (based on principal factor with varimax rotation)*

Low religiosity (0–3 *mitzvot*)

	Moroccans and Iraqis		Poles and Rumanians	
Type of identities	Factor 1	Factor 2	Factor 1	Factor 2
Jewish	.45	.36	.20	.74
Israeli	.36	.25	.04	.77
Broad ethnic category	.65	.18	.70	.15
Specific ethnic category	.92	.09	.80	.05
Class	.06	.62	.32	.22
Religious	.21	.42	.23	.30
Eigenvalue	2.44	1.07	2.29	1.26
Percentage of variance	40.6	17.8	38.1	21.0

Higher religiosity (4–5 *mitzvot*)

	Moroccans and Iraqis		Poles and Rumanians		
Type of identities	Factor 1	Factor 2	Factor 1	Factor 2	Factor 3
Jewish	.04	.68	.18	.66	.12
Israeli	.10	.44	.27	.33	.70
Broad ethnic category	.76	.18	.68	.07	.19
Specific ethnic category	.99	.07	.84	−.02	−.27
Class	.46	.17	.03	.03	−.13
Religious	.26	.44	−.35	.51	−.15
Eigenvalue	2.43	1.26	1.83	1.42	1.04
Percentage of variance	40.6	17.8	30.6	23.6	17.4

In both cases, perceptions of conflict between religious and secular Jews constitute the only variable which has no significant loading on the factor. Differently stated, it appears that different types of ethnic conflict, as well as conflict between social classes, have a common component, but this component is not responsible for the formation of perceptions of conflict between religious and secular Jews which appears to constitute a different dimension.

4 *Identifications (table 10.8)* Our analysis revealed that patterns of pride in the various identifications differed according to level of religiosity. We present, therefore, separate factor analyses for those in the category of zero to three observances and those who observe four or all five *mitzvot*. In the low religiosity Middle Eastern category, the first factor is loaded

Table 10.9. *Relative deprivation in political power: factor loadings (based on principal factor with varimax rotation)*

Social category	Moroccans and Iraqis		Poles and Rumanians	
	Factor 1	Factor 2	Factor 1	Factor 2
Ashkenazim	−.09	.14	.03	.53
Edot ha'Mizrach	.80	−.24	.19	.00
Respondents' country of origin	.71	−.26	.46	.45
Respondents' economic class	−.25	.76	−.48	−.08
Respondents' religious group	−.08	.33	−.19	−.07
Eigenvalue	2.07	1.00	1.48	1.03
Percentage of variance	41.4	20.0	29.5	20.6

mainly by both the subethnic identifications and the Jewish identification. The dominant variables in the second factor are pride in respondents' social class and in respondents' position on religion. In the high religiosity Middle Eastern category the pattern is quite different, especially in the second factor. The first factor can be interpreted as "ethnic," but for this category the Jewish identification, which appears to have a substantial loading among the lesser religious, is replaced by the class identification. The Jewish identification is the dominant component of the second factor, together with pride in religious position and the Israeli identification. It appears that in the low religiosity category the Jewish identification is related to the ethnic identifications, whereas in the high religiosity category it is related to the religious identification.

A different picture emerges among Europeans. In the low religiosity category the picture is quite straightforward; the first factor represents the broad and specific subethnic identifications, and the second factor represents the more general Jewish and Israeli identifications. The religious position is not significant in either factor. A different pattern is revealed in the high religiosity European category. Here we have a three factor solution. The first factor is parallel to the first factor found among their lesser religious counterparts. The second factor is loaded mainly by the Jewish and religious identifications, but the only variable significantly loaded on the third factor is pride in the Israeli identification. It appears that among respondents with high levels of religiosity, of whatever origin, pride in Jewish identification is related to pride in their identification as religious Jews. However, whereas among Moroccans and Iraqis both Jewish and religious identifications are related to the Israeli identification, among Poles and Rumanians the Israeli identification constitutes a separate factor.

5 *Relative deprivation in political power (table 10.9)* With regard to feelings of injustice or relative deprivation in the distribution of political power, the centrality of the feelings that relate to ethnic and class memberships is obvious. Among both Europeans and Middle Easterners, variables which pertain to ethnicity and social class are highly loaded on the factors. Feelings of relative deprivation in the political power of respondents' religious or secular allegiance seem to belong to a different domain.

6 *Support for political organization (table 10.10)* Factor analysis was not used in the analysis of this dimension since support for political organization constitutes only four variables. We present the correlations of support for political organization on a religious basis, on an ethnic basis, and on a class basis. Among Moroccans and Iraqis, there are moderate positive correlations among religious, ethnic, and class bases of political organization. However, it should be remembered that, even among Moroccans and Iraqis, only a small minority support political organization on any of these bases. Within that minority there is a tendency to positively respond to questions on support for political organization on more than one basis, but the meanings, if any, of these overlaps are not clear, and since only small numbers are involved, they would appear to have little significance.

Conclusions

Our findings may be summarized as follows:

1 There is a considerable overlap of religiosity with ethnic origin which has a high convergence with class. However, within each ethnic group there is some overlap of religiosity with class, and this convergence crosscuts the religiosity differences among some of the ethnic group.
2 The cultural differences, social distance, and conflict between religious and secular Jews are perceived by the majority to be greater than those among ethnic groups or classes.
3 Pride in identification with respect to religion (religious, traditional, secular) is less than pride in ethnic and class identifications among Moroccans and Iraqis and less than pride in class identification among Poles and Rumanians.
4 There is little relative deprivation regarding religious position among the majority. Among Moroccans and Iraqis it is much less than ethnic relative deprivation.
5 Only those with a high level of religiosity, who are disproportionately

Table 10.10. *Support for political organization on the basis of ethnicity, class, and religious position: product–moment correlation coefficients*

Correlated bases for organization	Moroccans	Iraqis	Poles	Rumanians	Total
Edah and broad ethnic category	.59	.44	*	*	.56
Broad ethnic category and class	.40	.38	*	*	.33
Broad ethnic category and religious position	.38	.48	*	*	.30
Class and religious position	.35	.49	.26	.22	.33

*Almost no Poles or Rumanians support political organization on the basis of ethnicity.

Moroccan, support political organization on a religious basis. Otherwise, support for this kind of political organization is on a par with support for ethnic or class political organization (a minority in all cases).

6 Most of the factor analyses show that the distribution of the religious images, identifications, and evaluations crosscut rather than converge with the distributions of the ethnic and class subjective dimensions which do converge at a number of important points (perceived social distance, perceived conflict, feelings of deprivation). There was no convergence of the religious and ethnic dimensions, and when there was some convergence of the religious and class dimensions, this applied only to one ethnic category and appears to be of minor significance.

7 In most of the factor analyses the solution for Middle Easterners required less factors than the solution for Europeans. This seems to indicate that the subjective dimensions of Europeans are more differentiated than those of Middle Easterners, and this conclusion obtains further support from the fact that in most of the analyses the most important first factor pertaining to Middle Easterners explains a higher proportion of the variance than the parallel factor among Europeans. Apparently, Middle Easterners reveal a greater tendency to base their various perceptions on common components.

These findings are hardly indicative of a religious-secular division that threatens Israeli society. Respondents may perceive that division to be of greater magnitude than ethnic and class divisions, but the greater weight of the religious factor in the cognitive dimension is not paralleled in the affective and evaluative dimensions, and the implications of the religious-secular division are blunted in all three subjective components (cognitive, affective, evaluative) by the crosscutting of important ethnic and class divisions.

Our sample includes religious Jews, but not *haredim* who are rarely found in Beer Sheva. It may be argued that the significant conflict in Israeli society is not between religious and secular Jews but between *haredim* and other Jews. But, although there are signs of polarization, with some sections of the religious population, including some from Middle Eastern *edot*, becoming "*hared*ized" or ultra-Orthodox, and some from traditional backgrounds becoming secular, the traditional section of the population is still by far the largest among Middle Easterners and it is by no means insignificant among Europeans.

If there is an increasing conflict between religious and secular Jews, the organization of the opposing groups is by no means symmetrical. The religious political parties and movements do not face political parties which focus their resources and policies on secularist issues nor strong secularist voluntary movements. The historical relationship between the Jewish religion and the Jewish people, the importance of a religiously conveyed history in the legitimation of the Israeli state, and the problem of expressing Jewishness without the use of symbols that are anchored in the Jewish religion have proved obstacles to the development of strong secularist movements in Israel. Secular Jews tend to form *ad hoc* groups in order to oppose religious Jews or *haredim* over various issues, but these groups have not developed into widely supported secularist movements.

IV

The impact of stratification

In part IV we look at the impact of stratification in two senses. The first sense is ethnic stratification: the differences among the groups of origin with respect to their socio-economic profiles and ethnic prestige. The second sense is the overall socio-economic or class stratification that cuts through the ethnic groups and categories. Both types of stratification are relevant in the analysis of voting in chapter 11. In chapter 12 ethnic stratification is shown to influence the amount of discrimination that is reported, but class stratification is shown to affect the consequences that are felt as a result of the discrimination. Chapter 13 brings many of the ethnic dimensions analyzed in this study together in order to show the effects of both types of stratification on the move toward assimilation or ethnic solidarity.

11

Voting

Explanations and the puzzle

The subject of ethnic voting in Israel has aroused strong interest both in the mass media and among social scientists. This interest stems principally from the clear statistical relationship between ethnic origins and support for the two largest political parties: Israelis of Middle Eastern origin have shown a strong preference, especially in the last few elections, for the Likud, and Israelis of European origin have continued to show a strong preference for the Labor Alignment or Ma'arach (Matras, 1965; Lissak, 1969; Arian, 1972; Peres, Yuchtman-Yaar, and Shafat, 1975; Shamir and Arian, 1983; Peres and Shemer, 1984; Peretz and Smooha, 1985). The correlation between ethnic origin and voting, and the feeling that the ethnic-political division has widened over the years have prompted investigations of the meanings and causes of the relationship.

The explanations that have been suggested by social scientists may be briefly summarized as follows:

1 The most common explanation of the support of Middle Easterners for the Likud is in terms of a protest vote (for example, Yishai, 1982; P. S. Cohen, 1983; Ben-Sira, 1988). It is argued that the feelings of deprivation, frustration, and bitterness that developed among Middle Easterners are directed against the Ma'arach, the party of the socio-political establishment, which they hold responsible for their relatively low economic distribution and status in Israeli society.

The Labor Party came to be the dominant party in the Yishuv, and as the party in power, from the establishment of the state until 1977, it controlled a large part of the society's resources and was held responsible for the consequences of the distribution. During the period of mass immigration it was the most important party involved in the system of exchange whereby the political parties allocated work, housing, and provided various other services in exchange for political support

(Shapiro, 1977). Azmon (1985) argues that the sense of disadvantage that developed among many immigrants was related less to what they had been given in housing, employment, and services than to the way in which they were given. The personification of dependency in the political patronage system generated bitterness and frustration, and once the system began to weaken, there was no longer any effective pressure for political returns. The negative reaction to the patronage system was directed especially toward the Labor Party which had used the system to its greatest effect, but failed to develop an alternative system which would have met the expectation of equal participation and representation of Middle Easterners within the political system.[1]

Although this explanation focuses on the Middle Easterners, it is seen to have implications for the electoral behavior of the Europeans who are believed to have reacted to the ethnic political bloc voting of the Middle Easterners by becoming more homogeneous in their support for the Ma'arach (Shamir and Arian, 1983; Peres and Shemer, 1984).

2 The class explanation presents the Ashkenazim and *edot ha'Mizrach* as social classes or socio-economic strata. The Middle Easterners, who are concentrated in the lower strata, reject the Ma'arach which, despite its self-definition as a labor party, has been associated for some time with the middle class (Swirski, 1981). The Europeans gained their privileged situation when the Labor Party was in power, and they continue to vote for it as the party that represents their interests.

3 Another explanation for the greater support among Middle Easterners for the Likud is the affinity between the attitudes toward Arabs among Middle Easterners, and the Likud's policies concerning Israel's relationships with Arab countries. As a consequence of their past as a minority in Arab countries and their images of Arabs, the Middle Easterners are more hawkish than the Europeans and prefer that party which takes a tougher stand in foreign policy and security (Peres, 1976; Yishai, 1982; Seliktar, 1984).

4 A cultural explanation emphasizes the distance between the religiously inclined Middle Easterners and the secular and socialist principles that characterize the Labor movement (Yishai, 1982). The emphasis on religion and tradition by some leaders of the Likud attracts the Middle Easterners.

5 An explanation which focuses on political culture notes that the Middle Easterners, who came from politically authoritarian societies, prefer the Likud in which there is a greater emphasis on the need for authority.

These explanations of the link between ethnic origins and voting patterns were developed principally at the theoretical level, and few investigators have tried to prove or falsify them empirically. The exceptions are the studies of Shamir and Arian (1983) and Peres and Shemer (1984). In both studies a number of possible intervening variables between ethnic origin and voting were investigated, but the authors did not find any variable or combination of variables that could account for the relationship. Shamir and Arian carried out a regression analysis which included explanatory variables derived from the propositions noted above. They found that "hawkishness" was the most significant factor (followed by religiosity), but the variables together accounted for only 12% of the variance. Separate regression analyses of Middle Easterners and Europeans did not bring a significant change in the picture. Peres and Shemer analyzed fewer variables and found that levels of education and income and the "hawkish"/"dovish" factor could explain only a small part of the divergent electoral behavior of Middle Easterners and Europeans.

Shamir and Arian account for their limited findings by the absence of adequate measures of ethnic deprivation and protest voting. Peres and Shemer argue that the factors which account for the support of the Likud among the Middle Easterners encompass such a large majority of this population that it is not possible to separate these factors from ethnic origin by statistical manipulation. This argument is unconvincing since a significant minority of Middle Easterners do vote for the Ma'arach: 24.6% in 1977, 22.5% in 1981, and 21.5% in 1984 (Peretz and Smooha, 1985).

The ethnic classification

The different approaches that attempt to account for the correlation of ethnic origin and voting pattern have one element in common: their dichotomous classification of Israeli Jews between Middle Easterners and Europeans. This classification has become so rooted in socio-political investigation in Israel that some investigators take it entirely for granted (e.g. Yishai, 1982; P. S. Cohen, 1983; Seliktar, 1984). In an attempt to deal with the issue of ethnic classification Peres and Shemer compared the voting patterns of Israeli Jews of Asian and African origins. The similarity of the patterns brought them to the conclusion that the common dichotomization is justified, at least in the analysis of electoral behavior. However, the distinction between African and Asian communities is not an appropriate test, since each continental category includes communities of origin which differ in many relevant respects.

179

There are, for example, important differences between the Iraqi and Yemenite communities.

We have shown in this study that, although there are substantial differences between the Middle Eastern and European categories, there is no justification in ignoring the variation that exists within each broad category. The following points which touch on these variations would appear relevant to an investigation of voting patterns:

1 Analyses of residential distribution according to different countries of origin (Klaff, 1977; Kraus, 1985) found a clear separation between the Middle Eastern and European categories, but also clear differences within each category. For example, the distribution of Jews from Iraq was closer to those of Rumanian origin than to those of Moroccan origin. Residential segregation is not generally analyzed as one of the differentiating factors in political behavior in Israel, but if, according to the argument of Peres and Shemer (1984), there are strong social pressures on individuals to vote in line with the dominant choice of their ethnic group especially in areas where the majority are from their group, this factor may well be relevant.

2 The analysis of political behavior according to the class perspective has assumed a clear class division between Middle Easterners, who make up the majority of the working class, and Europeans, who make up the majority of the middle class (Swirski, 1981; Yishai, 1982; Smooha, 1978). Weiker (1983) identifies a "middle grouping" of Jewish communities which have mostly been identified with a Judeo-Spanish or Ladino culture, and among the Jewish groups from Arabic countries a few, such as the Iraqis, have a similar occupational distribution to that of the middle category. Similarly, the occupational distribution of Rumanians is closer to the "middle category" than it is to other European groups.

3 It has been assumed that groups from Asia and North Africa are similar in their feelings of bitterness toward the "Ashkenazi establishment." Elhanani (1979) compared the explanations of inequality of Moroccans and Iraqis and showed that there are also clear differences between these two groups in their images of society. Whereas Moroccans are more inclined to account for the "ethnic gap" in terms of discrimination by the establishment or by Ashkenazim, Iraqis are more inclined to explain it as a consequence of the different periods of immigration of *edot ha'Mizrach* and Ashkenazim.

4 The argument of a cultural distance between the traditional religiosity of Middle Easterners and the secular Zionism of Europeans also assumed

that Middle Easterners displayed common cultural patterns and that differences according to the specific countries of origin were of little importance. However, there were secular Zionists as well as Communists among the Jews in Iraq, and among North African Jews there were groups who adopted French culture.

5 An emphasis on the contrast between the authoritarianism of Asian-African regimes and the liberal democracies of Europe has little relevance, since a large proportion of European immigrants came from authoritarian regimes in eastern Europe.

The findings summarized above indicate the existence of significant variations in residential patterns, socio-economic status, perceptions of discrimination, and cultural background according to country of origin within each broad category. This raises the possibility that the unsuccessful location of variables that would account for the correlation of ethnic origin and voting is a consequence of the neglect of distinctive factors which distinguish between Likud and Ma'arach voters in the different communities of origin. If the distribution of voters between the Likud and Ma'arach within the different communities of origin is the result of different factors, it would be impossible to locate these factors as long as the analysis is based on a dichotomous categorization of origins.

When we divide our sample of four groups of origin according to the broad categorization of Middle Easterners and Europeans, we find that the distribution of votes is similar to that which were found by investigations based on representative samples. We assume, therefore, that the sample reflects the distribution of voting in the Israeli-Jewish population, and that it is suitable for an analysis of those factors which account for that distribution. Respondents were asked which party they voted for in the elections of 1981. Of the 516 respondents who reported that they voted for one of the two large parties (20% refused to reveal their vote and the remainder voted for the smaller parties), 351 answered all the questions which constitute measures of the independent variables. The respondents represented a relatively low percentage of the total sample – the proportion was close to those of Peres and Shemer (1984), and Shamir and Arian (1983) – but the distribution of their demographic characteristics did not differ from that of the total sample.

Voting patterns: a discriminant analysis

The dependent variable is voting for the Likud or the Ma'arach. The independent variables were derived from the explanations reviewed above which attempt to explain the relationship between origins and voting. We note here the variables according to the explanations from which they were derived: (1) the ethnic factor or protest vote hypothesis was examined by respondents' perceptions of the extent of ethnic conflict between Ashkenazim and *edot ha'Mizrach*, (2) the class factor was examined by an objective measure of socio-economic position, (3) the extent to which traditionalism constitutes a factor in the distribution of voters between the two large parties was investigated by an index of respondents' religiosity, (4) the importance for respondents of a party's policies in foreign affairs and security was indicated when they were asked to note the most important reason they voted for their party. The answers to this question also indicated, (5) the importance of strong leadership or political authority for respondents.

Two additional variables are included in the analysis: age, and country of origin of friends. We include age because younger Israelis have been found to favor the Likud (Peres, Yuchtman-Yaar, and Shafat, 1975). Information on the origins of respondents' three best friends provides data which are relevant to examining the argument that an ethnically homogeneous social environment increases the tendency to vote in line with the dominant choice of one's ethnic group.

We used the method of discriminant analysis which enables us to make the best linear combination of independent variables in order to discriminate between Likud and Ma'arach voters. This method is preferred when the dependent variable is categorical and the independent variables are at least ordinal (Klecka, 1980; Swafford, 1980), especially in an analysis of political behavior (Vanneman and Pampel, 1977).

The statistical analysis was carried out in two stages. The first stage included thirteen explanatory variables. Since the categorization into specific communities of origin created relatively small groups, we carried out an additional analysis with the aim of reducing the number of variables. At the second stage only seven variables were included. Each one of the explanations suggesting a connection between origin and voting is represented by a variable whose discriminatory efficiency was found to be relatively large. The findings presented here relate to the second stage of the analysis. Although there were certain changes in the character of the functions that were obtained in the two stages, the general picture did not change substantially.

The statistical analysis was carried out for the total sample, and separately for the four groups of origin that composed it. In addition to the discriminant analysis, a series of tests were carried out in order to tape differences between Likud and Ma'arach voters according to the means of the discriminating variables.

Before turning to the findings of the discriminant analysis, we note the distribution of voters between the two large parties. The extent of the difference in the support for the two large parties in the country was reflected in our sample: 56% voted for the Likud and 44% for the Ma'arach. As expected, the Middle Easterners were more likely to vote for the Likud (65% of the Middle Easterners who indicated how they voted), and the Europeans for the Ma'arach (67%). However, an examination of the distribution of votes according to country of origin points to substantial differences between the two Middle Eastern groups. Whereas 73% of the Moroccans voted for the Likud, the distribution of Iraqi voters was more balanced, with 57% voting for the Likud. The distributions of the two European groups were much closer to each other: 68% of the Poles and 65% of the Rumanians voted for the Ma'arach.

The findings of the discriminant analysis in table 11.1 include three analyses of the total sample: the first does not include any reference to origin, the second includes a dummy variable which distinguishes between Middle Easterners and Europeans, and the third includes three dummy variables which distinguish among the specific countries of origin. The table also includes separate analyses of Middle Easterners and Europeans.

In the analysis which does not include origin (column 1), the discriminatory power of the function was fairly strong. Three variables were found to be significant in the discriminant function.[2] Firstly, socioeconomic status; higher socio-economic status increased the chances of support for the Ma'arach. Secondly, religiosity; higher levels of religiosity improved the chances of support for the Likud. And, thirdly, an emphasis on foreign policy and security as the principal reason for voting for a party improved the chances of support for the Ma'arach. It would appear that the "dovishness" of the Ma'arach rather than the "hawkishness" of the Likud is a factor in voters' choice.

Inclusion of the dichotomic categorization of Middle Easterners and Europeans in the discriminant analysis (column 2) did not result in a change in the efficiency of the function (the Lambda–Wilkes coefficient and canonical correlation remained the same). Nor was there a change in the meanings of the function. Thus, the Middle Eastern/European dichotomization would have appeared to have no independent influence on the pattern of voting beyond the variables that we have considered. Since the correlation coefficient between origin, as defined dichotomously, and voting was high, we may conclude that the variables included in

Table 11.1. *Discriminant analysis between Likud voters and Ma'arach voters for the total sample (N=423), Middle Easterners and Europeans (standardized coefficients of the discriminant functions)*[1]

Discriminating variables	Total (without origin) (N=423)	Total (dichotomous origin)	Total (country origin)	Middle Easterners (N=220)	Europeans (N=203)
Socio-economic status	.54	−.50	.50	.51	−.29
Perception ethnic conflict	−.08	−.09	.08	−.28	−.03
Importance leadership	−.30	−.29	.28	−.22	.30
Level religiosity	−.42	−.35	.25	−.27	.27
Importance foreign policy and security	.41	.39	−.38	.35	−.48
Age	.25	.22	−.21	.46	−.04
Social networks	−.09	−.12	.13	.31	.59
Dichotomous origin	—	.17	—	—	—
Morocco	—	—	.42	—	—
Iraq	—	—	.09	—	—
Poland	—	—	.14	—	—
Lambda–Wilkes coefficients	.79	.78	.77	.78	.83
Canonical correlations	.46	.47	.48	.47	.41
Centroids of groups					
Likud	−.49	−.49	.51	−.38	.56
Ma'arach	.46	.57	−.60	.76	−.36

1 All the functions are significant at the level of p<.01.

the analysis do intermediate between origin (i.e. Iraqis and Moroccans as opposed to Poles and Rumanians) and electoral behavior.

The division of the sample between Middle Easterners and Europeans and a separate analysis for each category (columns 4 and 5) reveals that the variables are a little more efficient in discriminating between Likud and Ma'arach voters among the Middle Easterners (canonical correlation .47) than among the Europeans (.41). The two functions are not identical in character. In the "Middle Eastern" function there are three significant factors: socio-economic status, the importance of foreign policy and security, and age. Higher socio-economic status, more advanced age, and an emphasis on foreign policy increase the chances of voting for the Ma'arach. In the European category the social network variable is dominant and foreign policy is important. Close social relations with Middle Easterners increase the chances of voting for the Likud, and noting foreign policy as the most important reason in the choice of a party increases the tendency to vote for the Ma'arach.

In summary, the use of the conventional method of dichotomization largely replicates the findings of previous studies. However, in comparison with previous studies, our variables account fully for the relationship between origin and voting, and we obtained relatively high percentages of the variance of the dependent variable.[3] This may be explained by our inclusion of a relatively extensive number of factors, but it should not be forgotten that each of the broad ethnic categories in our study includes only two groups of origin.

When we deviate from the conventional method of defining ethnic origin and analyze our sample according to the specific countries of origin, we discover a different picture which reveals neglected aspects of the relationship between origin and voting.

The importance of the distinction according to specific countries of origin is shown already in the analysis of the total sample (column 3). The new definition does not substantially improve the efficiency of the function, but there is a change in its meaning. "Moroccan" becomes the central discriminatory variable; belonging to the Moroccan group is found to be the most important determinant of the distribution of votes between the Likud and the Ma'arach. The different definition of "origin" results in religiosity losing the significance that it was found to have in the previous analyses (columns 1 and 2). The relationship between religiosity and voting derives from the combination of the high level of religiosity among Moroccans and their tendency to vote for the Likud.

Distinctive patterns

We turn to the central question of our analysis: the question of the existence of distinctive patterns of the communities of origin in accounting for
the distribution of support for the two large parties. The relevant findings
are presented in tables 11.2 and 11.3. Table 11.2 presents the means of the
variables that distinguish between Likud and Ma'arach voters in each
group of origin. These data are presented mainly in order to clarify and
validate the findings of the discriminant analysis in table 11.3.

A comparison of the discriminant functions according to specific
countries of origin (table 11.3) shows that the most efficient function is
found for the Moroccans (canonical correlation .54). In this group the
variables discriminate between Likud and Ma'arach voters more than in
the analysis of the general sample or in the separate analyses of the two
broad categories (Middle Eastern and European). However, in the other
groups the discrimination is less efficient, especially in the Iraqi and
Rumanian groups.

In order to facilitate an understanding of the discriminatory factors in
each group of origin, table 11.4 lists the variables that are significant in
determining the political distribution in each group, and the direction of
their influence. This table shows the existence of distinctive patterns for
each group of origin. We turn, therefore, to an examination of the
relevance of the different factors in accounting for the patterns of voting
in the different groups of origin.

Variables related to the ethnic factor are significant in all four groups of
origin. The existence of a protest vote may be indicated in the Moroccan
group, for only in this group does a perception of ethnic conflict increase
the chances of voting for the Likud. However, since the standardized
discriminant function coefficient of this factor is lower than the critical
value (.35), it has only relatively marginal significance in the Moroccan
function. In the other three groups, the ethnic factor is expressed in the
relationship between the origins of friends and electoral behavior.[4]
Friendship with individuals from the other broad ethnic category inclines
respondents to vote for the party which is supported by only a minority
of the category of origin to which they belong. Ethnic homogeneous
environments would appear, therefore, to be said to contribute to the
ethnic-political division. It should be noted that the social network factor
is especially prominent in the two Ashkenazi groups. Thus, the ethnic
factor, which has been assumed to have an important influence in the
shaping of the Middle Easterners' voting pattern, is shown here to be
significant among the Europeans.

Table 11.2. *Averages (x̄) and standard deviations (σ) of discriminating variables between Likud voters and Ma'arach voters, according to specific countries of origin*[1]

Discriminating variables	Type vote	M (N=121)		I (N=118)		P (N=91)		R (N=125)	
		x̄	σ	x̄	σ	x̄	σ	x̄	σ
Socio-economic status	Likud	-.94	1.22	-.82	1.28	.17	1.15	.26	1.42
	Ma'arach	.56*	1.37	-.23*	1.36	.73*	1.30	.62	1.09
Perception of ethnic conflict	Likud	4.09	1.46	3.83	1.65	3.70	1.31	3.98	1.50
	Ma'arach	3.48*	1.55	3.79	1.47	3.70	1.30	4.05	1.36
Importance of leadership	Likud	.21	.46	.26	.44	.21	.41	.10	.30
	Ma'arach	.07*	.27	.07*	.26	.08	.26	.03	.18
Level of religiosity	Likud	3.28	1.13	2.31	1.27	1.21	1.26	1.80	1.21
	Ma'arach	2.59*	1.37	2.13*	1.32	.73*	1.00	1.32*	1.04
Importance of foreign policy	Likud	0	0	0	0	0	0	0	0
	Ma'arach	.07*	.27	.04	.19	.10*	.30	.10*	.31
Age	Likud	35.57	5.40	38.68	5.46	40.03	9.55	38.77	5.70
	Ma'arach	38.50	4.92	39.70	5.08	42.57	9.38	40.08	4.54
Social network heterogeneity	Likud	.45	.75	.56	.70	1.51	1.09	1.28	1.02
	Ma'arach	1.00*	.82	.90*	.87	.71*	.87	.81*	.87

*Difference between the mean is statistically significant according to t-test (α≤.05).
1 Cell frequencies are not uniform due to small differences in the missing data pertaining to different variables. The frequencies presented are based on the variable with the largest "missing data." Deviations from these frequencies are only upwardly directed.

Table 11.3. *Discriminant analysis between Likud voters and Ma'arach voters, according to specific countries of origin. (Standardized coefficients of the discriminant functions)*[1]

Discriminating variables	Morocco (N=108)	Iraq (N=112)	Poland (N=84)	Rumania (N=119)
Socio-economic status	.73	.44	−.19	−.36
Perception of ethnic conflict	−.32	−.17	−.11	.08
Importance of leadership	.06	−.51	.18	.34
Level of religiosity	−.05	.15	.27	.34
Importance of foreign policy	.17	.44	−.50	−.44
Age	.45	.44	.10	−.23
Social network heterogeneity	.27	.35	.73 ·	.46
Lambda–Wilkes coefficients	.71	.84	.78	.85
Canonical correlations	.54	.40	.47	.39
Centroids of groups				
Likud	−.33	−.39	.62	.54
Ma'arach	1.22	.49	−.45	−.33

1 All the functions are significant at the $p<.001$ level.

Table 11.4. *Summary of the findings of the discriminant analysis*

Country of origin	Significant variables (ranked in importance)	Direction influence	
Morocco	1 Socio-economic status	Higher	→ Ma'arach
	2 Age	Older	→ Ma'arach
	3 Perception of ethnic conflict*	Conflictual perception	→ Likud
Iraq	1 Importance of leadership	Emphasis	→ Likud
	2 Foreign policy and security	Emphasis	→ Ma'arach
	Socio-economic status	Higher	→ Ma'arach
	Age	Older	→ Ma'arach
	3 Friendship network	Heterogeneous	→ Ma'arach
Rumania	1 Friendship network	Heterogeneous	→ Likud
	2 Foreign policy and security	Emphasis	→ Ma'arach
	3 Socio-economic status	Higher	→ Ma'arach
	4 Religiosity*	Higher	→ Likud
	Importance of leadership*	Emphasis	→ Likud
Poland	1 Friendship network	Heterogeneous	→ Likud
	2 Foreign policy and security	Emphasis	→ Ma'arach

*These standardized coefficients of the discriminant function are lower than the value of .35, but they are very close to it.

Socio-economic status is shown to be important in three of the four groups, the Moroccans, Iraqis, and Rumanians, and is especially prominent in the Moroccan group. In all three groups, higher socio-economic status increases the chances of voting for the Ma'arach.[5]

The political opinion factor is significant in the discrimination functions of the Iraqi and the two European groups. In all three groups those respondents who said that foreign policy and security were the major issues in determining their political choice were more inclined to support the Ma'arach. This finding indicates that there is a need to re-examine the common view that the "hawkishness" of the Likud appeals to the Middle Easterners.

The explanation that relates the preference among the Middle Easterners for the Likud to their traditionalism or religiosity is not supported by our findings. The only group in which religiosity has significant weight in the discriminant function is the Rumanian group. In all four groups the Likud voters have a higher mean level of religiosity than Ma'arach voters (table 11.2), but religiosity is found to have an independent influence on electoral behavior only in a European group.

In the Iraqi group, noting political leadership as the principal reason for supporting a party increases the chances of voting for the Likud. It should be noted that also among the Moroccans there is a clear difference between Likud and Ma'arach voters in emphasizing party leadership (table 11.2), but this difference is not found in the multivariate analysis. This is to be accounted for by the correlation between the leadership variable and socio-economic status $(-.21)$, and the dominance of the latter variable in the function. A relationship between emphasizing leadership and voting for the Likud among Rumanians was marginal (the coefficient is lower than .35). These findings would appear to confirm the argument of Shamir and Arian that the image of a strong leader of the Likud attracted voters (in the 1981 elections).

The last factor to be considered here is age. Although our sample is composed of a relatively narrow age range, our findings are in line with other studies (Arian, 1974; Peres, Yuchtman-Yaar, and Shafat, 1975). Youth increases the chances of support for the Likud in every group of origin, although the differences are small (table 11.2). In the multivariate analysis age was found to be dominant in the Moroccan group; only in this group does age have an independent effect on the distribution of voting.

Conclusions

The aim here was to examine the question of the relationship between electoral behavior and ethnic divisions among Jews in Israel. Most investigations on voting in Israel have found it difficult to locate the intermediary factors between origins and voting. Our findings indicate that this difficulty derives from the fact that there are distinctive patterns of factors which determine the distribution of voters between the two large parties in each group of origin. Some factors are found in some groups and not in others, and when there is a factor which is common to a number of groups its relative importance varies from group to group.

An examination of the factors that distinguish between voters of the two large parties within each group points to the dissimilarity of the two groups that, in terms of their overall socio-economic distribution, are found close to the top and bottom of the ethnic hierarchy in Israel: the Poles and the Moroccans. The patterns of voting of these two groups are determined by entirely different factors with only one factor common to them both. The groups that may be categorized as part of, or at least close to, a middle grouping in Israeli society, the Rumanians and Iraqis, are found to be intermediary also with respect to the factors that determine their electoral choices. They have some factors in common with each other, and they share factors with each of the two other groups.

The two European groups demonstrate clear similarities. In both, electoral behavior is related principally to the extent of primary social interaction with Middle Easterners, and to the foreign policies or images of leadership of the parties. Class factor and age are important in both Middle Eastern groups, but whereas these factors are dominant among the Moroccans, they are secondary among the Iraqis whose political distribution is determined more by the factors of political leadership and foreign policy. It should be noted that among the Iraqis, in contrast to the Moroccans, we did not find a relationship between electoral behavior and a perception of ethnic conflict.

A comparison of the patterns of voting in the four groups points to the Moroccans as an exception, for this is the only group in which the foreign policies and leadership of the parties do not have a direct influence on electoral behavior, and socio-economic status is the dominant factor in discriminating between voters of the two large parties. The Iraqi distribution is influenced by a combination of political issues, socio-economic status, and social networks, and this may indicate a greater potential for "floating voters" than among the Moroccans. In the two European groups, the major factor that distinguishes between the voters of the two large parties is the extent of social contacts with Middle Easterners. This fact, together with the influence of party characteristics, and the absence of the class factor, indicate that these groups may also include a potentially floating electorate.

We cannot pretend to have an explanation for all the differences with respect to influences on voting among the four groups, but our findings do throw doubt on the usefulness of dichotomizing the Israeli-Jewish population when investigating voting patterns. The particular characteristics of specific groups of origin within the two broad categories are relevant in analyzing electoral behavior.

12

Discrimination

The concept of discrimination

Discrimination is a phenomenon that is widely referred to and talked about in everyday life, but its recognition and meanings have rarely been investigated by sociologists. Sociologists have analyzed discrimination for the most part as a variable that can be defined and measured objectively, and they have given little attention to accounts by either the discriminators or the discriminated. Until recent years discrimination was discussed by sociologists almost exclusively in the field of racial and ethnic relations, and the focus of many studies was on the relationships between prejudice and discrimination (see Feagin and Eckberg, 1980, for a review). In recent years the topic of discrimination has shifted somewhat to a focus on discrimination against women. Discrimination is occasionally mentioned although rarely studied with reference to other areas of differentiation (for example, in the cases of the aged or physically disabled), but it is perhaps significant that the term has hardly ever been employed in the literature on class stratification. Since discrimination is often defined in terms of an inappropriate ascriptive orientation, its absence from the class literature would be understandable if it was generally agreed among sociologists that achievement determined class position. There is, however, considerable emphasis among many sociologists on differential treatment based on class origins; examples include children from the lower strata receiving inferior formal education, and individuals from the upper strata receiving preferential treatment in entering certain occupations.

One explanation of the fact that reference to discrimination is rarely encountered in the social class literature may be that it is a moralistic term; it implies a negative evaluation of a violation of a social norm. In attempting to measure and analyze discrimination in the areas of ethnic relations and gender inequality, sociologists have not freed themselves from the evaluative connotations of the term in everyday language. Sociologists of class, in comparison, appear to be far more successful in describing class practices in terms which do not imply deviations from ideal norms, which do not proportion blame, or refer to base motivations. Whether they support or oppose the class system, sociologists of class tend to view it as a recognized social order and to define classes in terms of structural "objective" characteristics. Discrimination, on the other hand, is seen as invidious and as something that can and should be stopped. In fact, in terms of motivations, the action itself, and its effects, what is understood as "discrimination" in ethnic and gender studies may be just as common or even more widespread in class practices.

The problems of treating discrimination in an objectivist fashion in ethnic studies begin with its definition. Discrimination may be defined in a weak "dictionary" sense as "differential treatment." Newman (1973: 199) writes: "Discrimination may be defined as any act of differential treatment toward a group or an individual perceived as a member of a group." Newman admits that all social relations involve some degree of differential treatment and discrimination must, therefore, refer to "an extremely high degree of differential treatment." But it is not clear who is to decide what is an "extremely high degree" and according to what bench mark. The decision must surely be essentially an arbitrary one.

Discrimination is more often defined in a stronger sense as a particular type of differential treatment that is based on certain codes rather than on others. One example will suffice. Pettigrew (1980) writes that discrimination is "an institutional process of exclusion against an out-group, racial or cultural, based simply on who they are rather than on their knowledge or abilities." In sum, most definitions of discrimination describe it as behavior that can be categorized on one side of Parsons' pattern variables rather than the other; collectivistic rather than individualistic, particularistic rather than universalistic, and ascriptive rather than achievement-oriented. It often appears to be assumed that in modern society the collectivistic-particularistic-ascriptive side is "irrational," "dysfunctional," "illegitimate," or "morally reprehensible." In fact, acts of discrimination may have clear rational intent on the part of the discriminator and may also be judged as rational by an observer using objective measures. Groups may obtain clear economic status and political benefits from discrimination. In cases of "statistical discrimination" discriminators attempt to reduce the costs of having to obtain information on individual applicants by excluding from consideration people from a given category who have a lower percentage of the attributes which the discriminator is seeking (Banton, 1983b).

One of the problems of these definitions is that there is not sufficient specification of contexts; in some institutional contexts the collectivistic-particularistic-ascriptive orientations might be considered quite legitimate. Another problem is that there is no consideration of the historical dimension. For example, according to these definitions, it would not be considered discrimination if individuals were rejected for jobs on the basis of a lack of formal qualifications. The individuals may, however, belong to a group whose experience of past discrimination did not allow them to obtain these formal qualifications. Appreciation of this has led to the concept of "total discrimination" which includes "past in the present" discrimination (Feagin and Eckberg, 1980).

The following definition of discrimination by the social philosopher Alan H. Goldman allows for the wide variety of the term's attributions by actors in society: discrimination "involves treating relevantly similar persons differently or relevantly different people the same" (Goldman, 1979: 23). This definition is not contextually or historically limiting and it is usefully encompassing because definitions of "relevantly similar" or "relevantly different" people may vary considerably among groups and in societal contexts.

For much the same reasons that discrimination has been difficult to define, it has also been difficult to measure. In many studies, indirect measures, particularly inequality and segregation, have been used. By a process of elimination, any inequality among groups in, for example, income that cannot be accounted for by other factors, such as education, experience, age, or religion, is explained by discrimination. Discrimination is inferred from unexplained variance, but although this may be a plausible hypothesis, other unexamined factors may be the causes (Burstein, 1985; Blalock, 1967: 15–18; Banton, 1983a: 367). Even if the inference is correct, it is only the effects of discrimination and not the actions themselves that are being examined.

Problems of measurement have led some investigators to treat discrimination as an inferred independent variable, but its theoretical status as an independent variable has been questioned by others. Schermerhorn (1970: 7) has argued that discrimination, like prejudice, is a dependent variable, and that a study of the structures of ethnic relations should focus on other areas. Newman (1973: 218–37) writes that once discrimination exists it may be a contributing factor in intergroup conflict, but that it represents "in the first instance" a weapon of conflict. The appropriateness of treating discrimination as a dependent variable or independent variable should depend on the research problem, but even if discrimination is assigned as a dependent variable, it remains an important problem.

Whether the focus of research has been on the discriminator or the discriminated, little attention has been given to their accounts or meanings of discrimination. Observers' accounts of the discriminators' motives may be divided into two broad categories: firstly, those that emphasize cultural and/or psychological factors such as prejudice or a "taste for discrimination," and, secondly, those that point to instrumental factors such as economic and status gains (Banton, 1983a: 367–77). With regard to the discriminated, sociologists have categorized minority "responses to discrimination," such as assimilation, pluralism, secession, or militancy (Kurokawa, 1970), but since the meanings of discrimination among the discriminated were not sought, it is not clear whether these are responses to discrimination or to possibly closely connected phenomena such as ethnic stratification. And without the accounts of the "discriminated," it is not clear why there should be a certain response to discrimination rather than another.

The recognition, meanings, and interpretations of the discriminatory event, its context, causes, and consequences should be obtained from participants. This does not mean that we need to restrict ourselves in an ethnomethodological fashion to a study of the accounting processes by which people construct a recognition of discrimination or to limit any account to its particular context, "the occasions of its use." The intention here is simply to suggest that a study of discrimination may profitably begin with considering the major images of discrimination by different groups or categories. The meanings evident in self-reported discrimination may then be categorized and related to the positions of respondents within the social structure.

Discrimination of Jews by Jews

Discrimination among Jewish groups of origin in Israel has been widely discussed both in the media and in social-scientific studies. The lower socio-economic profile of Jews from Asia and Africa and their weaker political representation have often been interpreted as consequences of discrimination practiced against them by Jews of European origins or Ashkenazim. It is argued that the earlier immigration of Ashkenazim and their control of resources enabled them to give preferential treatment to members of their own group (Smooha, 1978; Swirski, 1981). Inequality in income and occupational profiles that is not directly explained by such factors as education and period of immigration is often attributed to discrimination (see, for example, Smooha, 1978: 154–5, 191). There have, however, been few direct studies of discrimination and most of these have focused on institutional discrimination in the allocation of entitlements, especially among immigrants. Inbar and Adler (1977) reported differential treatment of Moroccan and Rumanian immigrants by public agencies in the 1950s. For example, a greater proportion of Rumanian immigrants were allowed to choose their area of residence upon arrival, and a greater proportion of Moroccan immigrants were sent to less urbanized areas.

Following the period of mass immigration there was a decline in institutional discrimination (Smooha, 1978: 189), but the policies of the 1950s and 1960s have had long-term effects, and the conviction that ethnic discrimination exists continues to be widespread (Lubel, 1983; Ashkhar, 1979; Khen, 1977; Anosh *et al.*, 1983). The proportion of respondents who have reported personal experiences of discrimination has varied widely in recent research. The conviction that discrimination exists appears to be far more widespread than reports of personal experience of it (Inbar and Adler, 1977; Elhanani, 1979; Lubel, 1983; Anosh *et al.*, 1983; Leslau *et al.*, 1988), and investigators have rarely attempted to categorize the discrimination acts, the contexts, the participants, and the effects. More crucially, they have not questioned the extent to which different patterns of discrimination may involve different categories of people in different positions in the social structure.

In chapter 8 we presented the distribution of respondents who believed that discrimination existed in Israel against certain groups. Respondents were also asked if they had personally experienced discrimination in Israel. About a third of the respondents (*N*=251) answered affirmatively to the latter question. As was expected a greater proportion of respondents from the two Middle Eastern groups, especially the Moroccans, reported that they had experienced discrimination, but significant minorities of Rumanians and Poles also reported having experienced discrimination. Our interviewers returned at a later date to the "discriminated sample" with an additional questionnaire focusing on discrimination. Only 128 persons were willing to co-operate further, but the distribution of these respondents was almost identical with those who had answered affirmatively to the discrimination question; it included individuals from all four groups of origin and from the higher and lower categories of socio-economic status that were distinguished for purposes of analysis.

The second interview began with a request from subjects to relate the discriminatory occurrence, and this was followed by questions about the "discriminator" and the context of the occurrence. Respondents were asked to expound their explanation of the event and to evaluate its consequences, if any, on their lives, such as on their job, economic situation, social relations, and family life.

Accounts of discrimination

Most accounts of the context of discrimination could be categorized as falling under two domains: work and relations with public bodies. The work domain encompassed 52% of all incidents reported: 33% of all incidents were related to promotion at work, 12% to obtaining a position, and 7% to social relationships in the work place. The following quotations illustrate the reports of discrimination in work settings:

I was usually refused the salary augmentations that other workers received from the boss. In one instance, the other workers received a 20% rise and I was given only 10%. The difference surely went to the boss's pocket (age thirty-five, Iraqi origin, low SES).

I was given the job of senior co-ordinator but a higher position was then created to control my work. The man who received the job was from another ethnic group. This was entirely unnecessary. I could have managed on my own (age forty-six, Moroccan origin, low SES).

The workers were divided by their support for the two political parties, the Likud and Ma'arach. Those who belonged to the Likud would throw you out of work. Middle Eastern Jews controlled several departments, and those who did not belong to them were constantly transferred from one department to another until they found themselves out of work (age forty-six, Moroccan origin, low SES).

A clear implication of these reports of discrimination in work-settings is that a principle of justice, the principle of the free job-market, had been violated. A free job-market may be defined as one where only qualifications and experience should be counted, and discrimination was attributed when "ascriptive" characteristics, especially ethnic membership, were considered.

Most descriptions of discrimination in work-settings may be characterized as a violation of merit, but a different meaning of discrimination, based on a violation of rights or fair distribution, was evident in most descriptions of discrimination by public institutions. The following reports illustrate this:

Discrimination was commonly practiced by the Ministry of Housing. Our numerous requests for housing in the state programs were always refused. We have eight children but other people with four children have received villas. Discrimination is a matter of governmental institutions (age forty-three, Moroccan origin, low SES).

After I was wounded during my military reserve service and following deep mental depressions, the doctors determined that I was free from any further army service obligation. The Ministry of Defense dismissed my repeated requests to be granted a disability status in my work, and my disability has not yet been officially recognized. I am hardly able to meet the job obligations that are imposed by my boss (age forty-two, Moroccan origin, low SES).

I was a student at the University preparatory course. Everyone learnt free because they were from *edot ha'Mizrach*. I am an Ashkenazi and I applied for an exemption from fees, but my application was turned down (age forty-six, Polish origin, high SES).

We wanted to move into an apartment allocated for young married couples . . . and we were eligible to receive one following army service. We filled in forms, but were told that we would not receive an apartment because we are not from *edot ha'Mizrach* (age thirty-seven, Rumanian origin, high SES).

This was at a time when there was a flood of immigrants. Preference in housing was given to families and not to single people like myself. Also, preference was given to immigrants from western countries (age forty-three, Moroccan origin, high SES).

The implication in these reports of discrimination in public settings is that a principle of equal or fair allocation had been violated. Respondents attributed discrimination when they did not receive what they believed they should have according to normatively defined needs and entitlements. The emphasis here is on equality of allocation to individuals in the relevant categories (cf. Homans, 1974; Yuchtman-Yaar, 1983).

Although most cases of reported discrimination occurred in the contexts of work and institutions, a minority of cases may be classed as discrimination in informal settings. For example, the parents of a prospective spouse opposed the marriage because of the ethnic origin of the respondent. These cases may also be classified as perceived violation of the principle of merit: the merit of sociability or the right to be accepted in an ideal free-market of friendship and marriage.

Discrimination in the realm of work tended to be reported more frequently by those of lower socio-economic status, both Middle Easterners and Europeans. Respondents of higher socio-economic status were more likely to report discrimination by public institutions. In many cases, the public-institution discrimination reported by Europeans was of the reverse discrimination type, similar to the complaints by whites in the United States.

The two major principles – merit and fair distribution – that respondents implied were violated in instances of discrimination, have been delineated in an explicit fashion by social philosophers and social theorists as the two common principles of justice in western capitalist societies (cf. Walzer, 1983; Homans, 1974; Moore, 1978). Violations of these principles may cut across various domains, such as work, housing, education, and welfare, but in modern capitalist welfare societies, certain domains, particularly that of work, are more likely to include violations of the merit principle, and other domains, particularly the provision of welfare services, are more likely to include violations of the allocation principle.

We found that violation of merit was rare outside the work sphere, but there were exceptions such as the following: "My application to the medical school was turned down in order to fill a quota of Arab students that was unrelated to talent" (age thirty-two, Polish origin, high SES). Violation of fair distribution was occasionally mentioned with respect to work. For example, one respondent told of a lay-off of several Middle Eastern Jews from a factory "without the full legally due financial reparation." In general, however, the attribution of discrimination as a violation of the merit principle was more likely to occur in market contexts where individuals and groups or both were in competition or in conflict with each other; discrimination as a violation of equal allocation was likely to occur in institutional contexts where distribution was expected to conform to legal codes or established procedures.

Whatever the domain, the characteristic of the respondents that was mentioned by them most frequently as related to their experiences of discrimination was their ethnic origin (either their specific country of origin or the broad category). Ethnicity was mentioned by 56% of the respondents, 6% mentioned their class, 8% their political allegiance, and the rest mentioned a wide variety of other factors. The ethnic factor is illustrated in some of the quotations above, and the following two quotations provide further clearcut examples:

I am religious and belong to *edot ha'Mizrach*. They [the municipal employers] wanted to lay me off and replace me with an Ashkenazi (age forty-five, Moroccan origin, middle SES).

When I went to the neighborhood kindergarten to register my daughter, I was told that it was after the deadline. But I know that the real reason is that I am an Ashkenazi (age thirty-seven, Rumanian origin, high SES).

Discrimination was especially likely to be interpreted in ethnic terms when the discriminator was seen to be acting in conformity with social norms. Nearly half of the respondents interpreted the discriminator's action in this way. However, an almost equal number accounted for the act in terms of the individual characteristics of the discriminator. Thus, a

Table 12.1. *Experience of discrimination, frequency of experience, and extent of damage of discrimination by SES and ethnic origin*

	SES[1] (average)	Ethnic origin[2].	N
Discrimination not experienced	.12	.54	522
Discrimination experienced	−.23	.35	232
Discrimination experienced			
Infrequently	.06	.39	170
Frequently	−1.10	.26	62
No financial damage or hardly any damage	.41	.38	59
Damage or severe financial damage	−.81	.31	56
No damage or hardly any damage at work	.30	.38	54
Damage or severe damage at work	−.75	.35	49
No damage or hardly any damage in family relationships	.26	.45	51
Damage or severe damage in family relationships	−.58	.23	61
Goal achieved later	.36	.43	49
Goal not achieved later	−.51	.28	50

1 The higher the index, the higher the socio-economic status. See n. 1 in chapter 9 for the construction of the index.
2 Ethnic origin: 0 – Middle Eastern, 1 – European.

respondent maintained that he was fired because the employer hated Moroccans, or another respondent claimed that he was not rewarded for his efforts because "my foreman does not like me . . . he is egoistic and wants to get credit for my achievements."

The class factor

The data that we have presented so far on discrimination have pointed to ethnicity rather than class or socio-economic status as the major focus. Respondents who believed that discrimination existed in Israel named the groups discriminated against in ethnic terms. And the accounts of respondents who said that they had been discriminated against emphasized ethnicity far more than any other factor. A comparison of the origins and socio-economic status of respondents who reported that they had been discriminated against with those who said they had not also indicated that it was the ethnic rather than the class factor that was important. However, when we turn to the frequency and the effects of discrimination that were reported by those discriminated against, it is the class factor that emerges as the important one (table 12.1).

Only a quarter of those who said that they had experienced discrimination reported that this had been a frequent experience, but the chances of lower status respondents reporting frequent experiences of discrimination were much greater than those of higher status respondents. Statistical tests showed that ethnic origin did not have an independent effect on whether discrimination was experienced frequently or infrequently. The importance of class also stood out when our subsample were asked the extent to which the discrimination had damaged them financially, at work, and in their family relationships. They were also asked if they had later achieved the object which, as a consequence of the discrimination, they had not at that time achieved. Lower status respondents were far more likely to report that the discrimination had affected or severely affected them financially, at work, and in their family relationships. They were also more likely to report that they had not been able to overcome the effects of discrimination. Again, statistical tests showed that ethnic origin had no independent effect on these variables.

Thus, although respondents were more likely to interpret the context of the discriminatory act and the motives of the discriminator in ethnic terms, their reports on the effects of the discrimination indicate that their class location was crucial in determining their experiences of it, and the extent to which the consequences were felt over the long term. These findings are in line with those in other societies (Miller and Riesman, 1972) where investigators have emphasized the importance of the struggle to achieve financial security among the lower socio-economic strata. The absence of financial security or suitable work is especially likely to affect family relationships in the lower strata because of the central importance of the family as a source of social relations.

Discrimination and social divisions in Israel

Israelis hold images of social divisions, not only between Ashkenazim and *edot ha'Mizrach*, but also between religious and secular Jews, Arabs and Jews, and socio-economic categories. However, these other divisions are less likely to be interpreted by Israeli Jews in terms of discrimination. The reservation of certain occupations to religious Jews, such as dietary law supervisors, is hardly likely to be considered discriminatory, and although ultra-Orthodox Jews have used various means to exclude secular Jews from their neighborhoods, the division of neighborhoods is mainly perceived in terms of voluntary preferences. Both religious and secular Jews are more likely to use the term "coercion" rather than "discrimination" in opposing what they perceive as unjust allocation to the advantage of the other.

Sociological studies have documented Jewish "control" of Arabs in Israel (Lustick, 1980; Zureik, 1979) and accounts of discrimination against Arabs (e.g., Smooha, 1978: 197–202) include both types of discrimination delineated in this chapter. However, the Israeli Jews' perception of Israeli Arabs as a minority that does not participate in the identity and culture of the society has meant that many do not perceive Arabs as "relevantly similar" and rarely discuss them in terms of discrimination.

As in other societies, class cleavages in Israel are rarely interpreted in terms of discrimination. We have noted that the term "discrimination" has moralistic connotations, and that sociologists of class have tended to distance themselves, more so than sociologists of race or ethnic relations, from such connotations. The class system may be described by some sociologists as a system of injustice and exploitation, but it is seen to be grounded in structural aspects and built on institutionalized rules and contracts which make the use of the term "discrimination" inappropriate.

Our findings suggest that in modern welfare societies, such as Israel, there may be varying aspects of attributional discrimination that are associated with different socio-economic strata. The features which may be found more frequently among the lower strata focus on the violation of the norm of merit and occur principally in the domain of work: the allocation of positions and the distribution of rewards are not perceived to be in accordance with the talents and skills of the individual. Other features, which may be found more frequently among the middle strata, focus on the violation of the norm of relevantly equal allocation and occur principally in the relationships between citizens and bureaucratic agencies. The allocation of services is not interpreted to be in accordance with the needs and entitlements of the individual.

The distribution of discrimination may be viewed within the context of the dynamics of inequality and the state in modern capitalist societies. Equality of opportunity is often asserted to be a value and even a fact, but class conditions are such that only a minority from the lower strata experience occupational mobility or advancement in their jobs. The hindrances and barriers experienced by the lower strata are interpreted by many as discrimination. Welfare politics have included policies of redistribution, but their formulations and implications are likely to raise conflictual interpretations of who are "relevantly unequal." For example, what is "affirmative action" for some is "reverse discrimination" for others, and in this context it will be the middle strata who are likely to attribute discrimination. Thus, discrimination is a phenomenon which takes on different meanings for different strata.

The finding that many aspects of discrimination are bound to class conditions raises the question of why people, whether or not they report having experiences of discrimination, account for discrimination in terms of ethnicity. There is, of course, a greater likelihood that discrimination will be viewed in terms of ethnicity in societies, such as Israel, where there is considerable overlap between class and ethnic origins. There is also the absence of a political tradition in which conflicts are formulated in class terms. More generally, it may be suggested that the structure of social classes in modern societies is viewed and justified by many, including the lower strata, in terms of universalistic and achievement orientations. In such a normative context, what seems unjust is accounted for in terms of illegitimate particularistic practices which focus on ethnicity, an appropriate primordial attribute.

We would not wish to give the impression that we are reducing discrimination to the class structure. Discrimination may refer to different kinds of occurrences and have a diversity of impacts. Many of its dimensions are bound to class realities rather than to ethnicity, but the phenomenon as a whole has been primarily understood as a reflection of ethnic relations. This has been the conviction of large sections of the population, as well as the victims of discrimination. Although sociologists have rarely investigated the meanings of discrimination, many have shared this common assumption. An investigation of the distribution of the meanings of discrimination has shown that it is time to question this conviction.

13

Assimilation or ethnic solidarity?

The span of theoretical possibilities

In chapter 1 we distinguished three theoretical perspectives ·that have dealt with the impact of socio-economic stratification on ethnicity: the assimilationist–developmental perspective, the cultural division of labor perspective, and the resource–competition perspective. These approaches imply divergent expectations with respect to the effects of stratification and socio-economic mobility in Israel. The assimilationist–developmental perspective, which emphasizes the relationship of cultural change to socio-economic mobility, would expect the more "modern" Israeli of European origin to exhibit a lower level of ethnicity, and that modernization would progressively eliminate ethnicity among the groups of Middle Eastern origin. From this perspective it might be argued that the comparatively recent immigration of many Israelis would account for the relative strength of ethnic allegiances (if such were found), but would expect the higher socio-economic strata of groups, such as Moroccans and Iraqis, to exhibit weaker ethnic solidarity than the lower strata.

The assimilationist perspective has its parallel in Israel in what has been referred to as the "absorption through modernization" approach of Eisenstadt and some of his students and colleagues (Eisenstadt, 1955; Bar-Yosef, 1968; Ben-David, 1953). The emphasis of this approach was on the absorption of "traditional" immigrants within the social framework of a modernizing society. A clear implication of this perspective was that those individuals of Middle Eastern origins who achieve high occupational status would be more acculturated, assimilated, and distant from particularistic identities based on origin.

Because there is considerable overlap of origins, subcultural differences, and socio-economic inequality among Jewish groups, the cultural division of labor model would not expect ethnicity to become attenuated, but because the Middle Easterners are concentrated in the lower strata and make up the great majority in peripheral communities, it would expect them, and particularly their lower ranks, to be the most ethnically minded. The Israeli advocates of the cultural division of labor perspective (Swirski, 1981) have paid little attention to middle-class Middle Easterners, but when mobiles from Middle Eastern *edot* were briefly considered, it was noted that they were often co-opted by the Europeans and that the potential leadership of the Middle Easterners was consequently weakened.

Like the cultural division of labor perspective, the resource–competition approach, which interprets ethnicity as a resource used to improve a competitive position, would not expect an attenuation of ethnicity, but it would expect socially mobile Middle Easterners, who are in greater occupational competition with Europeans, to be the most ethnically minded. The competition perspective has not been applied explicitly in the Israeli context, but Eisenstadt (1983) has argued that it is the mobile elements from the Middle East who have felt the greatest sense of deprivation from the predominantly European socio-political center, and that their dissatisfaction is being translated into political and possibly ideological expression. However, these arguments have had as yet little empirical grounding, and one aim of this study is to present evidence that will contribute toward an assessment of their validity.

A comparison of the two subordinate groups, the Moroccans and Iraqis, is made with reference to the corresponding traits of the Poles and Rumanians who represent here the dominant European category. A comparison of intragroup variations according to SES is made in all four groups. Four dimensions of assimilation and ethnic solidarity are analyzed. All the dimensions have been discussed in separate chapters, but here we bring them together in order to focus on the impact of stratification on the different facets of ethnicity. The first three dimensions largely parallel major dimensions of assimilation distinguished by Gordon (1964). The fourth dimension, perception of discrimination, represents a cognitive measure of ethnicity (Portes, 1984; Portes *et al.*, 1980).

1 *Cultural behavioral distance (acculturation)* This dimension is represented by two behavioral variables, voting and religiosity. We base our analysis of voting on the supporters of the two largest parties, the Ma'arach and the Likud, and for religiosity we use our index of five *mitzvot*.[1]

2 *Primary social distance (structural assimilation)* This dimension is represented by the ethnic homogeneity or heterogeneity of the three best friends of respondents. Because our data indicate only a marginal ten-

dency to homogeneous networks according to country of origin, we focus on whether the networks are homogeneous or heterogeneous according to the more general distinction between Middle Easterners and Europeans.[2]

3 *Identification*   This dimension is measured by the levels of identification with the specific community of origin and with the broad categories (Ashkenazim and *edot ha'Mizrach*).[3]

4 *Perception of discrimination*   We base our analysis of this dimension on respondents' perceptions of discrimination against *edot ha'Mizrach* as a whole.[4]

Because the Poles and Rumanians are associated with the dominant culture and share low levels of religiosity and ethnic identification, the differential effects of SES within these groups are expected to be of limited significance with respect to most of the dimensions. However, we showed in chapter 7 that blue-collar Europeans have a higher proportion of friends from Middle Eastern *edot* than white-collar Europeans.

If we simply set up the competition theory as an alternative to the assimilationist and cultural division of labor approaches, we would propose clear-cut conflicting hypotheses regarding the relative distances of Moroccans and Iraqis and their lower and higher socio-economic strata from the Europeans' patterns. The assimilationist and cultural division of labor approaches would predict that the more privileged subordinate group, the Iraqis, and the higher socio-economic strata of both the Iraqi and Moroccan groups would exhibit lower scores in religiosity, voting for the Likud, ethnically homogeneous friendship networks, identification with the community of origin and broad ethnic category, and perception of discrimination; the competition perspective would predict higher scores for these categories. However, the theories may attend to different facets or dimensions of ethnicity. More specifically, although mobiles from subordinate groups may assimilate into the dominant category and acculturate to its patterns of behavior and identification, in so far as mobiles enter into occupational and other competition with members of the dominant category, they may experience and/or perceive greater discrimination than the lower strata in their groups.

The data are analyzed by a series of regression equations, one for each variable representing the various dimensions.[5] Following our discussion, the main purpose of the analysis is to examine the effects of the interaction between SES and country of origin on the various dependent variables. The inclusion of a proper interaction term is not straightforward. In the present analyses the interaction effects are measured by six dummy variables, each representing an ethnic SES category. The categories are defined according to country of origin (Morocco, Iraq, Poland, and Rumania) and SES level (under and above the SES average of the total sample). The combination between the variables created eight categories (hereafter M, I, P, R represent country of origin, and higher and lower SES are signaled by "+" and "−" respectively). In the regression analyses M+ (higher status Moroccans) is coded "1," the rest of the sample "0." The additional dummy variables are coded similarly. The differences between the two lower status European groups (P−, R−) were found to be negligible. Hence, they were omitted from the analysis and serve as a base for comparison.

We are aware of the loss of information caused by the dichotomization of SES, and we have checked an alternative series of regression analyses which include multiplicative interaction terms; SES in its interval form is multiplied by four dummy variables representing the countries of origin. While the findings indicated by this kind of analysis are basically similar to those presented below, they were found to be less sensitive in showing the differentiation among the ethnic SES categories. Because this differentiation is crucial for testing the different perspectives, we have chosen to concentrate on the analyses which are based on the dichotomization of SES.

Besides the country-of-origin/SES combinations, two additional explanatory variables are included in the regression analyses: years of schooling and age. These variables are included mainly as controls. Obviously, years of schooling is highly correlated with SES ($r = .79$), but because the dichotomization of the latter still leaves substantial variance of the former in each SES category we preferred to control for it.[6]

Because we wished to examine the effects of the same independent variables on a number of dimensions of ethnicity, we considered the use of multivariate multiple regression which controls for the intercorrelations among the dependent variables (see, for example, Bock, 1975). We found, however, that with the exception of the correlation between the two ethnic identifications, the correlations among the dependent variables are either moderate or weak (see table 13.1). Multivariate multiple regression is expected, therefore, to produce similar solutions as ordinary multiple regression, and because the use of multivariate multiple regression results in a severe reduction of the number of cases,[7] we chose to base most of the analyses on ordinary multiple regression. We have used multivariate multiple regression only in the analysis of the two ethnic identifications which are highly correlated.

Table 13.1. *Product–moment correlation coefficients among the variables representing dimensions of ethnicity*

	Voting	Religiosity	Networks	Specific ethnic identification	Broad ethnic identification	Perceptions of discrimination
Voting	—	−.32	.02	−.20	−.19	−.19
Religiosity		—	−.20	.26	.23	.27
Networks			—	−.14	−.13	−.19
Specific ethnic identification				—	.66	−.20
Broad ethnic identification					—	−.19
Perceptions of discrimination						—
Average ($\bar{x}$)	.45	2.09	.89	2.76	2.85	1.38
SD (σ)	.50	1.49	.95	1.46	1.48	1.38

The variety of dimensions

Table 13.1 presents product–moment correlation coefficients among the six dependent variables. As noted, the two types of ethnic identification, representing together a single dimension, are highly correlated. The correlation between voting and religiosity, representing the behavioral dimension, is much lower, and the correlations among the variables representing different dimensions range from weak to moderate.[8] There is a weak pattern in which voting for the Likud Party, greater religiosity, ethnically homogeneous friendship networks, higher levels of ethnic identification, and perception of discrimination are somewhat associated with each other. However, the coefficients indicate that the dimensions are largely independent of each other, and that we can refer to different patterns of ethnicity.

We now focus on the links between the ethnic/SES categories and the dimensions of ethnicity. The main findings here are based on the regression analysis (table 13.2). The control variables, years of schooling and age, are either statistically insignificant or, when significant, negligible in magnitude. More years of education are associated with greater support for the "moderate" Labor Party and weaker ethnic identifications. Older respondents have higher degrees of religiosity, more ethnically homogeneous friendship networks, stronger ethnic identifications, and greater perception of discrimination. These relationships are of residual importance and, as noted, these two variables serve mainly as controls. The test of the different approaches is based mainly on the operation of the ethnic/SES combinations which we analyze in detail below, referring to each dimension separately.

(a) *The behavioral dimension (voting and religiosity)* The patterns revealed in both equations of the dependent variables representing this dimension are quite similar. Among Middle Easterners, the groups are differentiated both by country of origin and SES level. In voting, the main differentiation is between lower status Moroccans and all other Middle Eastern categories. M– is the only Middle Eastern category whose distance from lower status Europeans is large enough to reach statistical significance. The magnitude of the distance between both M+ and I– and the base comparative category brings the "b" values to the threshold of statistical significance. The fourth Middle Eastern category, I+, is the closest to the base category. The "b" effect pertaining to this category is nil, indicating the absence of any distance whatsoever.

The uniqueness of I+ is clearer in the second equation relating to

Table 13.2. *Metric (b) and standardized (β) regression coefficients of effects on variables representing dimensions of ethnicity*

Dimensions of ethnicity	Voting (N=485)[1]		Religiosity (N=756)[2]		Networks (N=682)[2]		Specific ethnic identification (N=794)[2]		Broad ethnic identification (N=794)[2]		Perceptions of discrimination (N=711)[3]		Average (x̄)	SD (σ)
Independent variables	b (SE)	(β)	b (SE)	(β)	b (SE)	(β)	b (SE)	(β)	b (SE)	(β)	b (SE)	(β)		
Years of schooling	.02* (.01)	.11*	.01 (.02)	.03	.00 (.01)	.01	−.07* (.02)	−.18*	−.04* (.01)	−.11*	.02 (.02)	.03	12.26	3.78
Age	.01* (.00)	.12*	.02* (.01)	.08*	−.03* (.01)	−.20	.00 (.01)	.00	−.03* (.01)	−.12*	.02* (.01)	.06*	39.62	6.52
Country of origin and SES combinations														
Iraq – higher SES	−.01 (.09)	−.01	−.04 (.20)	−.01	−.02 (.15)	−.00	.88* (.20)	.16*	.75* (.20)	.14*	1.83* (.23)	.29*	.08	.2
Morocco – higher SES	−.14† (.08)	−.08†	1.24* (.19)	.24*	−.51* (.14)	−.16*	1.04* (.19)	.21*	.75* (.19)	.15*	2.27* (.22)	.38*	.09	.29
Iraq – lower SES	−.12† (.07)	−.09†	.79* (.15)	.20*	−.78* (.12)	−.30*	.97* (.15)	.25*	−.89* (.15)	−.22*	1.90* (.18)	.42*	.17	.37
Morocco – lower SES	−.38† (.07)	−.09†	1.81* (.16)	.45*	−.98* (.12)	−.37*	1.35* (.15)	.34*	1.08* (.16)	.27*	2.20* (.18)	.48*	.16	.37
Poland – higher SES	.07 (.08)	.05	−.85* (.18)	−.21*	−.25* (.12)	−.10*	−.17 (.17)	−.04	−.52* (.17)	−.13*	−.13 (.21)	−.03	.15	.36
Rumania – higher SES	.10 (.08)	.07	−.13 (.17)	−.03	−.41* (.12)	−.16*	−.15 (.16)	−.04	−.28 (.17)	−.07	−.07 (.02)	−.02	.17	.37
R²	.18		.31		.16		.26		.25		.35			
a	3.49		.79		.47		3.17		4.13		1.48			

*b is more than twice its standard error (SE).
†b is almost twice its standard error.
1 Reduction in N is due to the fact that we analyze voters of the two big parties only.
2 Changes in N are due to missing data.

religiosity. In that equation I+ is the only Middle Eastern category whose distance from the base category does not reach statistical significance. However, a further differentiation is revealed among the remaining three Middle Eastern categories; I− is closer to the lower status European pattern than both Moroccan categories, although the distance between I− and both M categories lacks statistical significance. It appears that SES has stronger differentiating power among Moroccans in voting behavior, whereas it is especially effective in determining levels of religiosity among Iraqis. It is evident, however, that in both groups higher status diminishes both religiosity and the tendency to vote for the Likud.

The lack of statistical significance of P+ and R+ in the voting equation indicates that SES does not differentiate the Europeans in this respect. However, higher status Poles are differentiated from the lower status Europeans in religiosity. The effect of SES among Poles is similar in direction to its effect among the Middle Eastern groups: higher SES tends to diminish the level of religiosity.

We have noted that in Israel all Middle Eastern groups are attributed less prestige than any European group, but that there is differentiation within each broad category; Iraqis are attributed more prestige than Moroccans, and Poles more than Rumanians. The combination of ethnic prestige with the obvious prestige differentiation according to SES level provides an interpretation of the differences among the categories in voting and religiosity, but it appears that ethnic prestige is more important than esteem from SES in accounting for these differences. However, among the Middle Eastern categories, I+ stands out as having the closest pattern to that of the Europeans.

(b) *Structural assimilation – social networks* The uniqueness of I+ compared with the other Middle Eastern categories persists in this dimension. Because most "b" values are both negative and statistically significant, we can infer that lower status Europeans are relatively "open" to close relationships with Middle Easterners. The only Middle Eastern category which seems to be as open to interethnic friendship is I+. Here again the distance of both M+ and M− from the lower SES European pattern reaches statistical significance, but M+ is closer to the base category than both M− and I−. Thus, higher socio-economic status increases the likelihood that Middle Easterners will form friendships with Europeans, and this tendency is especially obvious among Iraqis.

Whereas in previous dimensions ethnic prestige and SES moved the tendencies of the categories in the same direction, in this dimension the categories differ according to whether there is a consistency between

211

their ethnic prestige and SES. Inconsistency between ethnic prestige and SES level is accompanied by relative ethnic heterogeneity of friendship networks. Both higher SES Middle Easterners and lower SES Europeans are more likely to encounter members of the opposite ethnic category as work associates and neighbors. But although within each broad ethnic category the status inconsistent groups are characterized by relative openness to interethnic friendships, there is a clear difference between M+ and I+, with the latter having by far the most heterogeneous networks.

(c) *Specific and broad ethnic identifications* The passage from variables representing acculturation and assimilation to the identificational variables is accompanied by a change in pattern. In accord with the previously analyzed dimensions, I+ is the closest of the Middle Eastern categories to the lower status Europeans in the specific ethnic identification. With respect to broad ethnic identifications, I+ and M+ are equally close to the lower status Europeans, but the distances are statistically significant. Thus, in this dimension, I+ is closer to other Middle Eastern categories than to any European category. It appears that SES has a stronger differentiating power among Moroccans than Iraqis, but the direction of the differentiation is similar for both groups; higher SES is associated with weaker ethnic identification. The distance between P+ and the base category with respect to the broad ethnic identification is statistically significant, indicating differentiation among the Poles according to SES level.

Similarly to voting and religiosity, the differences in identification among the categories can be interpreted in terms of the combined effects of ethnic prestige and SES. However, in this dimension, although there is a clear differentiation according to SES among the Middle Eastern categories, the major difference remains between all Middle Eastern and all European categories.

(d) *Perception of discrimination* When perception of discrimination is considered the groups are differentiated almost exclusively according to the broad ethnic category. All Middle Eastern groups are characterized by a relatively strong tendency to perceive discrimination against their broad ethnic category.

In this dimension, the previous pattern revealed among Moroccans is somewhat reversed. As with most of the previously analyzed variables, the distance between each Moroccan category and the base category is statistically significant, but only in this dimension are lower status

Moroccans closer to lower status Europeans than higher status Moroccans who perceive discrimination against Middle Easterners more than any other category. However, the differentiating power of SES among both Moroccans and Iraqis is negligible in magnitude.[9] The same is true for the Europeans who are not differentiated either by SES or by country of origin. It is evident that in spite of some differentiation according to country of origin and SES, both are secondary to the main source of separation – the broad ethnic category.

Socio-economic status and ethnicity: the outcome of the interaction

Stratification and mobility are by no means the only factors that influence assimilation and ethnic solidarity, but the analysis presented here has compared groups and strata within particular cultural parameters in order to shed light on the specific impact of stratification. It has been shown that stratification has differential influences with respect to different dimensions of ethnic allegiance and assimilation. Our data on Poles and Rumanians show that, among Europeans, both inter- and intragroup differences are less salient than among the Middle Easterners. Among Europeans the SES effect is negligible apart from its effect on friendship networks, and, among Poles, on broad ethnic identification and religiosity. Yet the effects of stratification, both between the two Middle Eastern groups and within each one, create substantial differences.

Most of our findings support the predictions derived from the assimilationist and the cultural division of labor approaches; higher SES Middle Easterners are closer to the Europeans' patterns of behavior and identifications than the lower SES Middle Easterners who have higher levels of religiosity, give more support to the Likud, and retain stronger ethnic identifications. The process of assimilation is selective in two ways, by country of origin and by socio-economic status. The Iraqis, who as a group have a higher socio-economic profile in Israel than the Moroccans, are overall closer to the Europeans. The higher SES Iraqis are the closest to the Europeans in their voting behavior, level of religiosity, and specific ethnic identification, and they also have the greatest proportion of European friends. The higher SES Moroccan pattern is similar in direction to that of the higher SES Iraqis, but apart from the broad ethnic identification and, to a lesser degree, voting behavior, its movement toward the Europeans is relatively moderate. Although class selectivity appears clearer than country of origin selectivity, differences between the two Middle Eastern groups are also found in the lower SES stratum; the lower SES Moroccans are more distant from the Europeans than the lower SES Iraqis in all dimensions.

The importance of treating ethnicity and assimilation as multidimensional phenomena is brought out clearly when we turn from the dimensions of behavior and identification to perceptions of discrimination. If the latter had been analyzed alone, it might have been concluded that empirical support had been found for the competition perspective. There is a clear dichotomy between the Middle Easterners, who perceive substantial discrimination against themselves, and the Europeans, who perceive much less discrimination against Middle Easterners. Among the Middle Easterners, the Moroccans perceive more discrimination than the Iraqis, the more so in the higher SES category. The differentiation among Moroccans according to SES is marginal compared with the difference between Europeans and Middle Easterners, but this pattern differs considerably from the pattern found in all other dimensions.

It is possible that change in perceptions may be slower than change in behavior, and that we have described a stage in a continuous process of the assimilation of mobile elements from the subordinate groups. On the other hand, feelings of belongingness to a discriminated group could promote, in certain circumstances, an increase in ethnic identification and ethnically based behaviors. Although mobile Middle Easterners move toward the Europeans' pattern at the individual level, they are aware that the majority of their group of origin remains concentrated in the lower strata, and whereas many Europeans are inclined to explain the overlap of origins and class as a consequence of cultural characteristics and lack of appropriate qualifications of Middle Easterners, the mobile Middle Easterners are more likely to explain this in terms of discrimination.

The evidence that we have provided from a single society will not be decisive in evaluating the relative qualities of the theoretical perspectives on ethnicity, but our analysis has indicated why apparently conflicting approaches have all secured empirical support. The perspectives have focused on different facets of ethnicity that do not necessarily move in the same direction. They may, in fact, move in opposite directions. Although this has occasionally been recognized, there are very few studies on the relationship between ethnicity and stratification that have analyzed more than one dimension of ethnicity, and the study of the relationships among the various dimensions of ethnicity has made little progress beyond Gordon's (1964) classic study.

Although we have focused in this chapter on the impact of stratification on ethnicity, we do not want to suggest that ethnicity is determined exclusively by socio-economic or class factors. There are cases where a variety of factors – cultural, demographic, political – account for strong ethnic boundaries in all dimensions, and these may be unaltered or strengthened by mobility and socio-economic differentiation. The ethnicity of Arabs in Israel would appear to be such a case. The case presented here of different groups of origin within the Israeli-Jewish population is only one possible pattern within a number of possibilities that were delineated in chapter 1. In this case, where the subordinate groups illustrate the same type of ethnicity, inter- and intragroup variations follow the same general pattern. This would not necessarily follow in a comparison of ethnic groups whose ethnicity takes different forms. Moreover, in other societal contexts, the behavioral and social distances, ethnic identifications, and images of discrimination among ethnic groups may evolve differently in relationship to each other.

The case studied here exemplifies a situation where the group and individual mobility of subordinate ethnics narrows the behavioral and social distances from the dominant category, somewhat diminishes the subordinate groups' ethnic identification, but does not weaken the images of discrimination that appear to persist beyond the situations in which the images arose. These findings constitute a comparative standpoint for further studies of the impact of stratification on ethnic solidarity and assimilation, the multidimensionality of which should structure the analysis.

V

Social cleavages: an overview of Israeli society and some theoretical implications

Part V is intended to bring together a number of our findings and to extend our analysis of Israeli society by incorporating into our discussion two populations that were not included in our sample: the ultra-Orthodox Jewish population and the Arab population. The wider theoretical relevance of our study is discussed in the final chapter.

Cleavages among Jews

The class cleavage

The cleavages of class, ethnicity, and religion have been analyzed along a number of dimensions, objective and subjective. Our findings have both corroborated what we know from other sources and thrown new light on the social divisions within the Israeli-Jewish population. With respect to class, we have confirmed that class consciousness is not strong in Israel, but we have also shown that class, quite independently of ethnic origin, is relatively important in the social life of respondents, including their friendship networks and in the ways that discrimination is felt.

Objective class position influences cognitive images of the class structure and levels of dissatisfaction with both the distribution of rewards among classes and with the individual's own socio-economic position. The weak politicized class consciousness appears to be related to the importance of the "socialist" or public economic sector in the political economy of Israel. Socialist ideology was one of the principal ideological forces that shaped Israeli society, but it came to be associated with elites, bureaucrats, or public servants who controlled and administered those parts of the economy belonging to the state or the Histadrut: the large industrial concerns, the co-operative transportation companies, the collective rural settlements, the public health organizations, and the highly centralized trade-union organization. The people who set up this formidable structure, and shared the ideology that legitimized it, enjoyed a high level of mobility at the same time that new immigrants, from a different cultural background than themselves, entered the blue-collar and lower white-collar positions.

Few immigrants from North Africa and Asia had supported socialist movements in their countries of origin, and the socialist ideology of a system in which they were placed in low positions was hardly likely to appeal to them. As in other societies, the relative absence among the lower strata of such assets as education and authority results in feelings of individual dissatisfaction and class deprivation, but in contrast with other societies, this has not led to the crystallization of classes as conscious collectivities. It is among the lower strata, in particular, that ethnicity rather than class has patterned social relationships, identity, and consciousness.

The tendency to closure based on class rather than ethnicity increases as one moves up the social scale, and it is associated in Israel with support for the political "left." This political allegiance among the privileged is, in part, a consequence of socialization to the values of Israel's historical Labor movement, conveyed in the past by the family and youth movements. The persistence of such political attitudes, despite the changes in social positions, indicates a recognition among the privileged that they achieved their present status within an opportunity structure erected on the basis of a "socialist" or Labor perspective (Matras, 1985). These benefits are not confined to those in authority in the public sector, but extend to the private sector where large companies have often been assisted by government agencies. Large owners in the private sector became so accustomed to state subsidies that their organization, the Manufacturers' Association, rejected the liberal or free-market policies introduced by the Likud government after it came to power in 1977 (Wolffsohn, 1987).

The middle class or middle strata of European origin is by no means homogeneous in support of the Labor Party. Sections of the lower middle class, especially the self-employed with small businesses, of European as well as Middle Eastern origins, have always been more inclined toward the Likud. In the 1977 elections many voters from the middle strata who had supported the Labor Party in the past voted for the new party Dash (the Democratic Movement for Change). Eisenstadt (1985) argues that, although the voters for Dash differed from the Middle Eastern supporters of Likud in their socio-economic characteristics, they shared the feelings of exclusion from the political center of the Labor establishment. The supporters of Dash included some who had been socialized into the Labor ideology but saw the movement as having become ossified and inefficient, and others who rejected the socialist premises of the Labor Party and its institutional manifestations, particularly the centralized economy and over-bureaucratization. Dash split up into factions (one faction joined the Likud-led government), and it did not survive to the following elections. Many of those who had voted for Dash returned to the Ma'arach in the 1981 elections, but in those and subsequent elections the political parties to the left of the Ma'arach attracted a significant section of the upper-middle, particularly professional, stratum. The Zionist left wing, represented by the Ratz and Mapam parties in the 1988 elections, see the Labor Party as moribund and ineffective, support a more "dovish" foreign policy, and stress the values of tolerance and democracy which some see as threatened in Israel's political climate.

The ethnic cleavage

The differences between European and Middle Eastern Israelis with respect to ethnicity are related to their cultural orientations that were shaped, in part, by their historical experiences in their countries of origin. It is misleading, however, to simply counterpoise Israelis from "modernized" European societies with Israelis from "traditional" Middle Eastern societies. The sociologists of the cultural division of labor school were correct to emphasize that most Israelis of European origin came from the relatively undeveloped societies of eastern Europe on the semi-periphery of the world capitalist system. They carried their argument too far when they minimized the importance of cultural factors in analyzing the development of Israeli society and relationships between European and Middle Eastern Israelis.

Modern nationalist and socialist ideologies spread from western and central Europe to eastern Europe in the latter part of the nineteenth century, and it was precisely the lack of economic modernization in eastern Europe that resulted in a more radical secularism among some sectors of eastern European Jewry than among western European Jews. Unlike western and central European Jews who experienced considerable socio-economic mobility, acculturated to the dominant cultures, and believed that they would finally be accepted socially into the wider societies, eastern European Jewry remained a predominantly poor, culturally distinct, and socially separated subsociety (Sharot, 1976, 1982). The majority of Jews in eastern Europe remained traditionally religious up to the interwar period, but it was from the minority of secular Zionists that came the pioneers of the New Yishuv in Palestine. Later immigrants from eastern Europe included some ultra-Orthodox who reinforced and revitalized the Old Yishuv, but the majority of immigrants, although not radical secularists, tended to be secularized.

Although the division in eastern Europe between Orthodox and secular Jews was transferred to the Yishuv, the relative numbers and power of these sectors were very different from what they had been in Russia prior to the Revolution and Poland prior to World War II. In the interwar Yishuv and the State of Israel the secular Jews from eastern Europe were the dominant element, and it was they who envisaged a unified nation of Jews from different origins.

Our data showed that the majority of European Israelis did not have a strong identification with their community of origin or as Ashkenazim, but they emphasized as much as Middle Easterners the social and cultural differences between the two broad categories. They did not translate their feelings of sharing cultural traits with others from Europe into an ethnic identification, but they tended to define Jews from the Middle East in ethnic terms, and they took it for granted that their own culture is *the* Israeli culture that was built in accordance with the Jewish version of European nationalisms and social democracy. They expected the Middle Eastern "ethnics" to "modernize" and to adopt their "non-ethnic" culture, but it was precisely this stance that contributed to the ethnization of Middle Eastern Israelis and their perception of the Ashkenazi establishment as a factor to be resisted.

The emergence of ethnicity among Middle Eastern Israelis, both as distinct *edot* and as part of *edot ha'Mizrach*, was largely a consequence of the contradiction between the Ashkenazi vision of Israeli-Jewish solidarity, based on a secularized nationalism, and the religiously informed vision of Israeli-Jewish solidarity among Middle Easterners. The interpretation of Zionism among Middle Easterners could not justify a desertion of values and norms that in their eyes were not just a particular legacy, but incorporated the essentials of the Jewish faith and collective identity. The notion of the "People of Israel" was at the very core of their group self-definition, and, as a "returning diaspora," they did not feel compelled to transform themselves in order to integrate into an "Israeli" society from which they felt culturally alienated. Thus, the first stages in the development of the Jewish state were characterized by a fundamental mutual misunderstanding concerning the meaning of the common endeavor. And it was the different meanings of "fusion of the exiles" that, together with the emergent ethnic stratification, resulted in the ethnization of Middle Eastern Israelis.

Public expressions of ethnicity among Middle Eastern *edot*, such as ethnic festivals, became more popular after Middle Eastern Jews had passed through the early stages of adaptation to their new society and attained a degree of security and self-respect. This flowering of ethnicity among Middle Easterners appears to have contributed to a renewal of interest among European Israelis in *their* cultural heritage. In the late 1980s groups studying the Yiddish language have multiplied, there is a wider use of Yiddish expressions in daily Hebrew speech, and there is a greater interest in aspects of Yiddish culture, such as the Yiddish theatre. This development is similar to the resurgence of white ethnicity in the United States, which was in part a reaction to the growth of black ethnic militancy, but Ashkenazi ethnicity is more limited in scope and is likely to remain so as long as the majority of European Israelis continue to hold to a secular form of nationalism.

These generalizations of the overall differences in cultural orientations and ethnic identifications between European and Middle Eastern Israelis need to be qualified by attention to differences according to country of origin, especially among Middle Eastern *edot*, and to differences within the groups according to socio-economic status. For example, more Iraqi immigrants than Moroccan immigrants had been influenced by secular trends and ideologies, including secular Zionism, prior to their immigration, and in Israel the Iraqis were less resistant to the predominantly secular culture of the Europeans. Those sectors of the Jewish population in Morocco who were closer to the French culture and were the least traditionally religious tended to migrate to France rather than Israel, and this selectivity in migration accounts, in part, for the relatively high levels of religiosity that we found in the Moroccan *edah*. Our data showed also that, whereas there was little difference between the Moroccans and Iraqis in the strength of their ethnic identification, only the Moroccan group included significant minorities whose ethnicity was culturally or politically salient, or both. In so far as their ethnicity was focused on the *edah*, it was found to be associated with religiosity. In so far as it was focused on *edot ha'Mizrach*, it was related to feelings of deprivation and being discriminated against.

The feelings of ethnic deprivation, that were especially prominent among the Moroccans but were also strong among the Iraqis, are clearly related to the overlap between socio-economic status and ethnic origin in Israel. Jews from North Africa and Asia make up the great majority of the poor and unemployed in the city slums and in the development towns of the country's periphery. The lower middle class has a more balanced ethnic composition, but the proportion of Europeans increases as one moves higher up the hierarchy, and in the highest stratum Europeans are clearly dominant.

Some sociologists have explained ethnic stratification in Israel principally by differences in human resources, such as the level of formal education, that immigrants brought with them from their countries of origin. Others have placed greater emphasis on the differential treatment and discrimination against Middle Easterners that was practiced by the state agencies and officials in the 1950s and 1960s. Both explanations can point to supporting evidence, but whatever their relative importance the resulting ethnic inequality has been viewed by many as a denial of the ideal of "fusion." Policies intended to "correct" this situation, such as

223

special educational programs for the underprivileged, have been implemented, but of greater importance in the development of ethnic stratification in Israel have been the changes in the economic and occupational structure that have resulted in considerable social mobility and the entrance of many Jews of Middle Eastern origins into the middle class. The overall economic gap between Europeans and Middle Easterners has not been reduced, and by some measures it has even widened, but the impact of a large middle class from Middle Eastern origins on ethnic relations should not be ignored.

In accord with the resource–competition school, the emergence of a middle class of Middle Eastern origins may have sharpened ethnic conflict; their command of resources and knowledge of the system could be major weapons in the management of a conflict strategy. However, these same attributes can be used to achieve successful assimilation into the dominant sectors of the society. In fact, a complex picture is suggested by our findings. In some dimensions, such as ethnic identification, mobile Middle Easterners remain closer to the dominant pattern of their ethnic groups than to their class; in others, such as friendship networks, they have distanced themselves from their ethnic groups and are similar to the dominant pattern of their class. There are also significant differences among mobiles from different Middle Eastern *edot*; in most dimensions middle-class Iraqis are much closer to the European pattern than are middle-class Moroccans who remain closer to the dominant pattern of their *edah*. However, even for middle-class Moroccans, the relative openness of ethnic boundaries and the recognition that belonging to the Ashkenazi-dominated sectors is a symbol of success, have meant that they have tended to assimilate into the higher strata and to refrain from shouldering the burdens of leading an ethnic struggle.

Whereas the ethnic identifications of middle-class Middle Easterners appear to have been weakened by their interaction with Europeans, the ethnic identifications of working-class Europeans appear to have been strengthened somewhat by their interaction with Middle Easterners. This statement should be qualified by noting that the effects of stratification among Europeans are more obvious with respect to the social dimension of friendship networks than with respect to the cultural dimensions such as ethnic identification. The friendship networks of blue-collar Europeans are far more ethnically heterogeneous than white-collar Europeans, but their *edah* and Ashkenazi identifications, although somewhat higher than among white-collar Europeans, are still modest compared with the equivalent identifications of Middle Easterners. Interaction with, and assimilation into, the other ethnic category make a difference, but neither middle-class Middle Easterners nor working-class Europeans detach themselves from the typical traits of their ethnic categories. And to the extent that there is a process of de-ethnization, it is a selective one that occurs particularly at the middle-class level and among certain *edot*, such as Iraqis, more than others.

Ethnicity and the political cleavage

The formation of ethnically defined groups and their stratification have had important political impacts that, in turn, have contributed to the development of ethnicity in Israel. Once again we need to emphasize that the state and its major institutions were formed under the leadership of a self-conscious elite of pioneers who came from eastern Europe and settled in Palestine during the first decades of the century. These founders and their sons remained at the highest levels of the various social and political hierarchies for many decades, and they were very selective in integrating others from outside their circles. The co-optation of a few non-Europeans into the political elite became a symbol of the political parties' representation of the "whole people," but this co-optation did not prevent, in fact it underlined, the unequal participation of Middle Easterners in political power. This inequality, together with the economic deprivation and the marginalization of Middle Easterners in the cultural life of the country, created a feeling of polarization that contradicted the ideal of fusion. Such a situation could not be without impact on political behavior.

In the first decade or so after their immigration, the majority of Middle Easterners accepted the leadership of the Labor-dominated establishment and voted for the Labor Party in the elections. Feelings of deprivation were expressed at an early date in the riots in Haifa in 1959 and later in Jerusalem in 1971, but the dominant Labor Party remained aloof from the culture of the Middle Easterners and made only token concessions. The transfer of Middle Easterners' political support to the nationalist Herut (the major component of what later became the Likud) was already evident in the early 1960s (Lissak, 1969: 76–97) and increased significantly in subsequent elections. Not only were the symbols of Herut closer to the national–religious cultures of the Middle Easterners, but also the party's long-standing confinement to the opposition made it a suitable vehicle for the Middle Easterners' protest against the establishment.

Our data showed that, unlike the Labor Party, which many identified as the party of the "workers," the Likud was not identified with any particular interest or sector. As such, it could be seen as more representative of the whole nation. It should be emphasized, however, that the support for the right is not equally strong among all Middle Eastern groups or at every socio-economic level within those groups. Support for the Likud was found to be especially strong among the Moroccans; many of whom saw the Labor Party as representing the interests of Ashkenazim.

The Likud gained the most from the erosion of the authority of the Labor Party among Middle Easterners. Support for the Labor Party also weakened, although to a much lesser extent, among the Europeans, especially after the setbacks during the first days of the Yom Kippur War in 1973, but this was mainly to the benefit of small centrist parties or parties to the left of Labor. Thus, Israel has become a country where the middle and upper strata are more often supporters of the left and the lower strata are more often supporters of the right.

The two major parties are divided in terms of the support that they receive from the different ethnic groups and categories, but they are not ethnic parties in the sense of presenting themselves as representing the interests of an ethnic sector. For nearly thirty years, from 1952 to 1981, the numerous attempts by ethnic lists to obtain a seat in the Knesset (Parliament) were of no avail in spite of the fact that, according to the proportional representation system in Israel, they had only to achieve 1% of the total votes to secure a seat. The ideology of fusion was strong enough to stigmatize the ethnic vote as divisive and anti-Zionist, and there was also a problem of leadership because the politicians from the mobile Middle Easterners were co-opted by the major parties.

A change began in 1981 when the newly formed party Tami, representing itself as a party of *edot ha'Mizrach* with an emphasis on its religious traditions, obtained about 4% of the votes and three seats in the Knesset. Tami was reduced to one seat in 1984 but another ethnoreligious party, Shas, gained four seats. The leaders of Shas had broken away from the ultra-Orthodox party, Agudat Yisrael, that was dominated by Europeans, and they presented the new party as a religious party of *edot ha'Mizrach* or Sephardim. By the 1988 elections Tami had disappeared (its leader had joined the Likud), but Shas obtained six seats, and its 5% of the total votes represented a significant 10% of the total votes of Middle Easterners.

An interpretation of the rise of the ethnic vote must, at this point, be somewhat speculative. The political behavior of Middle Easterners is often explained in terms of deprivation, and it might be contended that feelings of deprivation, as well as disillusionment with the Likud, have produced a growing determinedness to promote an independent political expression. The problem with such an interpretation is that Middle Easterners are much stronger politically than they were in the past. A consequence of their shift to the right was the creation of a situation of approximate equality between the two major parties, and an unprecedented sharpening of competition for votes between them. This has meant that the Middle Easterners have achieved a strong bargaining position, and the benefits from this situation are evident in the neighborhood renewal programs implemented in the 1980s in predominantly Middle Eastern areas, the new school programs emphasizing the cultural contributions of Middle Eastern Jewry, and the impressive growth of Knesset members and ministers of Middle Eastern origin. It may be argued, therefore, that the strengthening of independent ethnic politics is due less to feelings of deprivation than to the greater prominence of Middle Easterners on the public scene. Because they are less vulnerable to stigmatization and are courted politically, they are more inclined to support an ethnic party that clearly demonstrates their growth in power.

The stigmatization of political ethnicity is also less threatening when it is bound to religion. The only realm where pluralism within the Jewish population is officially recognized and institutionalized is religion as, for example, in the appointment of an Ashkenazi and a Sephardi rabbi at many levels of the rabbinate. Thus, it is at the junction of ethnicity and religion that the taboo against political ethnicity was broken down as Middle Easterners strengthened their position on the public scene.

The religious cleavage

Although Middle Eastern immigrants were the least inclined to accept the radical secularist Zionist vision of a new Israeli Jew, their experiences, and especially those of the younger immigrants and the second generation, in the relatively modernized educational, military, and political systems, resulted in considerable cultural adaptation. Cultural change included a weakening of religiosity, but for most Middle Easterners this did not mean a break from religion, but rather a departure from the high levels of religious observance of their parents. The majority of Middle Easterners depicted their new partly religious pattern in positive terms, referring to it as a "traditional" pattern, but some of those who have retained high levels of observance have been greatly concerned by the weakening of religiosity among Israelis of North

African and Asian origins. At first, those Middle Easterners who wished to stem the erosion of religiosity in their groups found that it was the Ashkenazim who provided them with a model of uncompromising Orthodoxy.

The ultra-Orthodox Ashkenazi sector has attracted especially that small proportion of Middle Easterners who seek a rabbinical career or wish to pursue traditional religious scholarship. The Ashkenazi *yeshivot* (religious academies) are the best financed, have the most renowned teachers, and are anchored in an unbroken tradition of religious scholarship. The ultra-Orthodox Ashkenazi sector is deeply divided by competing schools and dominant rabbinical figures, but, as the center of religious knowledge, it was bound to influence any segment of the population that defined itself as religious. Middle Eastern rabbis have become spiritually attached to certain Ashkenazi rabbinical leaders, and it was with the spiritual blessing of one such leader that ultra-Orthodox Middle Easterners established the Shas party. However, the emergence of Shas was, in large part, a response of religious Middle Easterners to feelings of being discriminated against by the Ashkenazi leaders of the ultra-Orthodox institutions, and in recent years there has been a development of ultra-Orthodox Sephardi *yeshivot* and other organizations with a clientele of Middle Easterners. The division of the ultra-Orthodox community along ethnic lines was signaled by the establishment of a Sephardi Council of Wise Sages of the Torah. The Council is the highest authority of the Shas party, and it is modeled on the Council of Torah Sages of Ashkenazi rabbis who decide the major policies of the Agudat Yisrael party.

Like Agudat Yisrael, Shas participates in elections and joins governmental coalitions in order to advance the interests of the ultra-Orthodox sector, such as aid for housing projects for the religious population and financial support for their schools, *yeshivot*, and community institutions. These parties also try to push forward legislation to regulate public life, and, although the non-religious population have often protested against what they commonly term "religious coercion," the appeal and influence of secularist movements, whose major aim is to reduce the power of the Orthodox religious establishment, have been very limited.

By defining their state and their society as "Jewish," even the most secularized Israeli Jews necessarily limit the potential of a secularist movement. The most secular forms of Zionism attempted to replace the Jewish religion by a concept of Jewish civilization, to strengthen Jewish solidarity as a modern form of nationalism, and to negate the *galut* (exile) by a return to the "Land of Israel." For its collective symbols Zionism had only a religiously infused Jewish heritage to draw upon: the Hebrew calendar, the traditional holidays, the biblical sites, and the rehabilitation of the sacred language as the vernacular. The traditional supernatural meanings of these symbols became irrelevant for many Israelis, but the symbols were still regarded as sacred, and their embedment in the sacred texts and myths meant that they could not be entirely separated from their religious meanings (Liebman and Don-Yehiya, 1984: 15–18). Moreover, however negative their view of the Jewish religion, the vast majority of Jews considered the embracing of another faith to signify a detachment from the Jewish people. A number of "Hebrew Christians" or "messianic Jews" have attempted to sustain a Jewish identity together with a belief in Jesus as the messiah, but no sector of the Israeli-Jewish population has been willing to accept them as part of "the people of Israel." It is this absence of separation of religion and state at the symbolic level that limits the appeal of secularist movements and provides the setting for the full participation of religious parties in political life.

Religion and the political cleavage

The general election in 1988 witnessed an impressive strengthening of the religious parties. Their percentage of the votes increased from 11% in 1984 to 15%, and from thirteen to eighteen seats in the Knesset. Only in one previous election, in 1961, did the religious parties achieve a slightly higher proportion of the votes, but at that time it was the "modern" Orthodox Zionist party, the Mafdal, that was dominant with twelve of the eighteen mandates, whereas in 1988 it was the *haredi* or ultra-Orthodox parties that obtained thirteen of the eighteen mandates.

The ultra-Orthodox camp in 1988 was represented by three parties. The most successful, Shas, obtained six seats. Its support came from Middle Eastern Israelis, and it presented itself in the election campaign as a revitalization of the sacred heritage and uplifter of the moral condition of *edot ha'Mizrach* who had been severely damaged by the "secular malaise" in Israeli society. The majority of its supporters are Zionists, but its leaders have been influenced by the "Lithuanian Orthodoxy," a non-Zionist trend in Judaism that has taken a moderate approach in what its leaders consider non-religious political issues, such as the status of the conquered territories. The "Lithuanians" participated as a separate party – Degel ha'Torah – for the first time and obtained two mandates. While it was understood between Shas and Degel ha'Torah that they would draw their support from different ethnic categories (*edot* ha'*Mizrach* and Ashkenazim), Degel ha'Torah was in fierce competition with the third ultra-Orthodox party, Agudat Yisrael, which obtained five seats. This competition resulted in an unprecedented mobilization of the ultra-Orthodox electorate that strengthened all the ultra-Orthodox parties. Agudat Yisrael was also helped by the support of the Habad Hasidim that takes a hawkish stand in Israel's conflict with the Arab countries, but the party has been mainly concerned with religious legislation and support for the educational and other institutions associated with it.

Whereas Agudat Yisrael began as an anti-Zionist party, Mafdal (the National Religious Party), represented the desire of a sector of religious Jewry to participate in the Zionist endeavor and endow it with religious significance. Up to the late 1960s the Mafdal was primarily concerned to achieve a coexistence with secular Zionists that would safeguard the full participation of religious people in the mainstream of Israeli society. One indication of this policy was the creation of religious *kibbutzim* and *moshavim*. The party was also concerned to build and to enlarge religious institutions (the Chief Rabbinate, rabbinical courts, burial societies, etc.) that were intended for all Jewish citizens.

These institutional concerns remain, but since 1967, and especially since 1973, they have increasingly taken second place to a concern to infuse the Jewish state with religious meaning and to promote Jewish settlement in the conquered territories. The younger generation of Mafdal politicians opposed the accommodative stance of their elders toward the dominant secular elite, fought for an active involvement in foreign policy, and condemned any territorial concession that would "betray" Israel's religious right to the "Promised Land." Gush Emunim (Bloc of the Faithful), a movement that began as a pressure group within the Mafdal interpreted the conquest of "Judea and Samaria" as part of the process of redemption, and promoted further the radical nationalist tendency within the Zionist religious population.

The increased support for the religious parties in 1988 was, in part, at the expense of the Likud, whereas the Ma'arach lost many of its former supporters to the parties on its left. The religious parties were then in a strong bargaining position because neither of the two largest parties, if they wished to exclude each other, could form a government without them. The Likud negotiated at first with the religious parties to form a coalition without the Labor Party, but the new strength of the religious parties, as well as the competition among them, pushed them to make far-reaching demands that produced an outcry among the secular population and were found unacceptable by the Likud leaders. After the two largest parties reached an agreement between themselves, the religious parties joined the wide coalition with much reduced demands. The fact that it was the demands of the religious parties that contributed to a coalition of the two major parties demonstrated the cleavage between the religious sector, especially the ultra-Orthodox, and the non-religious population. However, this polarization is mainly evident among European Israelis, and it is moderated by the continuous rather than polarized distribution of religiosity among Middle Easterners.

The religious–secular division, as well as the ethnic and class divisions within the Israeli-Jewish population, have both influenced and been influenced by the Jewish–Arab cleavage. This division, to which we now turn, has two components: the division between Israeli Jews and Israeli Arabs–Palestinians, and the cleavage between Israeli Jews and Arabs–Palestinians who live in the territories conquered by Israel in 1967.

15

Jews and Arabs

At the beginning of this study we distinguished between non-national forms of ethnicity, such as among Israeli-Jewish groups of origin, and ethnonationalism. It is the latter term that best denotes the cases of Jewish citizens and Arab or Palestinian citizens of Israel, and of Israeli Jews and the Palestinians in the West Bank and the Gaza Strip. The intra-Jewish cleavages and the Jewish-Arab cleavages differ in fundamental respects, but the framework of dimensions and perspectives in the sociology of ethnicity, discussed in the first chapter, can be applied to both. It is, in fact, the common conceptual framework that allows us to demonstrate the important differences between the two ethnic encounters and the relationships between them.

On the eve of the establishment of the State of Israel the Arab population of Palestine was about 1,200,000, nearly twice as large as the Jewish population. Only 156,000 remained after the first Israeli-Arab war, although there was some increase in the early fifties as a consequence of minor borderline changes with Jordan and a family unification policy. A high natural growth has gradually increased the proportion of Arabs in the population, and today the Arab citizens of Israel constitute 18% of the total population. They are themselves divided by ethnicity and religion: Sunni Muslims are the majority, the Christians belong to a number of churches, the Druze are an important group, and there are smaller groups of Samaritans and Karaites. Within the Muslim population, the Bedouin constitute a distinctive sector.

A large proportion of the Arab or Palestinian citizens of Israel have continued to live in villages, but their socio-economic and occupational profile has changed considerably. In the 1930s many were already making the transition from tenancy in feudal-like estates to wage labor, but the transition from peasant to proletarian was greatly accelerated after the establishment of the State of Israel. The mass flight in 1948 of Arabs from the territory that was to become Israel included the Arabic ruling class and the merchant and bureaucratic strata, and the majority of male workers who remained found wage labor outside their villages, as

232

agricultural laborers, in construction and transport, and in the lower status service jobs.

State planning and investment were almost exclusively directed to Jewish ventures, and the exclusion of Arab agriculture and industry from state support made it necessary for Arabs to commute daily from their villages to work for Jewish employers. Until 1967 agriculture was still the leading employment category of Israeli Arabs, followed by unskilled construction, industrial work, and menial service jobs. As the children of peasants with a high illiteracy rate, Arab workers did not have the resources to compete with Jewish immigrants, including those from the Middle East, who mostly came from urban environments and possessed many craft skills. The initial disadvantages of Arab workers were perpetuated by the unequal distribution of resources by the state, but from 1967, when Arabs from the West Bank and Gaza Strip entered the Israeli economy as cheap unskilled labor, Israeli Arabs moved into semi-skilled and skilled work. Construction became the predominant employment category until 1980 when it took second place to manufacturing industry. There was an increase in the number of self-employed as well as the development of an Arab middle class and intelligentsia (Rosenfeld, 1978; Makhou, 1982; Semyonov and Lewin-Epstein, 1987).

None of the theoretical perspectives in Israeli sociology would dispute that the changes in the economic character of the Arabic population were, in part at least, a consequence of governmental policies, but they differ in their interpretations of the Jewish-Arab ethnic encounter in the extent to which they emphasize economic or cultural factors, and in the extent to which they focus on these factors within the dominant or subordinate group.

The modernization-developmental perspective has paid relatively little attention to the Arab "minorities" in Israel, but when Eisenstadt has turned to the issue, he has emphasized the cultural facets on the Jewish side. Problems are seen to stem from a combination of attitudes or orientations among the Jews. On the one hand, Arabs are granted full citizenship and enjoy legal equality, as well as the special judicial and communal rights of religious minorities. Arabic is recognized as an official language, and the basic public services – education, health, and municipal services – are extended to the Arab population. On the other hand, the Jewish-Zionist character of the state has led to the exclusion of Arabs at a number of symbolic and material levels. When Arabs have been employed in manual work, this has been in contradiction with the value of Jewish labor that was held by socialist Zionism. The suspicion of Arabs as potential supporters of Israel's external enemies accounts for their exclusion from the army (apart from the Druze and some Bedouin) and the limitations that have been imposed on their movement and employment. This combination of Jewish attitudes results in a "relatively benign, but also restrictive, semi-colonial paternalism" (Eisenstadt, 1967, 1985: 337).

The mobility of Arabs has been restricted, both by their social and cultural background and by Jewish attitudes, but the processes of modernization have nevertheless brought about a weakening of tradition and the growth of an educated intelligentsia. These changes have led to new aspirations, greater frustration, and political radicalization. Thus, modernization is seen to exacerbate the situation of Arabs in Israel, but the basic problem is that of the Jewish state: how to allow Arabs a full and autonomous cultural and political participation (Eisenstadt, 1985).

The admission that Arabs were being radicalized rather than being absorbed through modernization necessarily meant that sociologists of the modernization school would deal with the Arab-Jewish encounter in entirely different terms from those with which they analyzed the European-Middle Eastern Jewish encounter. Smooha's pluralistic framework, in comparison, was intended to encompass both intra-Jewish and Arab-Jewish divisions in the same terms. The differences between the situations were presented by him mainly in terms of quantitative levels of pluralism, inequality, and conflict. In contrast with the subcultural pluralism among Jewish groups, the cultural pluralism of Jews and Arabs involved core-cultural differences: nationality, religion, first language, and basic ideologies. Arabs were exposed to the dominant values and life-styles of Jews and they have become increasingly bilingual and bicultural, but important cultural differences, such as in family roles, birth-rates, and popular music, remain.

Social pluralism is also much greater between Jews and Arabs than within the Jewish population. Legal separation pertains to the rights and autonomy of the religious communities in the regulation of such matters as marriage, divorce, and inheritance, but there are laws that benefit only Jews (the Law of Return, which entitles non-Israeli Jews to immigrate to Israel and become citizens, is probably the most important). Arabs are also separated from Jews in their ecological distribution: nearly 90% are concentrated in three areas, the Galilee, the "Little Triangle," and the Negev, and the vast majority live in Arab towns and villages. Only about 10% live in mixed Jewish-Arab towns, and in these most live in Arab neighborhoods.

Arabs are largely integrated into the economy, but there is a high level of separation in most other institutional spheres: there are separate

schools, Arabs have their own local governments, and in many governmental ministries and in the Histadrut there are special departments,
usually with Jewish heads, that deal with matters pertaining to the Arab
minority. The Zionist political parties have supported separate Arabic
lists, but since the appearance of Smooha's book (1978) there has been an
increase in the support for non-Zionist parties among Israeli Arabs.
Whereas in the past the majority of Arabs voted on the basis of
instrumental considerations, in the last few elections they have increasingly voted, like Jews, on an ideological basis (Shokeid, 1982). The
Israeli-Arab vote is still, however, far from homogeneous. In the 1988
elections, 40% of Israeli Arabs voted for the Zionist parties. The rest were
divided between three parties, two non-Zionist parties that included
some Jewish supporters and leaders but are understood by most Arabs
and Jews to be Arabic parties (a Communist party, Rakach, and the
Progressive List for Peace and Equality), and a pure Arabic party that
presented itself for the first time and gained one mandate.[1] None of these
parties have been considered by the major Zionist parties to be possible
coalition partners.

Contacts between Arabs and Jews are quite frequent at the impersonal
levels, at work and in public facilities, but close personal contacts are rare;
dating is taboo and there are very few intermarriages. The majority on
both sides discourage intimate contacts, and Arabs who have moved into
Jewish neighborhoods have sometimes been repulsed or made to feel
uncomfortable. Derogatory expressions, such as "Arab work," are
common among Jews, and a number of studies have shown that
prejudice against and negative stereotypes of Arabs are widespread. The
studies found that the majority of Jewish respondents agreed with
statements that it is impossible to trust Arabs, rejected the possibility of
having an Arab as superior to them at work, and said that they would be
bothered if their children befriended Arabs (Smooha, 1978: 199–201).

The state of belligerency with the Arab states has aggravated the
tension between Jews and Arabs in Israel, and, if anything, Jewish
attitudes toward Arab citizens have hardened in recent years. Tsemach
(1980) found that almost half of the Jewish respondents believed that
Jews should always receive preference in obtaining work, housing,
social-welfare allowances, and in acceptance to higher education. Discrimination is not institutionalized in this way, but laws that give
preference to army veterans and their families in obtaining governmental
assistance in housing, student loans, social welfare, and allowances,
amount to *de facto* discrimination. Beyond exemption from the army,
which most Arabs support, and other security considerations, which

justify exclusion of Arabs from military industries and diplomacy, Jews are reluctant to appoint Arabs to positions of pre-eminence or authority where other workers or clients are mostly Jews. Such practices limit the range of opportunities for Arabs who obtained a higher or professional occupation. As our data have shown, however, few Jews will mention Arabs as a category that is discriminated against. For most Israeli Jews, Arabs are not "relevantly similar."

Social pluralism is reinforced by inequality, and, as we have already indicated, inequality between Jews and Arabs is evident in income, occupational prestige, education, and political power. Although there has been an increase in the size of the middle class, Arabs are still underrepresented in all white-collar work, including the lower ranks, and overrepresented in manual work. Compulsory primary and secondary education has resulted in a considerable increase in educational levels in the Arab population, but they remain underrepresented in higher education. The frustrating effects of these limited improvements, together with the continuing absence of political appointments in national government, have increased dissatisfaction, but the extent of Jewish control is such that large demonstrations are infrequent and the majority remain law-abiding.

Smooha wrote that the appropriate model of Jewish-Arab relations in Israel is an "exclusionary domination model" in contrast with the "paternalism-co-optation model" of European-Middle Eastern Jewish relationships. Arabs have pushed for more independence and have shown greater readiness to challenge the status quo, but there has only been a moderate decrease in pluralism and inequality. Smooha designates Jews and Arabs quasi-castes: status is determined by birth, endogamy is the rule, and although passing from one group to another is theoretically possible by conversion, this is very rare. He argues that this structure is sustained by the overriding national objective of Israeli Jews to build a purely Jewish society in the Land of Israel.

The theme of the exclusion and subordination of the Arabs as a consequence of the Jewish-Zionist character of the state is emphasized even more by the political scientist Ian Lustick in his book, *Arabs in the Jewish State: Israel's Control of a National Minority* (1980). Lustick argued that the control of Arabs is accomplished by three strategies of Israeli Jews. Firstly, segmentation: the ethnic and religious divisions between Muslims, Christians, Bedouin, and Druze are encouraged, and pre-existing structural differences such as the competition between local *hamula*s (clans) are reinforced by, for example, giving support to two or three Arab lists. Secondly, co-optation: elders of the traditional *hamula*s have been encouraged to enter local politics and to serve as mediators for benefits, and other leaders are persuaded to work for the state by promises of comfortable jobs and personal advantages. Thirdly, dependence on the Jewish economy: government policies, such as the expropriation of Arab land and the absence of investment or assistance in economic ventures owned by Arabs, have meant that Arabs lack an autonomous basis of economic power and have no choice but to work for Jews. Economic dependence has made Arabs relatively easy to co-opt.

Rosenfeld (1983) has criticized Lustick for presenting a rigid theoretical framework that explains the domination and control of Arabs in terms of the essence of the Zionist state and does not pay heed to the internal divisions and potential developments within Zionism. In his reply, Lustick (1984) admitted that other versions of Zionism have existed but that the major institutions of the Israeli state have expressed and implemented that particular interpretation of Zionism which emphasizes the exclusively Jewish character of the state. It is not that Jews have made a calculated effort to discriminate against Arabs, but discrimination has been the inevitable consequence of institutions and practices that serve the ideological imperatives of the Zionist movement, such as the ingathering of the exiles and the Jewish settlement of the land. Thus, social scientists from a number of perspectives have argued that the exclusion and subordination of Arabs in Israel rest, at the most fundamental level, on the ideology or basic orientations of Israeli Jews.

An alternative materialistic perspective on the Jewish-Arabic encounter in Israel has been provided by the "dependency" or "internal colonialism" school. The economic dependency of Arabs on the Jewish economy is just one among a number of themes in the works of writers like Smooha and Lustick, but among some neo-Marxist writers it is far more central. There is a similar discussion by the dependency writers of the means used to subordinate and control Arabs, such as the expropriation of land, institutional separation, and discriminatory practices, but the fundamental level of explanation of such practices is that of material benefits rather than ideology.

Zureik (1979) argues that the colonial-capitalist mode of production introduced by the Jews, and supported by the British during the mandate, disrupted the socio-economic order of the native Arabs and transformed them into an "internal colony" of mainly wage-earners dependent on the dominant Jews. Zureik admits that the Zionist colonialization differed in some ways from classical colonialization, but the Labor Zionist policies of colonialization of the land (rather than its inhabitants), employing only Jewish labor, and buying only Jewish produce, not only resulted in the eviction of Arab peasants from their land, but also impeded the development of an Arab proletariat and bourgeoisie. The Palestinian peasantry was transformed into an easily manipulated marginal proletariat. The Jewish ideology is seen in this framework mainly as a justification of expropriation and exploitation.

Both Jewish-Arab relations and European-Middle Eastern Jewish relations have been analyzed in terms of dependency, but this has been done by different authors. No one work from this school has provided an overall or integrative analysis of these divisions, and it is difficult to see how this could be accomplished. Is the difference between the two cleavages that Arabs are simply more dependent than Middle Eastern Israeli Jews on the economy dominated by European Israelis? Zureik does, in fact, approve of the notion that dependency is not a dichotomous quality but can be understood as a continuum. Just as less developed countries may be seen as being in various degrees of dependence, so presumably might subordinate ethnic groups. Such a quantitative differentiation is unlikely, however, to account for the differences between the Arab-Jewish and Middle Eastern Jews-European Jews divisions, and without some inclusion of cultural or ideological factors at the level of explanation, it is difficult to see how this could be accomplished.

A somewhat different perspective has been presented by anthropologists who have given greater attention to cultural factors on the Arab side. Shokeid (1982), for example, emphasizes the relationship between ethnic identity and cultural orientations among Israeli Arabs. He notes the considerable change in sexual roles and behavior of Middle Eastern Jews in Israel compared with the continuing strength of traditional sexual roles and behavior among Israeli Arabs. Muslim Arabs have undergone much cultural change in Israeli society, but they have retained their traditional attitudes on sexual roles as an expression of their opposition to the influence of the culture of the wider society. Shokeid suggests that the strong ethnic identity of Muslim Arabs has disposed them to preserve distinctive core values as a form of cultural confrontation.

Socio-psychological studies of ethnic and other identities among Israeli Arabs have also contributed to our understanding of the subordinate group side of the ethnic encounter. These studies have shown that, when Israeli Arabs are asked to indicate the relative importance of their identities, the majority give the greatest weight to their national identities (Palestinian and Arab), and the least weight to their civic Israeli identity. Traditional identities, such as the *hamula* (clan) identity, have been replaced in importance by the national identities, and, since 1967, there has been a steady increase in the proportion of Israeli Arabs who say that the term "Palestinian" best denotes their collective identity. A recent survey (Rouhana, 1988) found that more than 75% of the Arab respondents chose the terms "Palestinian Arab," "Palestinian," or "Arab" to refer to their collective identity, and only 24% chose the terms "Israeli Arab" or "Israeli Palestinian." Class identity is relatively unimportant compared with the national identity, but it still comes before the Israeli identity.

It is clear that, not only the relative importance, but also the meanings of the Israeli identity are vastly different for Jews and Arabs in Israel. When Israeli Jews refer to their "Israeli identification," they are usually referring to their commonality with other Jewish citizens of Israel and not to the legal notion of citizen which they share with non-Jews. As we have shown, there is a close interrelationship between the Jewish and Israeli identities, and among Middle Easterners there are also highly positive correlations between these identities and the *edah* and *edot ha'Mizrach* identities. In contrast, high negative correlations have been found between the "Palestinian" and "Israeli" identities among Israeli Arabs. And whereas the terms "Palestinian" and "Arab" denote sentimental or affectively loaded identities, characterized by a strong feeling of belonging and closeness to others in the group, "Israeli" denotes for Israeli Arabs an identity limited to instrumental concerns such as equal rights and material improvements (Rouhana, 1988). Thus, even for that sizeable minority who incorporate an Israeli component in choosing an appropriate term to describe themselves (Israeli Arab, Israeli Palestinian), it would be misleading to conclude that there is an important common element between these identities and those of Israeli Jews.

As in other cases where both the dominant and subordinate ethnic groups support relatively closed social boundaries, the level of ethnicity within the subordinate group is unlikely to vary greatly according to socio-economic status. In contrast with the weakening of ethnic identity among the mobile Israeli Jews of Middle Eastern origin, the ethno-nationalism of Israeli Arabs is, if anything, heightened by socio-economic mobility. Exclusion by the dominant group has more important economic and social implications for members of the subordinate group than exclusion by the subordinate group has for members of the dominant group, and direct personal experiences of exclusion are likely to occur among the more highly educated sector of the subordinate group. Higher education does not necessarily enable Israeli Arabs to move into high-status occupations, and even though friendships may develop between Jews and Arabs there has been no crystallization of large integrated groups. Even in those rare cases where Arabs or Jews cross the boundary by religious conversion, they are likely to find themselves the objects of suspicion and to be labeled by their former identity.

With respect to their socio-economic profile and some elements of their culture, such as styles of cooking and family roles, Israeli Arabs are closer, and will acknowledge that they are closer, to Jews from the Middle East than to European Jews. But it is precisely these similarities that have made many Middle Eastern Jews the most determined to strengthen the boundary between Arabs and Jews. Arabs entered the low-paying jobs that had previously been manned predominantly by Middle Eastern Jews, and the combination of the Jewish Middle Easterners relative advantage over Arabs and relative deprivation *vis-à-vis* European Jews has meant that they have had the most to lose from a softening of the boundaries. European Israeli images of the "Oriental" Middle Eastern Jews and the often expressed views of the "Orientalization" of Israeli society have made Middle Eastern Jews particularly sensitive to their cultural difference from Arabs.

The reasons for the greater emphasis by Middle Eastern Jews on the ethnic boundary go deeper, however, than a reaction to the stigma of similarity. In so far as their subethnic identities (*edah, edot ha'Mizrach*) are convergent with their Jewish and Israeli identifications, and in so far as they retain the Jewish identity as their most valued one, they are more likely to emphasize the boundary than the more secular Europeans who put a greater emphasis on their Israeli identity. Middle Eastern Jews display the greatest convergence of nationality, ethnicity, and religion, but the point being made here can be extended to religious Israelis of European origins. Whereas it might be conceivable for secularized Jews to redefine the notion of "Israeli" as a purely civic identity divorced from a national component, for religious Jews it is difficult to conceive of a concept of "Israeli" that divorces it from the "People of Israel" and the "God of Israel." An attempt by a small number of Israeli-Jewish intellectuals to replace the Jewish identity with an Israeli or "Canaanite" identity was a failure, but for secular Jews there remains the possibility at least of retaining the Israeli and Jewish identities as important but separate identities. It has to be admitted, however, that developments, particularly since 1967, have been in the opposite direction: the Jewish and Israeli identifications have increasingly converged.

The development of a stronger Palestinian national identity among Israeli Arabs was related to their renewed contacts, from 1967, with the Palestinians in the West Bank and Gaza Strip, a population numbering

1,200,000. Violent confrontations between Jews and Palestinian Arabs intensified during the period of the British mandate, but from 1948 to 1967 the Israeli governments paid little attention to developments among the Palestinians living in the West Bank and Gaza. They conceived the "Palestinian question" as secondary to Israel's conflict with the neighboring Arab states and as an issue that would eventually be settled with those states, particularly Jordan. Since 1967 the confrontation between Jews and Palestinians has been renewed, and the mutual exclusivism of the two sides has produced a further radicalization of Jewish-Arab relationships that has had implications, not only for the cleavage between Jewish and Arab Israeli citizens, but also for intra-Jewish cleavages.

The Israeli occupation dislocated the pre-capitalist economy of small farms and crafts in the conquered territories, and the import of Israeli goods from across the 1967 borders meant that there was little possibility of developing industry. A large proportion of the male population of the territories was employed as unskilled wage laborers in the Israeli economy where they came to constitute 6% of the labor force. Nearly half of the non-citizen Palestinian workers were employed in construction, representing 35% of the work force in that sector, and the others were widely distributed in the agricultural, manufacturing, and service sectors. In the vast majority of cases they have filled unskilled and menial positions, and when Jews or Israeli Arabs have remained in these positions they have generally received higher remuneration than the workers from the occupied territories (Semyonov and Lewin-Epstein, 1987).

The effect of the economic incorporation of the non-citizen Palestinians has been to increase the overall levels of inequality among workers in the Israeli economy, but because it has enabled Jews and Israeli Arabs to move out of the lowest stratum, it has possibly softened the class divisions among Israeli citizens. As for the broad ethnic division within the Jewish population, surveys have found that a higher proportion of Middle Easterners than Europeans has taken a hawkish position and been less willing to envisage a withdrawal from the territories, but this is by no means a clear-cut division of opinion along ethnic lines, and the support for the extreme right-wing of the Jewish political spectrum has tended to come from Israelis of European or North American origin. It is the secular-religious division among Israeli Jews that is the most pertinent intra-Jewish cleavage for the Jewish-Palestinian conflict, but here the relevant division is not between secular Zionists and the ultra-Orthodox but rather between secular Zionists and religious Zionists.

241

There are, of course, hawkish secular Zionists and dovish religious Zionists, but it has been mainly secular Israelis on the center and left of the political spectrum that have expressed a willingness to withdraw from at least part of the territories, especially those parts heavily populated by Arabs, in exchange for secure boundaries and peace. The religious Zionists of the National Religious Party and the Gush Emunim movement cannot envisage withdrawal from the "sacred" land that they believe was given to the Jewish people by God, and from the religious sites that tie the sacred history of the past to the present endeavors of the Jewish people. For many religious Zionists, the meaning of withdrawal from the territories is a reversal of the process of redemption.

It should be noted, however, that the debate over the territories among the vast majority of Israeli Jews, including that between the religious and the most secular Jews, is not a dispute over the need to preserve the dominant Jewish character of the Israeli state but rather over the means of its preservation. In the 1988 election campaign the hawkish Likud party argued that only by holding on to the territories would they be able to guarantee the survival of the Jewish state. The dovish Labor Party argued that only by withdrawing from the territories, and thereby eliminating the Arabic "demographic threat," would Israel be preserved as a Jewish state. A binational or pluralistic state in which there would be a fundamental change in the relations of Jews and Arabs was not envisaged by any important Jewish political party or movement.

16

Toward a theory of social cleavages

In the first chapter we discussed major themes in the sociological literature on ethnicity including its relationship to class and religion. It was emphasized that, although the relative influence of instrumental and cultural factors on ethnicity may vary from case to case, neither material factors alone, nor cultural factors alone, are likely to explain the varying degrees and modes of integration and separation of ethnic groups. Socio-economic inequality of ethnic groups is often an important factor, but it has to be considered together with the nature and strength of ethnic symbols, often related to religion, among both the dominant and subordinate groups.

Ethnic inequality, the dominant group's orientations toward the subordinate group, and the latter's understanding of itself in relationship to the dominant culture and group are factors that are likely to be in dynamic interaction and to influence each other. Although one of these factors may in particular social or historical contexts be more determining than determined, it would be unwise to attempt a generalized reductionism whereby one factor – say a subordinate group's assimilationism or ethnic solidarity – is seen to be dependent on the other two, the level of ethnic inequality and the orientations of the dominant group. For example, although it can be argued that the Jewish communities of the diaspora became far more open to the wider non-Jewish environments as a consequence of the decline of economic differentiation between Jews and non-Jews and the greater openness of the non-Jewish society, an analysis of the level of openness reached by the Jewish communities needs to consider the independent influence of their religio-ethnic orientations.

This work has focused principally on the ethnic cleavages among Jews in Israel, but class and religious distinctions have also been analyzed, both in so far as they partially overlap with the ethnic divisions and as cleavages in their own right. We also reviewed briefly the ethnonational cleavages between Israeli Jews and Israeli Arabs–Palestinians and between Israeli Jews and the Arabs–Palestinians who live in the West

Bank and Gaza. The latter oppose the occupation by the Israeli state of the territories in which they live, but they may be considered part of an Israeli cleavage in so far as they participate in the Israeli economy as migrant workers, traveling daily across the 1967 borders.

Ethnicity, class, and religion have their own definitions, characteristics, dimensions, and problems of interest, and it makes sense that they should be studied in three subdisciplines. However, not only do they overlap empirically, they may also be conceptualized as having common features, and in this concluding chapter we present a conceptual framework that relates to all three cleavages. The intention here is to go beyond demonstrating the influence of one form of differentiation on another by comparing the cleavages within a single framework of concepts and ideas.

There have been a number of attempts in the sociological literature to reduce ethnic or religious differentiation to class differentiation, but there have been few attempts to present a non-reductionist framework that encompasses all three types of cleavage. The pluralist model has been applied to ethnic and religious divisions, but although inequality is considered as an important factor influencing ethnic and religious pluralism, class is not dealt with as a separate form of differentiation. Parkin (1979) has provided an interesting and potentially fruitful conceptual framework that is intended to encompass class, ethnic, and religious divisions. His major concern was class analysis, but one of his objections against other, particularly neo-Marxist, perspectives on class was that they made little attempt or were unable to explain other cleavages that often crosscut classes such as racial, ethnic, and religious groups. In place of conceptions of class as positions in formally defined structures, Parkin presents classes as determined primarily by modes of social closure and collective action, and he argues that these conceptions may equally well be applied to ethnic and religious groups.

Parkin has been criticized for abandoning the conceptual distinction in the class literature between structural position and collective action and focusing exclusively on the latter (Murphy, 1986), but although Parkin's focus may limit in some ways the questions related to classes, it does provide an appropriate conceptual framework for the analysis and comparison of different types of cleavage. His conceptualizations reflect, however, his primary interest in the class structure, and they require some modifications in order to encompass more adequately other types of cleavage. Parkin's starting-point is the notion of closure in the work of Max Weber (1968: 341–8). He develops Weber's ideas and introduces a number of useful conceptual distinctions, but he retains Weber's highly

244

instrumentalist conception of the central notion. Although Weber tended in general to emphasize the importance of cultural factors, his discussion of closure, which is part of a section on the economic relationships of organized groups, focuses on material interests.

Weber wrote that, in the competition for livelihood, one group of competitors will take an identifiable characteristic of another group of actual or potential competitors, such as their race or religion, as a pretext for excluding them. The driving force of closure or exclusion is the "monopolization of specific, usually economic, opportunities." Weber recognized that economic interests can favor the expansion of a group, but he noted that these may be countered by the economic interests of exclusiveness. Which particular economic interests will prevail will vary greatly empirically, but Weber did not provide a systematic framework to account for the varying degrees of openness or closure. It is evident from his examples, which include political parties and religious movements, that cultural and ideological factors would need to be considered, but his main concern in the section on closure was to focus on the influence of economic interests. His example of Islamic warriors who desired to have a non-Islamic population which would provide for the maintenance of the privileges of believers is an instance of economic interests promoting closure overriding a religious ideology emphasizing expansion.

Weber did not discuss closure with reference to classes, which he saw in terms of relationship to the market, but he did mention closure in his discussions of status groups in general and ethnic groups in particular. Status is the social estimation of honor connected with any shared quality of a group's members. Restrictions on social intercourse with others are linked to the specific style of life expected of members. Specific status honor "always rests upon distance and exclusiveness," and although material monopolies provide the most effective motives of the exclusiveness of a status group, they are rarely sufficient in themselves (1968: 932, 935). With respect to ethnic groups, Weber wrote that any cultural trait, no matter how superficial, can serve as a starting-point for the tendency to monopolistic closure (1968: 388).

The centrality of instrumental motives in Weber's fragmentary comments on closure cannot be denied, but there are suggestions that ideal or cultural factors are important in accounting for variations in closure. It is, however, the instrumental considerations that Parkin emphasizes, not only in his major focus on classes, but also in his discussion of ethnic and religious groups. His extension of the notion of closure beyond Weber relates mainly to the means of closure or forms of collective social action rather than to the ends of closure which are always, in Parkin's view, the maximalization of rewards and opportunities. We wish to question Parkin's claim that closure has never any other purpose but to serve or enhance material, social, or symbolic rewards. Perhaps symbolic rewards or interests can be understood to include almost any cultural facet of a group, but we submit that Parkin's formulation does not pay sufficient attention to the concerns of many ethnic and religious groups to preserve, through means of closure, their identities and cultural heritages. Such concerns may override the interests of a group with respect to its control of resources or attainment of rewards.

Parkin distinguishes two primary modes of social closure. Exclusionary closure, the only type noted by Weber, is typical of dominant groups and involves the exercise of power in a downward direction. Usurpationary closure is the typical mode of subordinate groups who attempt, by the exercise of power in an upward direction, to bite into the resources and benefits of dominant groups. Parkin's instrumentalist interpretation is evident in his argument that the usurpationary closure of subordinate groups represents a response to the exclusionary closure of the dominant groups. A subordinate group may be characterized by dual closure when its members attempt both to usurp resources from the dominant group, and to protect their own rewards and opportunities by excluding members of a group more subordinate than themselves. The white working class in the United States is given as an example, and in Israel Middle Eastern Israeli Jews also display a tendency to dual closure. Parkin does not appear to envisage, however, the possibility that a subordinate ethnic group may practice exclusionary closure against members of the dominant group, and that the subordinate group's mode of closure may be more than a response or countervailing action to the dominant group's closure. A situation of open dominant group and closed subordinate group is unlikely to be found in class stratification, but it does occur in the relationships of ethnic and religious groups. This is the situation of many religious sects, and in Israel sectors of the ultra-Orthodox provide an example. And where both dominant and subordinate groups practice closure against each other, it should not be assumed that the closure of the latter is only a reaction to the closure of the former. Muslim Arabs in Israel do not condemn intermarriage with Jews just because Jews condemn intermarriage with Arabs.

Parkin distinguishes two criteria of exclusion, individualistic and collectivistic. The individualistic type is typical of the modern class system; the monopolization by the modern bourgeoisie of productive property and credentials are justified as universalistic criteria. Inequalities of opportunity, as for example in the system of education, that favor the middle and upper classes are covert forms of collectivistic criteria, but the collectivistic forms of class exclusion based on lineage and the stigmatization of the lower orders have been eroded since the nineteenth century. As a new society without a feudal past Israel does not have a history of collectivistic class exclusion. Even the traditional form of exclusion in Jewish society was relatively individualistic: high status was based principally on religious scholarship, and although there was inequality of opportunity in the achievement of religious scholarship, the traditional educational system was open to all Jewish males. In modern Israel with its large public sector, credentials are the main form of exclusion, and this individualistic form is reinforced by the rhetoric of equality across almost the whole political spectrum.

Parkin compares the individualistic form of modern class exclusion with the purely collectivistic exclusion based on ethnicity and religion. He argues that collectivistic exclusion produces subordinate groups that are relatively integrated and communal in character, compared with the social fragmentation of subordinate groups that are excluded on an individualistic basis. We would argue, however, that groups may exclude others on an individualistic basis but, nevertheless, be highly integrated and communal in character.

Exclusion from religious groups or denominations within a religious tradition is often based on purely individualistic criteria. An individual may be admitted into a religious group on the basis of a purely formal qualification, such as a membership fee, but in some groups admission depends on meeting stringent requirements of individual beliefs and behavior. The former religious affiliation or qualities of the individual or his family may be disregarded; the criteria for exclusion and acceptance are purely individualistic. Such a religious group, based on individualistic exclusion, is likely to have a highly integrated communal character. Communal-type religious groups can be based on collectivistic exclusion, as is the case of introversionistic groups like the Amish, or on individualistic exclusion, as is the case of conversionist groups like the Jehovah's Witnesses. Some Jewish ultra-Orthodox groups have a highly communal nature and an individualistic form of exclusion. Although a very small proportion of secular Jews actually cross the boundary into the ultra-Orthodox community, the latter is open to any Jew who meets the requirements of stringent religious observance. In order to encompass such cases it is necessary to distinguish the relative closure of a boundary from its relative clarity or sharpness.

A boundary may be described as relatively open or closed depending on the amount of movement or mobility from one side to the other. A boundary may be described as relatively sharp or diffuse depending on the extent of differences, social, cultural, and identificational, between the two sides. These two qualities of boundaries are likely to be interrelated. Giddens (1980) has argued, for example, that mobility chances are an important determinant of the "structuration" of classes, and Parkin has been criticized for ignoring the importance of mobility in the process of class formation (Barbalet, 1982). However, there is no one-to-one relationship between the extent of mobility over a boundary and the boundary's clarity or, in Giddens' terminology, the group's structuration. One important additional consideration is whether mobility is in one direction or in both directions. Upward mobility out of a subordinate group without downward mobility into it may have little effect on the clarity of the group's boundary or may sharpen it even further. Moreover, the centrality of cultural and identificational components in some ethnic and religious groups can make their boundaries exceedingly resilient even if there is considerable movement over them.

To the extent that it is possible to speak about class boundaries in Israel, they are relatively open and diffuse. There has been considerable generational and intergenerational socio-economic mobility, both upward and downward. Moving from say blue collar to white collar may involve some changes in class identity (from wage-earner to middle class), but class identity is one of the least important identities among Israelis, both Jewish and Arab. Class culture, distinguished by accents, forms of language, patterns of leisure, and so on, is only likely to evolve if there is class reproduction over a number of generations, and because Israel is such a young society, class cultures are much less evident than in other countries, such as England. The relative absence of cultural class lines is no doubt both cause and consequence of the many friendships that we found to cross class differentiation. There are signs, however, that a lower class culture, largely independent from communities of origin, is emerging in poor neighborhoods where there has been a continuity of residence of two or three adult generations.

Intra-Jewish ethnic boundaries tend to be open, but they are less diffuse than class boundaries, especially among the lower strata. The frequent social movement across ethnic lines does not usually involve a substitution of ethnic identity (say from Easterner to Ashkenazi), but it often involves a weakening of ethnic identity. This movement does not necessarily make the boundaries less sharp. In fact, the crossing of mobile Middle Easterners into the predominantly middle-class European sector leaves the cultural contours of the boundary intact. Social movement across the secular-religious or ultra-Orthodox boundary is much less frequent than across the intra-Jewish ethnic boundaries, and in contrast to the ethnic boundary, it does involve a substitution of identity. Even if the crossing of the religious-secular boundary was far more frequent, it would be unlikely to affect the clarity of its contours. Lastly, the Jewish-Arab boundary is both relatively closed and relatively clear.

Parkin wrote that the usurpationary aims of the subordinate group can range from marginal redistribution to complete expropriation, and that in contrast with the exclusionary measures of the dominant group, the subordinate group relies heavily on the public mobilization of members. Complete expropriation would mean a change of the system rather than a change within the system, but Parkin makes clear in his discussion that the dominant tendency in subordinate classes in modern western societies is to seek some degree of redistribution. The major form of collective action at the disposal of subordinate classes to back up its claims is work sanctions or withdrawal from work. Parkin notes that the use of such means by subordinate ethnic groups is likely to be less disruptive because they are usually dispersed throughout the labor market, especially in low-paid jobs with weak industrial leverage. They have to rely more on political mobilization, and if a "liberal" group exists within the dominant group, to appeal to its moral sentiments.

In Israel, both the subordinate Jewish ethnic category, through their selective support of non-ethnic and ethnic parties, and the ultra-Orthodox, through their political parties, have achieved some redistribution of public funds in their favor. The political parties representing the interests of Israeli Arabs have been excluded as possible coalition partners and have not held a position of political leverage that might have enabled them to achieve a significant redistribution of the state's resources. The legally legitimate means available to Arabs living in the West Bank and Gaza to achieve their usurpationary aims are even more limited, because as non-citizens they are unable to exercise political leverage within the Israeli political institutions. During the *intifada* (uprising) some Palestinian workers have withdrawn from the labor market, but this economic action has been intermittent and sporadic, and although certain sectors of the Israeli economy have been affected by such action, it has not caused a serious crisis in the Israeli economy. The major form of collective action has been violent demonstrations. The "battles" with the Israeli army do have disruptive effects on the state's economic and human resources, but they are even more important at the symbolic level as powerful statements of the oppressed, exercising leverage upon the moral sentiments of some Israelis and, in the international scene, on governments that are in a position to influence or put pressure on the Israeli government.

Parkin writes that class may not be the most important cleavage in society, and this is clearly so in Israel. But because Parkin focuses on the different means of usurpation and pays little attention to the different aims of usurpation among class, ethnic, and religious groups, he does not provide a framework for evaluating the relative importance or depth of the cleavages in society. At the surface level of social reality and at any particular point of time, the disruption caused by strikes in class usurpation may be greater than the expressive forms of collective mobilization and activation of moral sentiments of ethnic or religious groups. Consideration of the different aims of usurpation may indicate, however, that at a deeper level of social reality, the ethnic or religious cleavage is the most important one.

The notion of depth has been a common one in structuralism. In the works of Levi-Strauss and others a dichotomy was presented between "surface" and "deep" structure, but some structuralist writers have preferred to speak of various levels of depth. We would hesitate to call our approach structuralist because we do not follow the distinction between an empirical or directly observable surface structure and invisible or non-directly observable deep structure. We do, however, wish to consider the cleavages in Israel with respect to their relative depths.

A deep cleavage may be the most visible in a particular time period, as the Israeli-Palestinian conflict has been during the period of the *intifada*, but at another point of time the deepest cleavage may be the least visible. The fundamental criterion of depth is the extent of change that would be required in order to meet the usurpationary claims of the subordinate groups and to delete the perceived disadvantages that arise from the forms of exclusionary closure. This requires consideration of the relationship of the meanings of the intrasocietal boundaries to the meanings that are attributed to the boundary and characteristics of the society as a whole. Whereas an intrasocietal boundary may be deleted or lose its significance by combining it with, or collapsing it into, the wider societal boundary, other boundaries may be irreducible to the wider one as long as it does not undergo a transformation. The elimination of an intrasocietal boundary may require more than the redistribution of rewards and resources. It may require redefinitions of the cultural contents and symbolic contours of the setting as a whole. The greater the transformation of the system that is required in order to eliminate the intrasocietal boundary, the deeper the level of social cleavage.

The aims of all subordinate groups in Israel, class, ethnic, religious, and ethnonational, include the redistribution of material resources and rewards, but only in the case of class divisions is this the single focus of usurpationary claims. As in other capitalist societies, industrial action is taken by workers in order to achieve some degree of redistribution, but the limited aims of class collective action are indicated by the focus on trade-union activities and the absence of determined class politics. Class cleavages are moderated by the rhetoric of equality by the right wing as well as the left wing, and by the support by large sectors of the dominant class for the Labor Party. The absence of class politics and the limitation of class usurpationary action to trade-union activities to achieve some degree of redistribution are also characteristics of the United States. The difference is that in the United States the capitalist ethos is shared by both dominant and subordinate classes, whereas in Israel a significant section of the dominant class subscribes to a socialist ethos. The outcome, an absence of politicized class conflict, is the same.

The overlap of socio-economic inequality with geographical origins in Israel has meant that claims of the disprivileged Jewish ethnic groups have been similar to those of subordinate classes, but inequality does not exhaust the meanings of the intra-Jewish ethnic cleavages. European and Middle Eastern Israeli Jews have held different understandings of "fusion" that relate to the overall meaning of a Jewish society in Israel. The demand for fusion among Middle Easterners is not just a demand for a social melting-pot, but one that involves the acceptance or integration of Middle Easterners' Judaisms into the dominant Israeli culture. The visits of political leaders to the yearly celebrations at the shrines of Middle Eastern Jewish saints represent at least a token change in this direction. But even if there were far more profound cultural transformations that would assure the elimination of intra-Jewish ethnic cleavages, this would not necessitate a drastic change in the principles of legitimation of the social order or a redefinition of the society's boundaries.

There is some degree of overlap between socio-economic divisions and the religious-secular division, but it is much less extensive or obvious compared with intra-Jewish ethnic inequality. The larger size of religious families, the religious education system, and the dedication to protracted sacred learning have contributed to the modest economic condition of many religious people. Instrumental claims, such as housing for the religious population and financial support for their religious and community institutions, have been among the major concerns of the religious political parties. The political balance of power has been such that the political parties have often had to limit themselves to promoting instrumental interests, but on those occasions when one of the major secular

parties has appeared to depend on their political support their usurpationary endeavors have presented a more radical challenge to the
secular population. The cleavage is deep because it is over the relationship of the social order to the ancestral religious legacy and the very
definition and meaning of being Jewish. Both religious and secular Israeli
Jews emphasize a common Jewish identity, but for the religious or
ultra-Orthodox Jews the secular Jew is missing an essential component of
that identity.

Religious Jews feel that it is their religious responsibility to transform
secular Jews into religious Jews, for they believe that the collective
redemption of all Jews depends on this transformation. When the
political situation permits they will activate their political resources to
promote this transformation, but they face a dilemma because they are
also an interest group concerned to promote the welfare of their own
members. Their "ultimate" aim of usurpation, involving a transformation of the very meaning of the social collectivity, is in tension with
their concern to defend the autonomy of their community and to gain for
it a larger share of the resources available in the existent order. In the
prevailing political context they pursue the more limited usurpationary
aims and these result in a further sharpening of the boundary between
them and the secular majority.

The inequality between the Arabic and Jewish populations in Israel is a
sharp one, and although the Arab citizens are represented by particular
parties in the political system, their exclusion from coalitions has meant
that they have been far less successful than religious Jews in realizing
their instrumental usurpationary aims. The overcoming of their subordination would require an unprecedented reallocation of resources, but
this would depend on a fundamental change, going beyond instrumental
matters, in the dominant Jewish group. It would mean a transformation
of the very meaning of being an Israeli so that it would no longer be
understood to be united with Jewishness. Such a transformation appears
a most unlikely development, as would a transformation of identity
among Israeli Arabs whereby the meaning of "Israeli" would go beyond
instrumental considerations to include a positive emotive dimension.

If the cleavage between Jewish and Arab citizens of Israel pertains to
the meaning of the civic identity, the cleavage between Israeli Jews and
Palestinians living in the West Bank and Gaza relates to the very
existence of the civic entity. The aim of usurpation here is full autonomy,
and the fundamental dispute is not only where the boundaries between
Israel and an autonomous Palestinian entity should be drawn, but
whether they should be drawn at all. On both sides there are large and

influential groups who wish to dominate a state that covers the whole territory. The concerns here include important questions of security, but beyond these the dispute is over a territory that carries deep symbolic meanings related to the historical and cultural endeavors of the two peoples.

The case of Israel is a case of multiple cleavages where the usurpationary claims of subordinate groups are in contradiction with each other. The transformation that would be required to overcome the Arab-Jewish cleavage is in opposition to the usurpationary aims, at the most general level, of the Jews of Middle Eastern origin, who wish to have their Judaisms incorporated fully into Israeliness, and, even more so, of the ultra-Orthodox Jews, who wish to make secular Israelis "genuine" Jews. These contradictions mean that there is no possibility that the subordinate groups will unify or push the society in the same direction. The likelihood is that the various groups will move the society in different directions. The subordinate groups will vary in the extent to which they achieve their usurpationary aims, but in evaluating their relative achievements it should be remembered that they differ with respect to the level of the social order that they are challenging. The pressures at the different levels bring about uncoordinated or inconsistent multilevel changes.

We have suggested in this concluding chapter that social differentiations such as class, ethnicity, and religion can be analyzed within a single conceptual framework as pertaining to different levels or depths of a particular social setting. The multiple cleavages present a complex picture of different interests, aims, and actions, but lack of co-ordination at the level of empirical reality does not prevent coherence at the level of theoretical elaboration.

Appendix A

The sample

Age   The mean age difference among the four groups of origin lacked statistical significance, although the age composition of the Poles was somewhat more heterogeneous than the other categories (table A.1).

Table A.1. *Age*

Country of origin	$\bar{x}$	σ	N
Morocco	39.21	65.62	216
Iraq	37.91	66.56	209
Poland	35.53	70.81	188
Rumania	38.01	65.96	213
Total	37.74	66.96	826

Age at migration   Out of the total sample 88% (731 respondents) were born outside Israel. The Poles were the only group with a sizeable proportion of Israeli born: 36% were born in Israel compared with no more than 5% in the other three groups. The Iraqis are characterized by an especially low age of migration (table A.2).

Table A.2. *Age at migration*

Country of origin	$\bar{x}$	σ	N
Morocco	18.55	66.34	212
Iraq	13.08	65.17	199
Poland	22.01	86.66	119
Rumania	20.82	68.13	203
Total	18.26	70.91	731

Socio-economic status An attempt was made to obtain about equal proportions of blue- and white-collar workers from each group of origin. However, the mean occupational prestige and the mean number of schooling years were higher for the two European groups (tables A.3 and A.4). The Rumanians and Poles had higher proportions in the higher

Table A.3. *Occupational prestige*

Country of origin	$\bar{x}$	σ	N
Morocco	51.40	21.05	210
Iraq	53.14	21.33	206
Poland	67.72	21.64	183
Rumania	64.98	22.30	208
Total	59.14	22.73	807

Table A.4. *Years of schooling*

Country of origin	$\bar{x}$	σ	N
Morocco	11.14	3.51	211
Iraq	10.84	3.97	202
Poland	13.70	3.74	183
Rumania	13.08	3.75	208
Total	12.16	3.94	804

status white-collar positions. In line with other studies in Israel, the correlation between years of schooling and occupational prestige was found to be lower for the Middle Eastern groups: for Moroccans .56, for Iraqis .61, for Poles .70, and for Rumanians .72. With respect to fathers' occupational prestige, the differences among the four groups were statistically significant but much less than for respondents (table A.5).

Socio-economic mobility Intergenerational mobility was characteristic of all four groups, but the correlations between respondents' and fathers' occupational status were low (table A.6). For three of the groups, the correlation between respondents' and fathers' educational attainment was greater (table A.6). The Poles demonstrated the greatest linkage between origins and destination. Since the Polish fathers were characterized by the highest levels of education and occupational prestige, this continuity may be a consequence of a ceiling effect.

Table A.5. *Fathers' occupational prestige*

Country of origin	$\bar{x}$	σ	N
Morocco	43.69	18.19	188
Iraq	41.61	21.21	196
Poland	49.92	22.25	174
Rumania	46.43	21.70	198
Total	45.29	21.05	756

Table A.6. *Correlation between fathers' and sons': 1 occupational prestige; 2 last school attended, for the four origin categories*

Country of origin	Prestige		School	
	γ	α	γ	α
Morocco	.13	.01	.23	.00
Iraq	.06	.14	.34	.00
Poland	.20	.00	.33	.00
Rumania	.19	.00	.17	.00

Appendix B

Deprivation index

The index was constructed according to respondents' answers to the following questions:

1 Is there discrimination against certain groups in Israeli society? If so, which groups are discriminated against. If respondent mentions his ethnic category (Ashkenazim or *edot ha'Mizrach*) or his *edah*, the answer is coded "1," otherwise, "0."
2 Have Ashkenazim got their proper share, less than their proper share, or more than their proper share in (a) economic area, (b) social esteem, (c) political power? For each of the three areas, Polish and Rumanian respondents who answered less than the proper share were coded "1": otherwise, "0."
3 Have *edot ha'Mizrach* got their proper share, less than their proper share, or more than their proper share in (a) economic area, (b) social esteem, (c) political power? For each of the three areas, Moroccan and Iraqi respondents who answered less than the proper share were coded "1": otherwise, "0."
4 Has your particular *edah* got its proper share, less than its proper share, or more than its proper share in (a) economic area, (b) social esteem, (c) political power? Answers coded as described in 2 and 3.

The index is the simple sum of the answers. Its range is from "0" (no felt deprivation) to "8" (highest level of felt deprivation).

Appendix C

Indexes of ethnic identification

The specific ethnic identification index was constructed by combining the following three measures:

1 Respondents who placed the specific ethnic identification above the broad ethnic identification in the hierarchy received "1," the others "0."
2 Respondents who expressed a high level of pride in the specific identification (points five and six on the six-point scale) received "1," the others "0."
3 Respondents who expressed a higher level of pride in the specific than in the broad ethnic identification (or expressed the maximum level of pride at point six on the scale in both identifications) received "1," the others "0."

Five levels of identification were distinguished. At the first level were placed the respondents who received zero on all three measures. At the second level were the respondents who did not express a high level of pride in the specific identification, but placed it before the broad identification either in the hierarchy or in terms of relative pride. The third level includes respondents who did not express a high level of pride in the specific identification, but placed it before the broad identification in both the hierarchy and in relative pride. It included also respondents who did not place the specific before the broad identification in either the hierarchy or in relative pride, but did express a high level of pride in it. At the fourth level respondents expressed a high level of pride in the specific identification and placed it before the broad identification in either the hierarchy or in relative pride. The fifth level (maximal identification) contained the respondents who received "1" on all three measures. An index of the broad ethnic identification was built on the same lines. Level of pride was given a weight twice that of place in hierarchy and relative pride; level of pride accounted for 80% of the divergence in the indexes.

Glossary

Agudat Yisrael: Federation of Israel; a predominantly Ashkenazi ultra-Orthodox party.

aliyah (plural, *aliyot*): literally "ascent," referring to Jewish immigration to the Land of Israel.

Ashkenazi (plural, Ashkenazim): Jews or descendants of Jews from central and eastern Europe.

bar mitzvah: literally "son of the Commandment"; a rite of passage held at the age of thirteen for boys who are called up in the synagogue to read a portion of the Law.

Bund: the major socialist, anti-Zionist Jewish party in eastern Europe.

Dash: the Democratic Movement for Change; a short-lived liberal, dovish party.

dati (plural, *datiim*): religious; referring in Israel to Jews who observe the *mitzvot* at a level and in a manner that is considered Orthodox.

Degel ha'Torah: literally "Flag of the Torah"; an Ashkenazi ultra-Orthodox party whose leaders and supporters seceded from Agudat Yisrael.

dhimmi (Arabic): term used by authorities in Muslim countries referring to Jews and Christians as subordinate, protected peoples.

edah (plural, *edot*): Jewish group from a particular country of origin.

edot Ashkenaz: all groups of Jews originating from central and eastern European countries.

edot ha'Mizrach: communities of the East; all groups of Jews originating from North Africa and Middle Eastern countries.

galut: exile; the Jewish dispersion outside Israel.

Gush Emunim: a religious, ultra-nationalist movement.

Habad: a Hasidic movement; unlike most other Hasidic movements it attempts to convert secular Jews to Orthodox Judaism.

halachah: the total body of Jewish religious laws.

hamula (Arabic): patrilineal Arab kinship group, usually comprised of a number of extended families.

Hanukkah: Festival of Lights, in commemoration of the rededication of the Second Temple by Judas Maccabeus and his followers after its desecration by the Syro-Greeks about 165 B.C.E.

haredi (plural, *haredim*): God-fearing or pious; ultra-Orthodox Jews.

hasid (plural, *hasidim*): follower of the mystical movement that emerged and spread among eastern European Jews in the eighteenth and nineteenth centuries.

Haskalah: the rationalist Enlightenment movement within Judaism.

hazan: cantor or reader of religious services.

heder: literally "room"; traditional religious school.

Herut: Freedom; right-wing party, now the principal component of the Likud.

hiloni (plural, *hilonim*): non-religious or secular.

Histadrut: General Federation of Labor in Israel; a federation of trade unions which is also a consortium of industrial enterprises, financial institutions, and agricultural co-operatives.

intifada: literally "awakening"; generally used to describe the recent civil uprising on the West Bank and the Gaza Strip.

Kabbalah: the mystical teachings of Judaism.

kehillah (plural, *kehillot*): Jewish community.

kibbutz (plural, *kibbutzim*): collective settlement based on collective ownership of the means of production.

kiddush: blessing over a cup of wine consecrating the Sabbath or religious holiday.

klitah: absorption of Jewish immigrants into Israeli society.

Knesset: assembly; the Israeli Parliament.

kuttab (Arabic): traditional elementary school among Moroccan Jews.

Landsmannschaften: Jewish organizations based on origin (countries, areas, or towns).

Likud: the principal right-wing party in Israel which emerged from a coalition of parties, including Herut, its principal component.

Little Triangle: a strip of land along Israel's "narrow waist."

lo-dati: non-religious or secular.

Ma'arach: the Labor Alignment Party which emerged from a coalition of labor parties, including Mapai, its principal component.

Mafdal: the National Religious Party.

Mapai: the Workers' Party of the Land of Israel; the historically dominant Labor Party that became the principal component of the Ma'arach.

Mapam: United Workers Party; small left-wing labor party.

mellah (Arabic): separate Jewish neighborhood in Islamic countries.

mesorati: traditionalist; term used in Israel to refer to those Jews who retain a number of religious observances but are not strictly observant.

mikveh: Jewish ritual bath.

mimuna: festival of Moroccan Jews, celebrated on the night which terminates the Passover holiday.

minhag (plural, *minhagim*): rite or custom.

mitzvah (plural, *mitzvot*): religious commandment.

Mizrachim: Easterners, usually translated in the literature as "Oriental"; identical in meaning to *edot ha'Mizrach*.

mizug ha'galuyot: "fusion of the exiles," referring to the fusion of all Jewish groups of origin into a unified nation.

moshav (plural, *moshavim*): co-operative smallholders' settlement.

oleh (plural: *olim*): Jewish immigrant to Israel.

Purim: festival commemorating the deliverance of Jews from the hands of Haman, the chief minister of Persia about 500 B.C.E.

Rakach: New Israel Communist Party, supported mainly by Israeli Arabs.

Ratz: Movement for Citizens' Rights; small left-wing dovish party.

rosh: head; referring to head of synagogue board, family, etc.

Rosh Hashanah: New Year, also known as Day of Judgment and Day of Memorial.

Seder: Order; the service and traditional meal of the family at Passover.

Sefer Torah: the Scroll of the Law read in the synagogue.

Sephardi (plural, Sephardim): descendants of the Jewish communities of Spain and Portugal.

Shas: Sephardi Torah Guardians; ultra-Orthodox party, supported by Jews from the Middle East.

shtetl: the small town Jewish community in eastern Europe.

Talmud: literally "lesson"; the rabbinical compendium made up of the Mishnah (the "Oral" Law) and the Gemara, the commentaries on the Mishnah.

Tami: Israel Tradition Movement; a religious party that was supported by Jews from the Middle East.

tephillin: phylacteries worn during the weekday morning services.

Yamim Noraim: Days of Awe between Rosh Hashanah and Yom Kippur.

yeshivah (plural, *yeshivot*): traditional educational institution of advanced religious study.

Yiddish: the Germano-Hebrew vernacular of eastern European Jews.

Yishuv: the pre-state Jewish community in Palestine.

Yom Kippur: Day of Atonement.

Zohar: literally, "Splendor," the major work of mystical Judaism.

Notes

6 Religiosity and secularization

1 We follow here Bryan Wilson's definition of secularization (Wilson, 1966: xiv; 1982: 149).
2 A recent survey of Israeli Jews found that only 64% expressed a belief in God and 35% said that they believed in the coming of the messiah, but 74% fasted on Yom Kippur, 88% lit Hanukkah candles, and 99% participated in the Passover Seder night meal (Ben-Meir and Kedem, 1979).
3 In Israel there are few non-Orthodox synagogues (on Reform and Conservative Judaism in Israel see Tabory, 1983), and Israeli Jews differentiate themselves mainly in terms of *dati* (religious, roughly equivalent to Orthodox in America), *mesoriti* (traditional), meaning a less Orthodox or less strict level of ritual observance, and *lo-dati* (non-religious) or *hiloni* (secular). On identification with respect to religion, see chapter 10. For overviews of religion in Israel see Deshen, 1978; Yaron, 1976.
4 In deciding which *mitzvot* to include in our questionnaire we had the benefit of the findings of a study in which Israelis were questioned regarding their performance of twenty *mitzvot* (Ben-Meir and Kedem, 1979). No clear-cut divisions in levels of religiosity were found; there was a continuum of religiosity ranging from the "strictly religious," 14% of the population who performed fourteen or more of the twenty *mitzvot*, to the "non-religious," 39% of the population who performed six or fewer of the *mitzvot*. Observance of the individual *mitzvot* ranged from 1% who did not use electricity on the Sabbath, to 99% who participated in the yearly Seder meal at Passover.
5 A problem with the Goldscheider and Friedlander study is that they had few questions on specific *mitzvot*, and they did not cover the range from those practiced by the Orthodox to those practiced by the majority. In constructing a typology of religiosity they combined both objective (specific *mitzvot*) and subjective measures (respondents' evaluations of the importance of religion in their homes and their parents' homes). Studies in Israel that have depended solely on respondents' evaluations, of their levels of religiosity include Herman (1970) and Antonovsky (1963).
6 Cohen's analysis of the Boston surveys is unusual in measuring the relationship of occupation (controlling for education and other factors) and religiosity, but his discussion is limited to a comparison between salaried and self-employed and professionals and all other occupations. As for income, Cohen found that this had little influence on ritual practice. Himmelfarb (1980) reported a small negative relationship between education and "total religiosity," but a larger positive relationship between income and "total religiosity."

7 The product–moment correlation coefficient between "Moroccan" as a dummy variable and religiosity is .46 indicating the relatively high religiosity of this group. The parallel beta coefficient has neither substantive nor statistical significance.

8 The product–moment coefficient between religiosity and years of schooling is nil, and the positive beta effect indicates the suppressive effect of the other independent variables.

7 Friendship networks

1 For somewhat different evaluations of the effect of intermarriage on ethnic integration in Israel see Peres and Schrift (1979) and Rosen (1982).

2 For discussion of the relationship of ethnic culture and the urban working class, see Gans (1982) and Yancey *et al.* (1976). A study of a relatively unassimilated Ukrainian group of the third and fourth generations in Canada found a negative correlation between education and ethnic homogeneity of friends (Borhek, 1970), but studies of white ethnic groups in the United States have found no significant relationship (Laumann, 1973; Yancey *et al.*, 1985). S. Cohen (1977) noted that the "old" ethnic groups in the United States have reached such a degree of assimilation that no relationship with socio-economic status was to be expected. Among the "new" Catholic immigrant groups he found an inverse relationship between education and in-marriage, but even among these groups there was no inverse relationship between education and intraethnic friendships.

3 Only 13.9% of the total sample reported that all three of their best friends were from their country of origin. According to country of origin of respondents: Iraqis, 6.7%, Poles 10.1%, Rumanians, 15.5%, and Moroccans, 22.6%.

4 Differences among the four groups of origin regarding their years of primary socialization in Israel do not account for the variation in their ethnic networks. The percentages of respondents who were in Israel or who immigrated to Israel before the age of fourteen were 45% of the Rumanians, 59% of Moroccans, 62% of Poles, and 86% of Iraqis.

5 An analysis of the odds of broad ethnically heterogeneous networks after controlling for primary socialization in Israel showed that the additional variable had no significant effect in the Moroccan and Polish groups. The odds among Iraqis decreased to some extent (1.03 compared with 1.20), but the effect of Iraqi origins had no statistical significance. Among Rumanians, control of primary socialization increased the odds of a heterogeneous broad ethnic network (1.55 compared with 1.31).

6 The interaction of Moroccan origin and class lacks statistical significance, but it is in the same direction as the interaction of class and Iraqi origin which is substantially as well as statistically meaningful.

7 The educational variable was dichotomized since the Israeli educational system is non-selective in terms of survival in the system until the age of eighteen. The system is selective in assigning pupils to the academic high-school track which is the avenue to higher education. Authority is dichotomized following Robinson and Kelley (1979).

8 The absence of rigid class and ethnic boundaries is, in part, a consequence of class and ethnic differences crosscutting each other; people from the same

ethnic group finding friends across class lines, and people from the same class finding friends across ethnic lines.

8 Ethnic consciousness

1 Ben-Sira (1988) found that 47% of his Middle Eastern respondents and 17% of his European respondents "agreed" or "absolutely agreed" with the statement that "the western *edot* prevented *edot ha'Mizrach* from entering high ranks." However, 24% of Middle Eastern respondents and 23% of European respondents "agreed" or "absolutely agreed" that "equality would be achieved if *edot ha'Mizrach* worked as hard as the western *edot*."

2 Similar differences between Moroccans and Iraqis were found in a study (Elhanani, 1988) carried out in 1975 in two "development" towns where the populations were from the lower socio-economic strata. Whereas 41% of the Moroccan respondents were of the opinion that there was no need to partially change or abandon the customs of their *edah* in order to adjust to the customs of the country, only 14.6% of the Iraqis were of this opinion.

9 Class consciousness

1 The SES index was based on the sum of the standardized scores of the three components – years of schooling, occupational prestige (coded by Hartman's 1975 Israeli occupational prestige scale), and housing density (number of rooms in house divided by household members). Each component was weighted by its factor loadings using the method of principal factor. A single factor accounted for 55.8% of the items' variance. The items' loadings were: .42 for years of schooling, .83 for occupational prestige, and $-.47$ for housing density.

2 A regression analysis shows that the SES components and the blue-collar/white-collar classification account together for 5.8% of the variance in the number of classes perceived; the factor with clear influence is occupational prestige (beta coefficient is .13) and the blue-collar/white-collar classification does not add to the explanation.

3 The correlation between the blue-collar/white-collar distinction and class conflict was .22; between occupational status and class conflict $-.21$; between housing density and class conflict .21. When SES was dichotomized the correlation with class conflict was .27.

4 An index of class deprivation was constructed based on three questions, each one referring to a different aspect of deprivation. The respondents were asked to evaluate whether their social class had received less than it deserved, its proper share, or more than it deserved in (a) the economic area, (b) social esteem, and (c) political power. Respondents who said "less than it deserved" in all three areas were defined as "deprived."

5 The support for the Labor Alignment among the five class categories was as follows: lower blue collar 20%, higher blue collar 28%, independents 27%, lower white collar 31%, higher white collar 38%.

10 Religious, ethnic, and class divisions: convergent or crosscutting?

1 The term "factor analysis" refers to several statistical techniques with one common denominator – they enable the presentation of a set of variables by a smaller number of hypothetical variables usually named factors. Hence, factor analysis is based on the assumption that some underlying factors are responsible for the covariation among the observed variables. In the present analysis the transformation of the given sets of observed variables into other sets of variables is based on principal factor solutions. The rotation does not improve the quality of the solution, and it is used only in order to obtain simpler and more readily interpretable results. We use the varimax method of rotation which assumes orthogonality among the various factors. It simplifies the structure of each factor by maximizing the variance of its squared loadings. In our tables we present: (a) factor loadings which are equivalent to correlations between factors and variables, (b) eigenvalues which give an indication of the relative importance of the different factors, and (c) percent of variance. We base our interpretation of the substantive meaning of the various factors on the assumption that loadings below the value of .40 indicate relative marginality of the variables. For detailed discussion on factor analysis see, for example, Kim and Mueller, 1982a, b.

11 Voting

1 Ben-Sira (1988) found that 51% of his respondents of Middle Eastern origin and 38% of the European respondents "agreed" or "agreed absolutely" with the statement that, "the absorption by the political parties in the 1950s caused the ethnic gap"; 28% of the Middle Easterners and 12% of the Europeans "agreed" or "agreed absolutely" with the statement that, "the workers' movement caused the ethnic gap because they wanted *edot ha'Mizrach* to be dependent on them."

2 In the absence of unambiguous criteria for evaluating the size of standardized coefficients of the discriminant function, we determined that a coefficient with a lower value than .35 be judged as marginal in its importance.

3 In addition to discriminant analyses, we carried out regression analyses with the aim of comparing our findings with those of Shamir and Arian (1982). We preferred to base our conclusions on discriminant analysis because of the problems in evaluating regression analysis when the dependent variable is dichotomous (Blalock, 1979). However, in comparison with Shamir and Arian, who accounted for 12% of the variance in their total sample and also in the separate analysis of Middle Easterners and Europeans, the variables in our analysis account for 22% of the variance of the total sample, 21% in the separate analysis of Middle Easterners, and 17% in the separate analysis of Europeans.

4 Also among the Moroccans Ma'arach voters have a higher mean number of European friends than Likud voters. The correlation coefficient between social network heterogeneity and the function is high (.45), but the standardized coefficient is low. This is accounted for by the relatively high correlation between social network heterogeneity and socio-economic status ($-.36$). The

fact that the latter variable is dominant in the discriminant function leaves only a marginal weight to social network heterogeneity.

5 Also among the Poles Ma'arach voters are characterized by high socio-economic status, but the correlation coefficient between this factor and the function is low (−.28). Since the discriminant function is built in a way that would create a distinction among the groups, it is evident that this factor is marginal in the creation of the distinction in comparison with other variables.

13 Assimilation or ethnic solidarity?

1 Categories range from "0," no practice observed, to "5," all five practices observed.

2 Categories range from "0," all three best friends from respondents' broad ethnic category, to "3," all three best friends from the other broad ethnic category.

3 For the identification indexes, see appendix C.

4 An index composed according to respondents' answers to the following questions: (a) Is there discrimination in Israel against certain groups? If respondent answered affirmatively, he was coded "1," otherwise "0." (b) Do *edot ha'Mizrach* receive their proper share, economically, in social esteem, in political power? For each of these three areas respondents who answered "less than their proper share" were coded "1," otherwise "0." The categories range from "0" to "4."

5 We are aware of the fact that voting, a dichotomous variable, is not an ideal dependent variable in regression analysis. However, Hanushek and Jackson (1977) comment that, in models with dichotomous dependent variables, Ordinary Least Squares (OLS) estimates do not differ greatly from those of more appropriate methods (probit and logit) when the sample is not skewed. We decided to use the OLS model for the analysis of voting because this analysis enables a more comprehensive comparison of the variables that represent the various dimensions.

6 The coefficient of variability of "years of schooling" for the whole sample is .31, for the higher SES category (N=393) .22, and for the lower category (N=390) .25.

7 The reduction in N is caused by the fact that we only included voters of the two large parties in our analysis. Because pairwise deletion of missing data is not available in Manova (the program we have used for the multivariate multiple regression), it is evident that in our case the deficiencies of the multivariate multiple regression prevail over its merits.

8 The correlation coefficient between voting behavior and friendship networks is nil. This is due to the suppressive effect of a third variable – ethnic origin. It appears that heterogeneous friendship networks effect the voting behavior of Europeans and Middle Easterners in opposite directions. They weaken the tendency of Middle Easterners to prefer the Likud whereas among Europeans they enlarge support for the Likud (see chapter 11).

9 In a study of North Africans and Iraqis carried out in 1976 in three urban areas in Israel, Leslau *et al.* (1988) also found no statistically significant differences between the two groups in their perceptions of discrimination. They found

that, among Iraqis, more educated respondents were somewhat less likely to perceive discrimination, but, among North Africans (mainly Moroccans), perceived discrimination was the same for all educational levels.

15 Jews and Arabs

1 In the 1989 local elections Muslim fundamentalist groups defeated for the first time the established secular parties in some Arab municipalities, and it is likely that the fundamentalists will put themselves forward as a party in the next general elections.

References

Abramov, S. Zalmon 1976. *Perpetual Dilemma: Jewish Religion in the Jewish State.* Rutherford, N.J.: Fairleigh Dickinson.

Adler, Israel, and Robert Hodge 1983. "Ethnicity and the process of status attainment in Israel." *Israel Social Science Research* 1: 5–23.

Adorno, T. W., Else Frenkel-Brunswick, Daniel J. Levinson, and R. Nevitt Sanford 1950. *The Authoritarian Personality.* New York: Harper & Row.

Alba, Richard D. 1985. "The twilight of ethnicity among Americans of European ancestry: the case of Italians." *Ethnic and Racial Studies* 8: 134–58.

Alexander, Jeffrey C. 1980. "Core solidarity, ethnic outgroup and social differentiation: a multidimensional model of inclusion in modern societies" pp. 5–28 in J. Dofny and A. Akiwowo (eds.), *National and Ethnic Movements.* Beverly Hills, Calif.: Sage.

Allan, Graham 1977. "Class variation in friendship patterns." *British Journal of Sociology* 28: 389–93.

Amilianer, Avraham 1979. "Aspects of self-suppression as a function of acculturation processes experienced by Moroccan origin parents of Beer Sheva high school students" (in Hebrew). Unpublished Ph.D. thesis. Jerusalem: Hebrew University of Jerusalem.

Anosh, N., A. Laslau, and Y. Shaham 1983. *Youth in Underprivileged Neighborhoods* (in Hebrew). Tel Aviv: Tel Aviv University.

Antonovsky, Aaron 1963. "Israeli political-social attitudes" (in Hebrew). *Amot* 6: 11–22.

Arian, Asher 1972. "Electorate choice in a dominant party system" in A. Arian (ed.), *The Elections in Israel – 1969.* Jerusalem: Academic Press.

Arjomand, Said Amir 1986. "Social change and movements of revitalization in contemporary Islam" pp. 87–107 in J. A. Beckford (ed.), *New Religious Movements and Rapid Social Change.* London: Sage.

Arnold, F. W. 1984. "West Indians and London's hierarchy of discrimination." *Ethnic Groups* 6: 47–64.

Ashkhar, C. 1979. *Class, Ethnicity, Groups of Pupils and Deprivation Feeling* (in Hebrew). Tel Aviv: Tel Aviv University.

Azmon, Yael 1985. "Urban patronage in Israel" pp. 284–94 in E. Cohen, M. Lissak, and U. Almagor (eds.), *Comparative Social Dynamics: Essays in Honor of S. N. Eisenstadt.* Boulder, Colo.: Westview Press.

Baker, Donald G. 1983. *Race, Ethnicity and Power: A Comparative Study.* London: Routledge & Kegan Paul.

References

Banton, Michael P. 1983a. *Racial and Ethnic Competition*. Cambridge: Cambridge University Press.

1983b. "Categorical and statistical discrimination." *Ethnic and Racial Studies* 6: 269–83.

Barbalet, J. M. 1982. "Social closure in class analysis: a critique of Parkin." *Sociology* 16: 484–97.

Baron, Salo Wittmayer 1930. *The Jews in Roumania*. New York: Columbia University Press.

Barth, Frederick 1969. "Introduction" pp. 1–38 in Frederick Barth (ed.), *Ethnic Groups and Boundaries*. Boston, Mass.: Little Brown.

Bar-Yosef, Rivkah 1968. "Desocialization and resocialization: the adjustment process of immigrants." *International Migration Review* 2: 27–43.

1970. "The Moroccans: background to the problem" pp. 419–28 in S. N. Eisenstadt, R. Bar-Yosef, and C. Adler (eds.), *Integration and Development in Israel*. Jerusalem: Israel Universities Press.

Beer, William R. 1980. *The Unexpected Rebellion: Ethnic Activism in Contemporary France*. New York: New York University Press.

Bell, Daniel 1975. "Ethnicity and social change" pp. 141–74 in N. Glazer and D. P. Moynihan (eds.), *Ethnicity: Theory and Experience*. Cambridge, Mass.: Harvard University Press.

Bell, Wendell, and Robert V. Robinson 1980. "Cognitive maps of class and racial inequalities in England and the United States." *American Journal of Sociology* 86: 320–49.

Ben-David, Joseph 1953. "Ethnic differences or social change?" pp. 33–52 in C. Frankenstein (ed.), *Between Past and Future: Essays and Studies on Aspects of Immigrant Absorption in Israel*. Jerusalem: Szold Foundation.

Ben-Meir, Yehuda, and Peri Kedem 1979. "Index of religiosity of the Jewish people of Israel" (in Hebrew). *Megamot* 14: 353–62.

Ben-Porat, Amir 1985. "An ontological model of class consciousness." *International Journal of Comparative Sociology* 26: 60–74.

1986. *Between Class and Nation: The Formation of the Jewish Working Class in the Period Before Israel's Statehood*. Westport, Conn.: Greenwood Press.

1989. *Divided We Stand: Class Structure in Israel from 1948 to the 1980s*. Westport, Conn.: Greenwood Press.

Ben-Porath, Yoram 1983. "The conservative turnabout that never was." *Jerusalem Quarterly* 29: 3–11.

Ben-Rafael, Eliezer 1982. *The Emergence of Ethnicity: Cultural Groups and Social Conflict in Israel*. Westport, Conn.: Greenwood Press.

1985. "Ethnicity: theory and myth" (in Hebrew). *Megamot* 29: 190–204.

Ben-Sira, Zeev 1988. *Alienated Identification in the Jewish-Israeli Society: Interethnic Relations and Integration* (in Hebrew). Jerusalem: Magnes Press.

Benski, Tova 1988. "Acculturation and musical taste patterns: a sociological analysis" pp. 35–64 in A. Deutsch and G. Tulea (eds.), *Social and Cultural Integration in Israel*. Ramat-Gan: Bar-Ilan University, Sociological Institute of Community Studies.

Berger, Peter L. 1967. *The Sacred Canopy*. Garden City, New York: Doubleday.

Bernstein, Deborah 1980. "Immigrants and society – a critical view of the dominant school of Israeli sociology." *British Journal of Sociology* 31: 246–64.

1981. "Immigrant transit camps: the formation of dependent relations in Israeli society." *Ethnic and Racial Studies* 4: 26–43.

1984. "Conflict and protest in Israeli society: the case of the Black Panthers of Israel." *Youth and Society* 16: 129–52.

Bernstein, Deborah, and Shlomo Swirski 1982. "The rapid economic development of Israel and the emergence of the ethnic division of labour." *British Journal of Sociology* 33: 64–85.

Blalock, Hubert M. Jr. 1967. *Toward a Theory of Minority Group Relations*. New York: Wiley.

1979. *Social Statistics*. New York: McGraw-Hill.

Blau, Peter M. 1977. "A macrosociological theory of social structure." *American Journal of Sociology* 83: 26–54.

Blauner, Robert 1972. *Racial Oppression in America*. New York: Harper & Row.

Bock, R. Darrell 1975. *Multivariate Statistical Methods in Behavioral Research*. New York: McGraw-Hill.

Body, Monica, David L. Featherman, and Judah Matras 1980. "Status attainment of immigrants and immigrant origin groups in the United States, Canada and Israel." *Comparative Social Research* 3: 199–228.

Bonacich, Edna 1972. "A theory of ethnic antagonism: the split labor market." *American Sociological Review* 37: 547–59.

1980. "Class approaches to ethnicity and race." *Insurgent Sociologist* 10: 9–23.

Borhek, J. T. 1970. "Ethnic group cohesion." *American Journal of Sociology* 76: 33–46.

Bowser, B. P. 1985. "Race relations in the 1980s: the case of the United States." *Journal of Black Studies* 15: 307–22.

Britten, Nicky 1984. "Class imagery in a national sample of women and men." *British Journal of Sociology* 25: 406–34.

Burgess, M. Elaine 1978. "The resurgence of ethnicity: myth or reality?" *Ethnic and Racial Studies* 1: 265–85.

Burstein, P. 1985. "On equal employment opportunity and affirmative action." *Race and Ethnic Relations* 4: 91–112.

Central Bureau of Statistics 1972. *Demographic Characteristics of the Population: Population and Housing Census, 1972*. Series no. 14. Jerusalem.

1984. *Census of Population and Housing Publications: Localities, Population and Households*. Jerusalem.

1988. *Statistical Abstract of Israel*. Series no. 39. Jerusalem.

Chouraqui, A. 1952. *Les Juifs d'Afrique du Nord*. Paris: Presses Universitaires de France.

Cohen, Erik 1972. "The Black Panthers and Israeli society." *Jewish Journal of Sociology* 14: 93–109.

1983. "Ethnicity and legitimation in contemporary Israel." *Jerusalem Quarterly* 28: 111–24.

Cohen, Hayyim J. 1973. *The Jews of the Middle East, 1860–1972*. New York: John Wiley & Sons.

Cohen, Percy S. 1983. "Ethnicity, class and political alignment in Israel." *Jewish Journal of Sociology* 25: 119–30.

Cohen, Steven M. 1977. "Socioeconomic determinants of intraethnic marriage and friendship." *Social Forces* 55: 997–1005.

1983. *American Modernity and Jewish Identity*. New York: Tavistock.

Coleman, Richard P. and Lee Rainwater 1978. *Social Standing in America*. New York: Basic Books.

Confino, Michael 1953. "Conflicts and changes in Northern Africa" (in Hebrew). *Mibifnim* 16: 56–81.

Connor, Walter 1977. "Ethnonationalism in the first world: the present in historical perspective" in M. J. Esman (ed.), *Ethnic Conflict in the Western World*. Ithaca, N.Y.: Cornell University Press.

1978. "A nation is a nation is a state, is an ethnic group is a . . ." *Ethnic and Racial Studies* 1: 377–400.

Coser, Lewis 1956. *The Functions of Social Conflict*. New York: Free Press.

Cox, Oliver C. 1948. *Caste, Class and Race*. New York: Monthly Review Press.

Curran, J. 1979. "Separation in Northern Ireland" pp. 145–51 in R. L. Hall (ed.), *Ethnic Autonomy – Comparative Dynamics*. New York: Pergamon.

Dahrendorf, Ralf 1959. *Class and Class Conflict in Industrial Society*. Stanford, Calif.: Stanford University Press.

Deshen, Shlomo 1972. "Ethnicity and citizenship in the ritual of an Israeli synagogue." *Southwestern Journal of Anthropology* 28: 69–82.

1974. "Political ethnicity and cultural ethnicity in Israel during the 1960s" pp. 281–309 in A. Cohen (ed.), *Urban Ethnicity*. London: Tavistock.

1976. "Ethnic boundaries and cultural paradigms: the case of Tunisian immigrants in Israel." *Ethos* 4: 271–94.

1978. "Israeli Judaism: introduction to the major patterns." *International Journal of Middle East Studies* 9: 141–69.

1980. "Religion among Oriental immigrants in Israel" pp. 235–46 in A. Arian (ed.), *Israel: A Developing Society*. Assen: Van Gorcum.

Deshen, Shlomo, and Moshe Shokeid 1974. *The Predicament of Homecoming: Cultural and Social Life of North African Immigrants in Israel*. Ithaca, N.Y.: Cornell University Press.

Dillingham, Gerald L. 1981. "The emerging black middle-class: class conscious or race conscious." *Ethnic and Racial Studies* 4: 432–51.

Efrat, Elisha 1987. *Development Towns in Israel: Past or Future* (in Hebrew). Tel Aviv: Achiasaf Publishing House.

Eisenstadt, S. N. 1955. *The Absorption of Immigrants: A Comparative Study Based Mainly on the Community in Palestine and the State of Israel*. Glencoe, Ill.: Free Press.

1967. *Israeli Society: Background, Development, Problems*. New York: Basic Books.

1969. "The absorption of immigrants, the amalgamation of exiles and the problems of transformation of Israeli society" (in Hebrew) pp. 6–13 in *The Hebrew University: The Integration of Immigrants from Different Countries of Origin in Israel*. Jerusalem: Magnes.

1970. "Israel: traditional and modern social values and economic development" pp. 107–22 in S. N. Eisenstadt, R. Bar-Yosef, and C. Adler (eds.), *Integration and Development in Israel*. Jerusalem: Israel Universities Press.

1983. "Some comments on the 'ethnic' problem in Israel." *Israel Social Science Research* 1: 20–9.

1985. *The Transformation of Israeli Society*. London: Weidenfeld and Nicolson.

1986. "The development of the ethnic problem in Israeli society: observations and suggestions for research." Research paper no. 17. Jerusalem: The Jerusalem Institute of Israel Studies.

Elhanani, Edith 1979. "Deprivation feeling and patterns of response among two ethnic communities in Israel" (in Hebrew). Unpublished M.A. thesis. Ramat-Gan: Bar-Ilan University.

1988. "Between two cultures: the attitudes of members of two oriental groups in Israel towards their cultural integration in society" pp. 16–55 in A. Deutsch and G. Tulea (eds.), *Social and Cultural Integration in Israel*. Ramat-Gan: Bar-Ilan University, Sociological Institute for Community Studies.

Eliav, Mordechai 1982. "Ethnic relations in the Jewish community in Palestine in the 19th century" (in Hebrew). *Pe'amim* 11: 118–34.

Encyclopaedia Judaica 1972. Jerusalem: Keter Publishing House.

Enloe, Cynthia H. 1976. "Religion and ethnicity" pp. 347–71 in P. F. Sugar (ed.), *Ethnic Diversity and Conflict in Eastern Europe*. Santa Barbara, Calif.: A.B.C-Clio.

Feagin, J. R., and D. L. Eckberg 1980. "Discrimination: motivation, action, effects, and context." *Annual Review of Sociology* 6: 1–20.

Fernea, R. A. 1973. *Nubians in Egypt*. Austin: University of Texas Press.

Fischer-Galati, Stephen 1981. "The radical left and assimilation: the case of Romania" pp. 89–103 in B. Vago (ed.), *Jewish Assimilation in Modern Times*. Boulder, Colo.: Westview Press.

Fishelson, Gideon, Yoram Weiss, and Mark Nili 1980. "Ethnic origin and income differentials among Israeli males, 1969–1976" pp. 253–76 in A. Arian (ed.), *Israel: A Developing Society*. Assen: Van Gorcum.

Frazier, Franklin E. 1957. *Black Bourgeoisie*. New York: Free Press.

Friedlander, Dov, and Calvin Goldscheider 1979. *The Population of Israel*. New York: Columbia University Press.

Friedman, Georges 1967. *The End of the Jewish People*. New York: Doubleday.

Gallie, Duncan 1983. *Inequality and Class Radicalism in France and Britain*. Cambridge: Cambridge University Press.

Gans, Herbert 1979. "Symbolic ethnicity: the future of ethnic groups and cultures in America." *Ethnic and Racial Studies* 2: 1–20.

1982. *The Urban Villagers: Groups and Class in the Life of Italian Americans*. 2nd edn. New York: Free Press.

Geertz, Clifford 1963. "The integrative revolution: primordial sentiments and civil politics in new states" pp. 105–57 in Clifford Geertz (ed.), *Old Societies and New States: The Quest for Modernity in Asia and Africa*. New York: Free Press.

George, H. Jr. 1984. *American Race Relations Theory: A Review of Four Models*. Lanham, Md.: University Press of America.

Giddens, Anthony 1980. *The Class Structure of the Advanced Societies*. 2nd edn. London: Hutchinson.

Ginor, F. 1983. *Socioeconomic Disparities in Israel* (in Hebrew). Tel Aviv: Am Oved.

Glazer, Nathan 1983. *Ethnic Dilemmas, 1964–1982*. Cambridge, Mass.: Harvard University Press.

Glazer, Nathan, and Daniel P. Moynihan 1975. "Introduction" pp. 1–26 in N. Glazer and Daniel P. Moynihan (eds.), *Ethnicity: Theory and Experience*. Cambridge, Mass.: Harvard University Press.

Gleason, Philip 1979. "Confusion compounded: the melting pot in the 1960s and 1970s." *Ethnicity* 6: 10–20.

Goldberg, Harvey E. 1978. "The mimuna and the minority status of Moroccan Jews." *Ethnology* 17: 75–87.

Goldman, Alan H. 1979. *Justice and Reverse Discrimination*. Princeton: Princeton University Press.

Goldscheider, Calvin, and Dov Friedlander 1983. "Religiosity patterns in Israel." *American Jewish Year Book* 83: 3–39.

Goldstein, Sidney, and Calvin Goldscheider 1968. *Jewish Americans: Three Generations in a Jewish Community*. Englewood Cliffs, N.J.: Prentice Hall.

Gonen, Amiram 1985. "The changing ethnic geography of Israeli cities" pp. 25–38 in A. Weingrod (ed.), *Studies in Israeli Ethnicity: After the Ingathering*. New York: Gordon and Breach.

Goodman, L. A. 1972. "A general model for the analysis of surveys." *American Journal of Sociology* 77: 1035–86.

Gordon, Milton M. 1964. *Assimilation in American Life*. New York: Oxford University Press.

Goyder, John C. 1983. "Ethnicity and class-identity: the case of French- and English-speaking Canadians." *Ethnic and Racial Studies* 6: 72–89.

Gradus, Yehuda, and Eliezer Stern 1979. *Beersheva* (in Hebrew). Jerusalem: Keter Publishing House.

Graetz, Brian R. 1983. "Images of class in modern society: structure, sentiment and social location." *Sociology* 17: 79–96.

Hanushek, E. A., and J. E. Jackson 1977 *Statistical Methods for the Social Sciences*. New York: Academic Press.

Hartman, Moshe 1975. *Occupation as a Measure of Social Class in Israeli Society* (in Hebrew). Tel-Aviv: Tel-Aviv University.

    1980. "The role of ethnicity in married women's economic activity in Israel." *Ethnicity* 7: 225–55.

Hartman, Moshe, and Hanna Ayalon 1975. "Ethnicity and social status in Israel" (in Hebrew). *Megamot* 21: 124–39.

Hechter, Michael 1975. *Internal Colonialism: The Celtic Fringe in British National Development, 1536–1966*. London: Routledge & Kegan Paul.

    1978. "Group formation and the cultural division of labor." *American Journal of Sociology* 84: 293–318.

Heiberg, M. 1979. "External and internal nationalism: the case of the Spanish Basques" pp. 180–200 in R. L. Hall (ed.), *Ethnic Autonomy – Comparative Dynamics*. New York: Pergamon.

Heller, Celia S. 1977. *On the Edge of Destruction: Jews of Poland Between the Two World Wars*. New York: Schocken.

Herberg, Will 1960. *Protestant, Catholic, Jew*. Garden City, New York: Doubleday.

Herman, Simon J. 1970. *Israelis and Jews: The Continuity of an Identity*. New York: Random House.

    1977. *Jewish Identity: A Social Psychological Perspective*. Beverly Hills: Sage.

Herzog, Hanna 1984. "Is there political ethnicity in Israel" (in Hebrew). *Megamot* 28: 332–52.

Hiller, Peter 1975. "Continuities and variations in everyday conceptual components of class." *Sociology* 9: 255–81.

References

Himmelfarb, Harold S. 1980. "The study of American Jewish identification: how is it defined, measured, obtained, sustained, lost." *Journal for the Scientific Study of Religion* 19: 48–60.

Hirschman, Charles 1983. "America's melting pot reconsidered." *Annual Review of Sociology* 9: 397–423.

Hoetinck, H. 1972. "National identity, culture and race in the Caribbean" in E. Q. Campbell (ed.), *Racial Tensions and National Identity*. Nashville, Tenn.: Vanderbilt University Press.

Homans, G. C. 1974. *Social Behavior: Its Elementary Forms*. New York: Harcourt Brace Javanovich.

Horowitz, Dan, and Moshe Lissak 1989. *Trouble in Utopia: The Overburdened Polity of Israel*. Albany, N.Y.: State University of New York Press.

Hundert, Gershon David, and Gershon C. Bacon 1984. *The Jews in Poland and Russia: Bibliographical Essays*. Bloomington, Ind.: Indiana University Press.

Hurwic-Nowakouska, Irena 1986. *A Social Analysis of Postwar Polish Jewry*. Jerusalem: The Zalman Shazar Center for Jewish History.

Inbar, Michael, and Chaim Adler 1977. *Ethnic Integration in Israel*. New Brunswick, N.J.: Transaction.

Jackson, Mary R., and Robert W. Jackson 1983. *Class Awareness in the United States*. Berkeley, Calif.: University of California Press.

Keyes, Charles F. 1981. "The dialectics of ethnic change" pp. 4–30 in Charles F. Keyes (ed.), *Ethnic Change*. Seattle, Wash.: University of Washington Press.

Khen, Michael 1977. "Achievement and ascriptive factors in deprivation feeling" (in Hebrew). *Social Research Quarterly* 12/19: 149–66.

Kim, Jae-On, and Charles W. Mueller 1982a. "Introduction to factor analysis." Paper no. 13. Beverly Hills, Calif.: Sage.

　1982b. "Factor analysis; statistical methods and practical issues." Paper no. 14. Beverly Hills, Calif.: Sage.

Klaff, Vivian Z. 1977. "Residence and integration in Israel: a mosaic of segregated peoples." *Ethnicity* 4: 103–27.

Klecka, W. R. 1980. *Discriminant Analysis*. Beverly Hills, Calif.: Sage.

Klorman-Eraqi, Bat-Zion 1981. "Messianism in the Jewish community of Yemen in the nineteenth century." Unpublished Ph.D. thesis. Los Angeles: University of California.

Knoke, David, and Peter J. Burcke 1980. *Log Linear Models*. Beverly Hills, Calif.: Sage.

Korpi, Walter 1983. *The Democratic Class Struggle*. London: Routledge & Kegan Paul.

Kraus, Vered 1982. "Ethnic origin as a hierarchical dimension of social status and its correlates." *Sociology and Social Research* 66: 452–66.

　1985. "Social segregation in Israel as a function of objective and subjective attitudes of the ethnic groups." *Sociology and Social Research* 69: 50–71.

Krausz, Ernest 1986. "Edah and 'ethnic groups' in Israel." *Jewish Journal of Sociology* 28: 5–18.

Kuper, Leo 1965. *An African Bourgeoisie: Race, Class and Politics in South Africa*. New Haven, Conn.: Yale University Press.

Kurokawa, M. (ed.) 1970. *Minority Responses*. New York: Random House.

References

Lal, Barbara Ballis 1983. "Perspectives on ethnicity: old wine in new bottles." *Ethnic and Racial Studies* 6: 154–73.

Landecker, Werner S. 1981. *Class Crystallization.* New Brunswick, N.J.: Rutgers University Press.

Laumann, E. O. 1969. "The social structure of religious and ethno-religious groups in a metropolitan community." *American Sociological Review* 34: 182–97.

1973. *Bonds of Pluralism: The Forms and Substance of Urban Social Networks.* New York: John Wiley & Sons.

Lavi, Th. 1974. "The background to the rescue of Romanian Jewry during the period of the Holocaust" pp. 177–86 in B. Vago and G. L. Mosse (eds.), *Jews and Non-Jews in Eastern Europe 1918–1945.* New York: John Wiley & Sons.

Lazerwitz, Bernard 1977. "The community variable in Jewish identification." *Journal for the Scientific Study of Religion* 16: 361–9.

Leifer, Eric M. 1981. "Competing models of political mobilization: the role of ethnic ties." *American Journal of Sociology* 87: 23–47.

Leslau, Avraham, Ernest Krausz, and Sara Nussbaum 1988. "Feelings of discrimination among Iraqis and North Africans in Israel" pp. 156–80 in A. Deutsch and G. Tulea (eds.), *Social and Cultural Integration in Israel.* Ramat-Gan: Bar-Ilan University, Sociological Institute for Community Studies.

Lewis, Arnold 1979. *Power, Poverty and Education.* Ramat Gan: Turtledove.

1985. "Phantom ethnicity: 'Oriental Jews' in Israel's Society" pp. 133–58 in A. Weingrod (ed.), *Studies in Israeli Society: After the Ingathering.* New York: Gordon and Breach.

Lewis, Herbert S. 1984. "Yemenite ethnicity in Israel." *Jewish Journal of Sociology* 26: 5–24.

Liebman, Charles S., and Eliezer Don-Yehiya 1983. *Civil Religion in Israel: Traditional Judaism and Political Culture in the Jewish State.* Berkeley, Calif.: University of California Press.

1984. *Religion and Politics in Israel.* Bloomington, Ind.: Indiana University Press.

Lipset, S. M., and S. Rokkan 1967. "Cleavage structures, party systems and voter alignments" pp. 1–64 in S. M. Lipset and S. Rokkan (eds.), *Party Systems and Voter Alignments.* New York: Free Press.

Lissak, Moshe 1969. *Social Mobility in Israeli Society.* Jerusalem: Israel Universities Press.

Loeb, Lawrence D. 1985. "Folk models of Habbani ethnic identity" pp. 201–16 in A. Weingrod (ed.), *Studies in Israeli Society: After the Ingathering.* New York: Gordon and Breach.

Lopreato, Joseph, and Lawrence E. Hazelrigg 1972. *Class, Conflict, and Mobility.* San Francisco, Calif.: Chandler Publishing Company.

Lotan, Michael 1983. "On Ashkenazic identity" (in Hebrew). *Mahbarot Lemehkar Velebikoret* 8: 5–19.

Lubel, S. 1983. *Religious and Ethnic Behaviors and Deprivation Feelings in Two Communities* (in Hebrew). Ramat-Gan: Bar-Ilan University.

Lustick, Ian 1980. *Arabs in the Jewish State: Israel's Control of a National Minority.* Austin, Tex.: Texas University Press.

1984. "Being explicit on the limitations of a Jewish state – a reply to Henry Rosenfeld." *Israel Social Science Research* 2: 73–6.

Machover, Moshe, and Akiva Orr 1971. "The class nature of Israeli society." *New Left Review* 65: 3–26.

Makhou, Najwa 1982. "Changes in the employment structure of Arabs in Israel." *Journal of Palestine Studies* 11: 77–102.

Mann, Michael 1973. *Consciousness and Action among the Western Working Class*. London: Macmillan.

Marcus, Joseph 1983. *Social and Political History of the Jews in Poland, 1919–1939*. Berlin: Mouton.

Marger, Martin N. 1985. *Race and Ethnic Relations: American and Global Perspectives*. Belmont, Calif.: Wadsworth.

Martin, David 1978. *A General Theory of Secularization*. Oxford: Basil Blackwell.

Matras, Judah 1965. *Social Change in Israel*. Chicago: Aldine.

    1985. "Intergeneration social mobility and ethnic organization in the Jewish population of Israel" pp. 1–24 in A. Weingrod (ed.), *Studies in Israeli Society: After the Ingathering*. New York: Gordon and Breach.

Matras, Judah, and Andrea Tyree 1977. "Ethnic and social origin dominance in occupational attainment in Israel." Paper presented at A.S.A meeting, Chicago.

Matras, Judah, and Dov Weintraub 1977. "Ethnic and other primordial differentials in Israel." Discussion paper. Jerusalem: Brookdale Institute.

McKay, James 1982. "An exploratory synthesis of primordial and mobilizationist approaches to ethnic phenomena." *Ethnic and Racial Studies* 5: 395–420.

McKay, James, and Frank Lewis 1978. "Ethnicity and the ethnic group: a conceptual analysis and reformulation." *Ethnic and Racial Studies* 1: 412–27.

McRoberts, Kenneth 1979. "Internal colonialism: the case of Quebec." *Ethnic and Racial Studies* 2: 293–318.

Mendelsohn, Ezra 1974. "The dilemma of Jewish politics in Poland: four responses" pp. 203–19 in B. Vago and G. L. Mosse (eds.), *Jews and Non-Jews in Eastern Europe*. New York: John Wiley & Sons.

Meyer, Peter, *et al.* 1953. *The Jews in the Soviet Satellites*. Syracuse, N.Y.: Syracuse University Press.

Meyers, Allan R. 1982. "Patronage and protection: the status of Jews in precolonial Morocco" pp. 85–104 in S. Deshen and W. P. Zenner (eds.), *Jewish Societies in the Middle East*. Washington, D.C.: University Press of America.

Miles, Robert 1982. *Racism and Migrant Labour*. London: Routledge & Kegan Paul.

Miller, S. M., and Frank Riesman 1972. "The working-class subculture: a new view" pp. 186–98 in P. Blumberg (ed.), *The Impact of Social Class*. New York: Thomas Y. Crowell.

Mol, Hans 1972. *Western Religion*. The Hague: Mouton.

Moore Jr., Barrington 1978. *Injustice: The Social Bases of Obedience and Revolt*. New York: M. E. Sharpe.

Murphy, Raymond 1986. "The concept of class in closure theory: learning from rather than falling into the problems encountered by neo-Marxism." *Sociology* 20: 247–64.

Nagel, Joane, and Susan Olzak 1982. "Ethnic mobilization in new and old states: an extension of the competition model." *Social Problems* 30: 127–43.

Nahon, Yaakov 1984a. *Trends in Occupational Status: The Ethnic Dimension* (in Hebrew). Jerusalem: Jerusalem Institute of Israel Studies.

1984b. "Ethnic gaps – the situation over time" (in Hebrew) pp. 23–43 in N. Cohen and O. Ahimeir (eds.), *New Directions in the Study of Ethnic Communities*. Jerusalem: Almog Press.

1987. *Patterns of Educational Extension and the Structure of Occupational Opportunities – The Ethnic Dimension*. Jerusalem: Jerusalem Institute of Israel Studies.

Newman, W. M. 1973. *American Pluralism: A Study of Minority Groups and Social Theory*. New York: Harper & Row.

Nielsen, François 1980. "The Flemish movement in Belgium after World War II: a dynamic analysis." *American Sociological Review* 45: 76–94.

1985. "Toward a theory of ethnic solidarity in modern societies." *American Sociological Review* 50: 33–49.

Novak, Michael 1972. *The Rise of the Unmeltable Ethnics*. New York: Macmillan.

Olzak, Susan 1982. "Ethnic mobilization in Quebec." *Ethnic and Racial Studies* 5: 253–75.

1983. "Contemporary ethnic mobilization." *Annual Review of Sociology* 9: 355–74.

Orans, M. 1971. "Caste and race conflict in cross-cultural perspective" in P. Orleans and W. E. Russel (eds.), *Race Change and Urban Society*. Beverly Hills, Calif.: Sage.

Palloni, Albert 1979. "Internal colonialism or clientelistic politics? The case of southern Italy." *Ethnic and Racial Studies* 2: 360–77.

Park, Robert E. 1928. "Human migration and the marginal man." *American Journal of Sociology* 33: 881–93.

Parkin, Frank 1972. *Class Inequality and Political Order*. St Albans: Paladin.

1979. *Marxism and Class Theory: A Bourgeois Critique*. London: Tavistock.

Parsons, Talcott, and Neil Smelser 1956. *Economy and Society*. New York: Free Press.

Patai, Raphael 1971. *Tents of Jacob*. Englewood Cliffs, N.J.: Prentice-Hall.

Patterson, G. James 1979. "The new ethnicity." *American Anthropologist* 81: 103–5.

Pavlak, Thomas J. 1976. *Ethnic Identification and Political Behavior*. San Francisco, Calif.: R. & E. Research Associates.

Peres, Yohanan 1969. "Ethnic identity in Israel" (in Hebrew), pp. 74–87 in The Hebrew University: *The Integration of Immigrants from Different Countries of Origin in Israel*. Jerusalem: Magnes Press.

1971. "Ethnic relations in Israel." *American Journal of Sociology* 76: 1021–47.

1976. *Ethnic Relations in Israel* (in Hebrew). Tel Aviv: Sifriat Poalim.

Peres, Yohanan, and Sara Shemer 1984. "The ethnic factor in the elections" pp. 89–111 in D. Caspi, A. Diskin, and E. Gutmann (eds.), *The Roots of Begin's Success*. London: Croom Helm.

Peres, Yohanan, and Ruth Schrift 1978. "Intermarriage and interethnic relations." *Ethnic and Racial Studies* 1: 428–51.

Peres, Yohanan, Ephraim Yuchtman-Yaar, and R. Shafat 1975. "Predicting and explaining voters' behaviour in Israel" pp. 189–203 in A. Arian (ed.), *The Elections in Israel – 1973*. Jerusalem: Academic Press.

Peretz, Don, and Sammy Smooha 1985. "Israel's eleventh Knesset election." *The Middle East Journal* 39: 86–103.

Pettigrew, T. F. 1980. "Prejudice" pp. 820–9 in S. Thernstrom (ed.), *Harvard*

Encyclopedia of American Ethnic Groups. Cambridge, Mass.: Harvard University Press.

Phizacklea, Annie, and Robert Miles 1980. *Labour and Racism*. London: Routledge & Kegan Paul.

Portes, Alejandro 1984. "The rise of ethnicity: determinants of ethnic perceptions among Cuban exiles in Miami." *American Sociological Review* 49: 383–97.

Portes, Alejandro, Robert Nash Parker, and Jose A. Cobas 1980. "Assimilation of consciousness: perceptions of U.S. society among Latin American immigrants to the United States." *Social Forces* 59: 200–11.

Poulantzas, Nicos 1975. *Classes in Contemporary Capitalism*. London: New Left Books.

Rabinowicz, Harry M. 1965. *The Legacy of Polish Jewry: A History of Polish Jews in the Inter-War Years, 1919–31*. New York: Thomas Yoseloff.

Ragin, Charles 1979. "Ethnic political mobilization: the Welsh case." *American Sociological Review* 44: 619–35.

Roberts, K., F. G. Cook, S. C. Clark, and Elizabeth Semeonoff 1977. *The Fragmentary Class Structure*. London: Heinemann.

Robinson, Robert V., and Wendell Bell 1978. "Equality, success, and social justice in England and the United States." *American Sociological Review* 43: 125–43.

Robinson, Robert V., and Jonathan Kelley 1979. "Class as conceived by Marx and Dahrendorf: effects on income inequality and politics in the United States and Great Britain." *American Sociological Review* 44: 38–58.

Roche, J. P. 1984. "Social factors affecting cultural, national, and religious ethnicity: a study of suburban Italian-Americans." *Ethnic Groups* 6: 27–46.

Rofe, Yacov, and Leonard Weller 1981. "Ethnic group prejudice and class in Israel." *Jewish Journal of Sociology* 23: 101–13.

Rosen, Sherry 1982. "Intermarriage and the 'blending of exiles' in Israel." *Research in Race and Ethnic Relations* 3: 79–102.

Rosenfeld, Henry 1978. "The class situation of the Arab national minority in Israel." *Comparative Studies in Society and History* 20: 374–407.

1983. "History, political action and change as 'aberrations' and Zionism as an irremediable 'contradiction.'" *Israel Social Science Research* 1: 69–76.

Rosenfeld, Henry, and Shulamit Carmi 1976. "The privatization of public means, the state-made middle class, and the realization of family value in Israel" pp. 131–59 in J. G. Peristiany (ed.), *Kinship and Modernization in Mediterranean Society*. Rome: Center for Mediterranean Studies.

Rosenstein, Carolyn 1981. "The liability of ethnicity in Israel." *Social Forces* 59: 667–86.

Rouhana, Nadim 1988. "The civic and national subidentities of the Arabs in Israel: a psychopolitical approach" pp. 123–53 in J. Hofman (ed.), *Arab-Jewish Relations in Israel*. Bristol, Ind.: Wyndham Hall.

Roumani, Maurice 1979. *From Immigrant to Citizen: The Contribution of the Army to National Integration in Israel: The Case of Oriental Jews*. The Hague: Foundation for the Study of Plural Societies.

Sandberg, Neil C. 1974. *Ethnic Identity and Assimilation: The Polish-American Community*. New York: Praeger.

Scase, Richard 1974. "English and Swedish concepts of class" in F. Parkin (ed.), *The Social Analysis of Class Structure*. London: Tavistock.

References

Schermerhorn, R. A. 1970. *Comparative Ethnic Relations: A Framework for Theory and Research*. New York: Random House.

Schwartz, Sharon R., Bruce G. Link, Guedalia Naveh, Itzhak Levav, and Bruce P. Dohrenwend 1989. "Oriental Jews in Israel: separating class and ethnic prejudice." Unpublished manuscript.

Seliktar, Ofira 1984. "Ethnic stratification and foreign policy in Israel: the attitudes of Oriental Jews towards the Arabs and the Arab-Israeli conflict." *The Middle East Journal* 38: 34–50.

Semyonov, Moshe, and Noah Lewin-Epstein 1987. *Hewers of Wood and Drawers of Water*. Ithaca, N.J.: Cornell Institute of Labor Studies.

Semyonov, Moshe, and Andrea Tyree 1981. "Community segregation and the costs of ethnic subordination." *Social Forces* 59: 649–66.

Shamir, Michal, and Asher Arian 1983. "The ethnic vote in Israel's 1981 elections" pp. 99–111 in A. Arian (ed.), *The Elections in Israel – 1981*. Tel Aviv: Ramot Publishing Co.

Shapiro, Yonathan 1977. *Democracy in Israel* (in Hebrew). Ramat-Gan: Masada.

Sharot, Stephen 1973. "The three-generation thesis and the American Jews." *British Journal of Sociology* 24: 151–64.

1976. *Judaism: A Sociology*. Newton Abbot: David & Charles.

1982. *Messianism, Mysticism, and Magic: A Sociological Analysis of Jewish Religious Movements*. Chapel Hill, N.C.: University of North Carolina Press.

Shavit, Yossi 1984. "Tracking and ethnicity in Israeli secondary education." *American Sociological Review* 49: 210–20.

Shilhav, Joseph, and Menachem Friedman 1985. *Growth and Segregation – The Ultra-Orthodox Community of Jerusalem* (in Hebrew). Jerusalem: Jerusalem Institute for Israel Studies.

Shokeid, Moshe 1982. "Ethnicity and the cultural code among Arabs in a mixed town: women's modesty and men's honor at stake" pp. 32–52 in M. Shokeid and S. Deshen, *Distant Relations*. New York: Praeger.

1985. "Cultural ethnicity in Israel: the case of Middle Eastern Jews' religiosity." *A.J.S Review* 9: 247–71.

Shokeid, Moshe, and Shlomo Deshen 1982. *Distant Relations: Ethnicity and Politics among Arabs and North Africans in Israel*. New York: Praeger.

Shuval, Judith T. 1956. "Class and ethnic correlates of casual neighboring." *American Sociological Review* 2: 453–8.

1962. "The micro-neighborhood: an approach to ecological patterns of ethnic groups." *Social Problems* 9: 272–80.

Simmel, Georg 1955. *Conflict and the Web of Group Affiliations*. New York: Free Press.

Sklare, Marshall, and Joseph Greenblum 1979. *Jewish Identity on the Suburban Frontier*. 2nd edn. Chicago: University of Chicago Press.

Smith, Anthony D. 1981. *The Ethnic Revival*. Cambridge: Cambridge University Press.

1984. "Ethnic myths and ethnic revivals." *Archives Européennes de Sociologie* 25: 283–305.

Smooha, Sammy 1978. *Israel: Pluralism and Conflict*. London: Routledge & Kegan Paul.

1985. "A critique of an updated establishmentarian formulation of the cultural perspective in the sociology of ethnic relations in Israel" (in Hebrew). *Megamot* 29: 73–92.

1987. *Social Research on Jewish Ethnicity in Israel, 1948–1986*. Haifa: Haifa University Press.

Smooha, Sammy, and Vered Kraus 1985. "Ethnicity as a factor in status attainment in Israel." *Research in Social Stratification and Mobility* 4: 151–75.

Smooha, Sammy, and Yohanan Peres 1975. "The dynamics of ethnic inequality: the Israeli case." *Social Dynamics* 1: 63–80.

Spilerman, Seymour, and Jack Habib 1976. "Development towns in Israel: the role of community in creating ethnic disparities in labor force characteristics." *American Sociological Review* 81: 781–812.

Stahl, Abraham 1976. *Cultural Fusion in Israel* (in Hebrew). Tel Aviv: Am Oved.

Stein, Howard F., and Robert F. Hill 1977. *The Ethnic Imperative: Examining the New White Ethnic Movement*. University Park, Pa., and London: Pennsylvania State University Press.

Steinberg, Stephen 1981. *The Ethnic Myth: Race, Ethnicity, and Class in America*. Boston, Mass.: Beacon Press.

Sternberg, Ghitta 1984. *Stefanesti: Portrait of a Romanian Shtetl*. Oxford: Pergamon Press.

Swafford, M. 1980. "Parametric techniques for contingency table analysis." *American Sociological Review* 45: 664–90.

Swirski, Shlomo 1981. . . . *Lo Nehkshalim Ela Menuhkshalim* ("Orientals and Ashkenazim in Israel: The Ethnic Division of Labor") (in Hebrew). Haifa: Mahbarot Le'Mehkar U'Lebikoret.

Tabory, Ephraim 1983. "Reform and Conservative Judaism in Israel." *American Jewish Year Book* 83: 41–61.

Tabory, Ephraim, and Bernard Lazerwitz 1983. "Americans in the Israeli reform and conservative denominations: religiosity under an ethnic shield?" *Review of Religious Research* 24: 177–87.

Theriault, G. F. 1979. "Separatism in Quebec" pp. 102–36 in R. L. Hall (ed.), *Ethnic Autonomy – Comparative Dynamics*. New York: Pergamon.

Thompson, John L. P. 1983. "The plural society approach to class and ethnic political mobilization." *Ethnic and Racial Studies* 6: 127–53.

Tsemach, M. 1980. *The Attitudes of the Jewish Majority Towards the Arab Minority* (in Hebrew). Jerusalem: Van Leer Institute.

Vago, Bella 1981. "Communist pragmatism toward Jewish assimilation in Romania and in Hungary" pp. 105–26 in B. Vago (ed.), *Jewish Assimilationism in Modern Times*. Boulder, Colo.: Westview Press.

van den Berghe, Pierre L. 1978. *Race and Racism: A Comparative Perspective*. 2nd edn. New York: Wiley.

1981. *The Ethnic Phenomenon*. New York: Elsevier.

Vanneman, R. D. 1980. "U.S. and British perceptions of class." *American Journal of Sociology* 85: 759–90.

Vanneman, Reeve, and Fred C. Pampel 1977. "The American perception of class and status." *American Sociological Review* 42: 422–38.

Wade, P. 1985. "Race and class: the case of South African blacks." *Ethnic and Racial Studies* 233–49.

Walzer, Michael 1983. *Spheres of Justice: A Defense of Pluralism and Equality*. Oxford: Martin Robertson.

Weber, Max 1968. *Economy and Society*. 3 vols., edited by G. Roth and C. Wittich. New York: Bedminster Press.

Weiker, Walter F. 1983. "Stratification in Israeli society: is there a middle category?" *Israel Social Science Research* 1: 30–56.

Weimann, Gabriel 1983. "The not-so-small world: ethnicity and acquaintance networks in Israel." *Social Networks* 5: 289–302.

Weingrod, Alex 1979. "Recent trends in Israeli ethnicity." *Ethnic and Racial Studies* 2: 55–65.

Weinryb, Bernard D. 1972. *The Jews of Poland: A Social and Economic History of the Jewish Community in Poland from 1100 to 1800*. Philadelphia, Pa.: Jewish Publication Society of America.

Weintraub, Dov, and Vered Kraus 1982. "Social differentiation and place of residence: spatial distribution, population compositions and stratification in Israel" (in Hebrew). *Megamot* 27: 367–81.

Weissbrod, Lilly 1983. "Religion as national identity in a secular society." *Review of Religious Research* 24: 188–205.

Willie, Charles V. 1983. *Race, Ethnicity and Socioeconomic Status*. New York: General Hall Inc.

Wilson, A. 1984. "Mixed race children in British schools: some theoretical considerations." *British Journal of Sociology* 35: 42–61.

Wilson, Bryan R. 1966. *Religion in Secular Society*. London: Watts.

1982. *Religion in Sociological Perspective*. Oxford: Oxford University Press.

Wolffsohn, Michael 1987. *Israel, Polity, Society, and Economy, 1882–1986*. Atlantic Highlands, N.J.: Humanities Press International.

Yancey, W. L., E. P. Eriksen, and G. H. Leon 1985. "The structure of pluralism: 'We're all Italian around here, aren't we, Mrs. O'Brien?'" *Ethnic and Racial Studies* 8: 94–116.

Yaron, Zvi 1976. "Religion in Israel." *American Jewish Year Book* 76: 41–90.

Yatziv, Gadi 1979. *The Class Basis of Party Affiliation – The Israeli Case* (in Hebrew). Papers in Sociology. Jerusalem: The Hebrew University.

Yishai, Yael. 1982. "Israel's right wing Jewish proletariat." *Jewish Journal of Sociology* 24: 87–97.

1984. "Responses to ethnic demands: the case of Israel." *Ethnic and Racial Studies* 7: 283–300.

Yuchtman-Yaar, Ephraim 1983. "Expectations, entitlements, and subjective welfare" pp. 89–108 in S. E. Spiro and E. Yuchtman-Yaar (eds.), *Evaluating the Welfare State*. New York: Academic Press.

1986. "Differences in ethnic patterns of socio-economic achievement in Israel: a neglected aspect of structural inequality" (in Hebrew). *Megamot* 29: 393–412.

Zamir, Rinah 1966. "Beer Sheva 1958–1959 – social processes in a development town" (in Hebrew) pp. 335–65 in S. N. Eisenstadt *et al.* (eds.), *Social Structure of Israel*. Jerusalem: Academon.

Zureik, Elia T. 1979. *The Palestinians in Israel: A Study of Internal Colonialism*. London: Routledge & Kegan Paul.

Index